THE IVP NEW TESTAMENT COMMENTARY SERIES

Revelation

J. Ramsey Michaels

Grant R. Osborne
series editor

D. Stuart Briscoe
Haddon Robinson
consulting editors

INTERVARSITY PRESS
DOWNERS GROVE, ILLINOIS, USA
LEICESTER, ENGLAND

InterVarsity Press
P.O. Box 1400, Downers Grove, IL 60515, USA
38 De Montfort Street, Leicester LE1 7GP, England

InterVarsity Press® is the book-publishing division of InterVarsity Christian Fellowship®, a student movement active on campus at hundreds of universities, colleges and schools of nursing in the United States of America, and a member movement of the International Fellowship of Evangelical Students. For information about local and regional activities, write Public Relations Dept., InterVarsity Christian Fellowship, 6400 Schroeder Rd., P.O. Box 7895, Madison, WI 53707-7895.

Inter-Varsity Press, England, is the book-publishing division of the Universities and Colleges Christian Fellowship (formerly the Inter-Varsity Fellowship), a student movement linking Christian Unions in universities and colleges throughout the United Kingdom and the Republic of Ireland, and a member movement of the International Fellowship of Evangelical Students. For information about local and national activities write to UCCF, 38 De Montfort Street, Leicester LE1 7GP.

USA ISBN 0-8308-1820-0

UK ISBN 0-85111-683-3

Printed in the United States of America 

Library of Congress Cataloging-in-Publication Data

Michaels, J. Ramsey.
Revelation/J. Ramsey Michaels.
p. cm.—(The IVP New Testament commentary series: 20)
Includes bibliographical references.
ISBN 0-8308-1820-0 (alk. paper)
1. Bible. N.T. Revelation—Commentaries. I. Title.
II. Series.
BS2825.3.M46 1997
228'.07—dc21 *97-5276*
CIP

British Library Cataloguing in Publication Data

A catalogue record for this book is available from the British Library

19 18 17 16 15 14 13 12 11 10 9 8 7 6

12 11 10 09 08

For Bill Lane

General Preface

In an age of proliferating commentary series, one might easily ask why add yet another to the seeming glut. The simplest answer is that no other series has yet achieved what we had in mind—a series to and from the church, that seeks to move from the text to its contemporary relevance and application.

No other series offers the unique combination of solid, biblical exposition and helpful explanatory notes in the same user-friendly format. No other series has tapped the unique blend of scholars and pastors who share both a passion for faithful exegesis and a deep concern for the church. Based on the New International Version of the Bible, one of the most widely used modern translations, the IVP New Testament Commentary Series builds on the NIV's reputation for clarity and accuracy. Individual commentators indicate clearly whenever they depart from the standard translation as required by their understanding of the original Greek text.

The series contributors represent a wide range of theological traditions, united by a common commitment to the authority of Scripture for Christian faith and practice. Their efforts here are directed toward applying the unchanging message of the New Testament to the ever-changing world in which we live.

Readers will find in each volume not only traditional discussions of authorship and backgrounds, but useful summaries of principal themes and approaches to contemporary application. To bridge the gap between commentaries that stress the flow of an author's argument but skip over exegetical nettles and those that simply jump from one difficulty to another, we have developed our unique format that expounds the text in uninterrupted form on the upper portion of each page while dealing with other issues underneath in verse-keyed notes. To avoid clutter we have also adopted a social studies note system that keys references to the bibliography.

We offer the series in hope that pastors, students, Bible teachers and small group leaders of all sorts will find it a valuable aid—one that stretches the mind and moves the heart to ever-growing faithfulness and obedience to our Lord Jesus Christ.

Author's Preface

Before I ever taught the book of Revelation, I took two courses on it at two different seminaries. The first got as far as chapter 12 and ran out of time. The second reached chapter 12, jumped to chapter 20, and then ran out of time. Later, I learned of a graduate course that managed to cover only the first five verses of chapter 1!

Writers of commentaries have no such luxury, nor can they get away with skipping chapters 8-9 or 15-16, as I was in the habit of doing during the many years I taught the book in seminary, college, and church. Writing a commentary is no easy task because one has to say a little something about every page, every paragraph, almost every verse. A commentary is a continuous reading of the whole book, in which I try to put myself in the place of the biblical writer and visionary, John, and at the same time in the place of a modern reader—any reader.

Jim Hoover of InterVarsity Press, has helped me a great deal with the reader. Jim had earlier been my student in seminary, and in a wonderful role reversal he has gently reined in my professional tendencies to leave nothing unsaid. Writing a book, like making fine sculpture, is about knowing what to leave out. A commentary should not become so long and formidable that it gets in the way of hearing and obeying the biblical text itself. The biblical book must speak with its own voice, not ours. Only the Holy Spirit can accomplish this, but editors like Jim help encourage us to let it happen.

I am indebted to others as well. Neglected in the church, the book of Revelation is alive and well in the academy. I learned a great deal from participating in the Society of Biblical Literature Seminar on "Reading the Apocalypse" from the standpoint of both literary and social science criticism. At the purely practical level, I want to thank my son David for helping me become semi-literate with Windows 95, and my friend Alan Waterman for transferring my old Wordstar files to Microsoft Word without mishap. This was a part of a major passage in life, from full-time teaching to a pleasant and active partial retirement, with writing as a thread of continuity between the two. I am grateful above all to my wife Betty, our children and grandchildren, and our many friends, for making that transition a happy one. Their love has little directly to do with the book of Revelation, but much to do with the One revealed there.

All of us who venture to interpret the book of Revelation stand poised between the joyful promise of Revelation 1:3 and the terrible warnings of 22:18-19. Only with the help of those who have shared with us "in the suffering and kingdom and patient endurance that are ours in Jesus" (Rev. 1:9) can we claim the promise and heed the warnings.

To one such friend of many years I have dedicated this book.

Introduction

Ambrose Bierce (1947:347), in *The Devil's Dictionary,* included the following tongue-in-cheek definition: "REVELATION, *n.* A famous book in which St. John the Divine concealed all that he knew. The revealing is done by the commentators, who know nothing." We who presume to write commentaries on the book of Revelation need to take Bierce's words to heart so as not to take our own words or opinions too seriously. On the other hand, it is not quite true that "St. John the Divine concealed all that he knew." John was told at the end of his series of visions, "Do not seal up the words of the prophecy of this book, because the time is near" (Rev 22:10). The book is written to be understood, and blessings are pronounced on "the one who reads the words of this prophecy" and "those who hear it and take to heart what is written in it" (Rev 1:3).

For better or worse, the book of Revelation has become a public book, a part of our cultural heritage that belongs even to those who have never read it. We are reminded almost daily that we are on the threshold of a new millennium. For decades we have been warned of the danger of a nuclear holocaust called "Armageddon." Popular books and movies make use of the magical number 666 to play on people's fears, whether of science or religion, ancient witchcraft or modern technology.

Those who read this ancient book attentively and resist the popular tendency to trivialize it are unlikely to remain neutral about it. They will either love it or hate it—attitudes that have little to do with understanding. We can be repelled by the book of Revelation either because we have misunderstood it or because we have understood it all too well. Alternatively, we can love the book and its message for all the wrong reasons. It is a difficult book because of its imagery and symbolism and because it persists in asking questions many of us are unable or unwilling to answer: "Where do you stand? Which side are you on?"

No commentary can answer those questions for anyone. Reading a biblical commentary is no substitute for reading and rereading the biblical text. All the commentator can do is remove some of the roadblocks to understanding and otherwise try to stay out of the way.

□ The Genre and the Author of the Book of Revelation

Much has been written lately about the genre of biblical books, including the book of Revelation. *Genre* is a French loan word that refers to classifying artistic or literary works. To ask about the genre of the book of Revelation is to ask what kind of literature it is. To what writings, ancient or modern, is it similar? To what order or grouping does it belong? Regarding Revelation, these questions find no consensus. Our first impulse is to call it an *apocalypse,* for that is what it calls itself in its title (Rev 1:1, where the Greek word *apocalypsis* is translated "revelation" in the phrase "revelation of Jesus Christ"). Its title seems to place it in a class of writings that scholars call "apocalypses," such as 1 and 2 Enoch, 4 Ezra and 2 Baruch in early Judaism, or the Apocalypse of Peter and the Apocalypse of Paul in post-New Testament Christianity. But these writings were called apocalypses precisely because their imagery resembled that contained in the book of Revelation! Can we say that these works are apocalypses because they are similar to the book of Revelation and at the same time say that the Revelation is an apocalypse because it is similar to them?

The argument sounds circular, and it is. Moreover, most apocalypses pretended to be written by revered figures from the biblical past (see

Michaels 1992:23-27), while the author of the book of Revelation identifies himself only as "John" (Rev 1:4, 9; 22:8), a contemporary of his readers who was known personally to at least some of them. If his book calls itself an apocalypse once, it calls itself a prophecy at least five times (1:3; 22:7, 10, 18, 19), possibly six (see 19:10). Clearly the term *prophecy* in these instances defines what is meant by *apocalypse* or *revelation* in 1:1 (compare 1 Cor 14:6, where Paul uses the terms *revelation* and *prophecy* almost interchangeably).

The book of Revelation is a written prophecy, like the prophetic books of the Hebrew Bible, or Old Testament. It is the only book of prophecy in the New Testament. Revelation fits the genre of prophecy because it claims to predict the future (what "must soon take place," 1:1; 22:6; "what will take place later," 1:19), and it consists of visions and oracles from God that are delivered by a prophet to a specific community. Like many of the Old Testament prophets (notably Jeremiah and Ezekiel), John is a definite personality, an "I" who addresses a specific "you." At the same time, like most prophetic books of the Hebrew Bible, the book of Revelation is introduced by a heading, or title (1:1-3), that refers to the prophet in the third person ("his servant John," 1:2; compare Is 1:1; Jer 1:1-3; Ezek 1:2-3; Hos 1:1; Joel 1:1; Amos 1:1, etc.).

This creates a certain ambiguity about authorship that illustrates how closely questions of genre and authorship are intertwined. Is John the author? Or is the author the anonymous person or persons who composed Revelation 1:1-3 and then proceeded to quote what they claimed John saw and heard and eventually wrote down? Of course, John *could* have written 1:1-3, referring to himself in the third person in order to give his book universality and credibility in preparing it for a wider audience than the one he first intended. In any event, we shall refer to John as the author.

If we leave 1:1-3 out of the picture, a third possibility in regard to the question of genre presents itself. Revelation 1:4—22:21, or at least the beginning and the ending of the section, has the formal characteristics of a *letter*, like the letters of Paul. It begins with an identification of both the letter's writer ("John") and its recipients ("the seven churches that are in Asia," v. 4). This is followed by a formula that begins with "grace to you and peace" (vv. 4-5) and by a doxology (vv. 5-6) that corresponds to Paul's characteristic blessing or thanksgiving. It ends with a benediction, also echoing many of Paul's letters: "The grace of the Lord Jesus be with God's people. Amen" (22:21).

The "I" that pervades the book of Revelation can therefore be understood as either the "I" of a prophet like Jeremiah or Ezekiel, or the "I" of a letter writer like Paul. The book's prophecies occur within the framework of a very long letter, the longest in the New Testament. The title or heading of the work (1:1-3) signals the reader that the letter to follow is no ordinary letter, but a prophetic communication from God through Jesus Christ to John, and through John to the seven congregations of Asia Minor.

In short, no one genre identifies the book of Revelation perfectly. If a label must be attached to it, perhaps it is best called a "prophetic letter." Whether Revelation is taken as prophecy, letter or prophetic letter, however, the "I" style of this work should be taken seriously. Whatever else it may be, the book of Revelation is a kind of spiritual autobiography, a *testimony* or *personal narrative* of what one man saw and heard on the island of Patmos over an unspecified period of time (see 1:2, "who testifies to everything he saw").

The first-person style of narration differentiates the work from the four Gospels (where it surfaces only in Lk 1:3 and Jn 21:25). It finds its closest parallel in Paul's account of his own religious experience in Galatians 1:11—2:14. John, like Paul, received "a revelation of Jesus Christ" (Rev 1:1; Gal 1:12), but was willing, in contrast to Paul, to describe what he saw in great detail. Paul's caution and reserve about revealing what he had seen and heard is evident in 2 Corinthians 12:1-4, where he shuns the first person and speaks only of "a man in Christ" who "heard inexpressible things." John, by contrast, punctuates his narrative with "I saw" and "I heard," so that the reader sees heaven and earth, present and future, through John's eyes and hears the trumpets, the thunders and the voices of the book of Revelation through John's ears. Yet we never learn to know him as well as we know Paul, for his letter does not reveal his own personality. Whereas Paul is eager to reveal himself but reticent to describe his visions, John is explicit about his visions but slow to inject himself into his account.

When John does appear in the story, it is as a stand-in for the reader, not as an omniscient author fully in control of what is happening. Probably because he is a well-known authority figure to the congregations of the seven churches, he identifies himself at the outset as one who stands alongside them, not one who stands over them: "I, John, your brother and companion in the suffering and kingdom and patient endurance that are ours in Jesus, was on the island of Patmos because of the word of God and the testimony of Jesus" (1:9). John is our guide to the visions, but because he is on our level, as "brother and companion," he is as amazed as we are at what he sees and hears. He knows some things we do not, but he misunderstands other things and has to be corrected, even rebuked, by the heavenly beings who appear to him. He does exactly what he is told, whether it is taking a little scroll from the hand of a gigantic angel and eating it (10:8-9) or measuring the temple of God, all but the outer court (11:1-2). He writes only what he is told to write (10:4).

John responds emotionally to what happens. When he sees that no one is worthy to open the seven-sealed scroll in chapter 5, he weeps bitterly, and one of the elders in heaven tells him, "Do not weep! See, the Lion of the tribe of Judah, the Root of David, has triumphed. He is able to open the scroll and its seven seals" (5:5). Later, when he takes the little scroll, he finds it (just as he was told) "sweet as honey in my mouth, but when I had eaten it, my stomach turned sour" (10:10). When he sees the great multitude in white robes in chapter 7, an elder asks him who they are and where they have come from. He pleads ignorance, leaving the elder to answer his own question (7:13-14). When he first sees Babylon the prostitute seated on the scarlet beast in chapter 17, John wonders "with great admiration" (17:6 KJV), just as a deluded world had "wondered after the beast" in an earlier passage (13:3 KJV). He comes to his senses only when the angel who showed him the vision says, "Why are you astonished?" (17:7).

Later, when the vision has come to an end, John falls down to worship the angel and has to be told, "Do not do it! I am a fellow servant with you and with your brothers who hold to the testimony of Jesus. Worship God!" (19:10). At the end of his last vision, not having learned his lesson, John tries to worship the angel *again* and hears the angel's rebuke a second time (22:8-9).

These are some of the passages in which John functions, at least in part, as *our* surrogate. *We* are intended to share his wonder and his fears. *We* are told—twice—to worship God alone, not angels. *We* are warned not to be deceived by the splendor of Rome or any other worldly power. It is for *our* sake that the visions are explained. Sometimes John himself does the explaining, even as he narrates what he sees (4:5; 5:6, 8; 14:4-5), but other times he too is in the dark. When the visions are explained to him, *we* benefit as well (as in 7:14-17 and 17:7-18).

In short, the author has presented himself not in a formal way, as if he were writing a real autobiography, but as a literary character telling a story over which he himself has only limited control. We get to know him only as what literary critics call an "implied author," for we know only as much about him as he wants us to know. At the same time, he wears the mantle of an "implied reader" by reacting to what he sees and hears in the way he expects *us* to react. Reading his work, we follow in his tracks, learning from both his example and his mistakes.

"John," then, is the implied author and doubtlessly the real author as well. But who is "John"? The simple answer is that we do not know. Church tradition as far back as the second century identified him as John the apostle, brother of James and son of Zebedee, one of four fishermen whom Jesus called by the Sea of Galilee when he began his ministry (see Mk 1:16-20). Justin Martyr called him "one of the Apostles of the Christ" (*Dialogue with Trypho* 81.4), and Irenaeus cited him as "John the Lord's disciple" (*Against Heresies* 4.20.11). An anonymous second-century prologue to Luke's Gospel claimed that "John the Apostle, one of the Twelve, wrote the Apocalypse in the Isle of Patmos and after this the Gospel." Around A.D. 200, Hippolytus asked rhetorically, "Tell me, O blessed John, Apostle and pupil of the Lord, what have you seen and what have you heard about Babylon?" (*On Antichrist* 25-26).

John does *not* so identify himself. His original readers needed no further introduction, and he supplied none. At least one ancient Christian writer, Dionysius, a fourth-century bishop of Alexandria, concluded that the book of Revelation was the work of another John who lived in Ephesus, "a holy and inspired person," but not the apostle (Eusebius, *Ecclesiastical History* 7.25.1-26). John's own vision of "the twelve names of the twelve apostles of the Lamb" on the twelve foundations of the holy city (21:14) implies a certain generational distance between him and the original apostles. Clearly he regarded himself as one of the "saints and prophets" (16:6; 18:24) and consequently "a holy and inspired person." If he was not from Ephesus, he was at least known to the Christian communities in that part of the world. To this extent Dionysius's conclusion fits the facts as we know them.

□ The Social World of the Revelation

Church tradition has spoken about the date as well as the author of Revelation. Irenaeus claimed that John's great vision was "seen not long ago, but almost in our own time, at the end of the reign of Domitian" (*Against Heresies* 5.30.3; compare Eusebius, *Eccesiastical History* 3.18.3). Since Irenaeus wrote toward the close of the second century, and the emperor Domitian's reign ended in the last decade of the first, the testimony sounds exaggerated. But Irenaeus is probably comparing John's "recent" prophecy with those of such ancient biblical prophets as Jeremiah and Daniel.

In any event, the testimony of Irenaeus has tended to fix the date of Revelation at around A.D. 96. The book has seemed to many readers to presuppose the active persecution of Christians by the Romans. This reading fosters the assumption that widespread oppression or persecution took place during the reign of Domitian (between A.D. 81 and 96; see, for example, Case 1920:1-54). Yet there is no historical evidence for such oppression. This could mean either that the book of Revelation was not written at that time or that the book does not presuppose an actual, ongoing crisis.

The latter conclusion is finding increasing acceptance among recent interpreters. Any minister who has preached a series of sermons on the messages to the seven churches knows that these congregations were not unlike Christian congregations today, whether in the situations they faced or in the prevailing attitudes with which they faced them. Persecution was a possibility (though not yet an actuality) for three of the congregations (Smyrna, Pergamum and Philadelphia), but divisions and false teaching *within* the respective faith communities seem to have posed a more serious threat (at Pergamum, for example, and Thyatira), with complacency representing the worst threat of all (especially at

Ephesus, Sardis and Laodicea).

Complacency is rarely a problem for a persecuted community. The fact that one martyr from the recent past can be singled out by name in one congregation (Antipas at Pergamum, 2:13) is a clue that martyrdom was not yet a common experience among the book's first readers. Something close to a consensus exists that "Revelation does not seem to have been written in response to an obvious, massive social crisis recognized as such by all Christians, not even a regional one" (Yarbro Collins 1984:98; also Thompson 1990:171-201). Instead of an actual persecution or crisis, the book addresses a *perceived* crisis, and the author's perception is not even shared by all his readers. To a considerable extent, it is a wake-up call to Christians who do not sense that they are in any particular danger—a tract for our times no less than John's.

The enemies of God—the dragon of chapter 12, the two beasts of chapter 13, and Babylon the prostitute in chapter 17—are within as well as outside the Christian congregations. It is not a matter of "us against them," in which all who are within the Christian community are secure and all who are outside it are doomed. Such a scenario would only foster the complacency John is trying to undermine. Rather, John's visions describe the last chapter of the ancient conflict between good and evil, inviting the readers to stand beside God and the Lamb against the forces of evil, even to the point of martyrdom. The book of Revelation promises victory not to everyone in the Christian congregations, but to "those who overcome," or conquer (2:7, 11, 17, 26; 3:5, 12, 21; 21:7; compare 12:11; 15:2), just as Jesus conquered (3:21; 5:5; compare 17:14).

But how did Jesus conquer? In two ways: through being "slaughtered" as God's sacrificial Lamb (5:6 NRSV) and through his own "testimony," whether understood as the testimony he bore or the testimony of his followers about him (see 1:2, 9; 12:17; 19:10; 20:4). Jesus himself is "the faithful witness," or martyr (1:5; 3:14). In his final victory over the armies of the beast and the false prophet he is called "Faithful and True" (19:11) and bears the name "the Word of God" (19:13; compare 19:9; 21:5). Accordingly, "those who overcome," or conquer, are those who "follow the Lamb wherever he goes" (14:4) and are "called, chosen and faithful" (17:14). Having been conquered at first by the forces of evil (13:7), they become conquerors in turn "by the blood of the Lamb and by the word of their testimony" (12:11). They are redeemed by Jesus' blood (1:5; 7:14), not their own, and yet the book provides ample evidence that many of them, like the Lamb, are "slain," or slaughtered (6:9; 18:24; compare 16:6; 17:6; 20:4). Their "testimony" (Greek *martyria*), like that of Jesus, is a testimony sealed by death. Whether all of them are actually martyred or not, their faithfulness must be proven in a setting in which martyrdom is a distinct possibility.

This conclusion leads many to assert that the situation presupposed in the book is more like the one faced by persecuted Christians in the Third World than the one experienced by Christians in the industrialized West, but there is no clear evidence that this is the case. The fact that John views his readers as potential martyrs and as combatants in a great war between God and Satan does not mean that they saw themselves in those terms, any more than most Western Christians do today. Martyrdom for Christ is not high on our list of fears or aspirations at the close of the twentieth century. We are more worried about random violence in the streets, and certainly more worried about our health and our financial security than about bloody persecution at the hands of some anti-Christian tyrant.

It is easy to assume that the situation of John's original readers differed sharply from our own, that they lived out their lives in the world of John's apocalyptic visions. This is most unlikely. Despite obvious differences between John's time and our own, his visions were probably as strange to many of his first readers as they are to us. These visions are by no means a picture of the social world that John actually lived in, but rather a prolonged piercing glance *through* that world to the cosmic struggle between good and evil taking place just behind or beyond it. There is every reason to believe that if he experienced his visions today, John would look through, or beyond, our more secular, scientific world in much the same way, issuing us a similar wake-up call, however different his imagery might be.

In short, the book of Revelation gives us little information about the *actual* social world in which it was written, and consequently little information about the date of its composition. It is difficult to either prove or disprove the traditional date near the end of the reign of

Domitian. The book could have been written any time between A.D. 70 and 100, or even a bit later. Its social world is not unlike the one presupposed in 1 Peter, except that where Peter sees stern challenges to live for Christ in a hostile culture, John sees deadly dangers. Where Peter shows flashes of optimism about the possibility of being good Christians and good Roman citizens at the same time (for example, 1 Pet 2:12-17), John sees church and empire on a collision course.

Probably the differences between Revelation and 1 Peter lie as much in the authors' perceptions as in the social realities. Even Peter, after all, had his less optimistic moments in which he envisioned a showdown between faith and unbelief, with a "fiery trial" (4:12 KJV) of suffering and persecution (see 1 Pet 3:13-17; 4:12-19; 5:8-9).

In the cities of Asia Minor to which John wrote, Christians were being pressured to participate in certain social and religious activities of the trade guilds. And some of their very own prophets—supposedly in the Spirit—were doing the pressuring. To John, this meant compromising their faith in violation of the Jerusalem Council's decree (Acts 15:20, 29) forbidding Gentile Christians from "eating food sacrificed to idols and . . . committing sexual immorality" (Rev 2:14; compare 2:20). John's concern as a prophet is to combat such false prophecy by urging faithfulness to "the word of God and the testimony of Jesus Christ," probably equivalent in John's mind to the tradition handed down from "the twelve apostles of the Lamb" (21:14). Beyond this, there is little to distinguish the social world of Revelation from that of 1 Peter or most other Christian writings of the last decades of the first century. John's social world remains largely a mystery to us because it is not the subject of his book.

□ Traditional Interpretations

What then *is* the book of Revelation about? Modern historical critical scholarship has assumed it is indeed about the author's social world. This used to be called the *preterist* interpretation of the book. But we have just seen that the book sheds less light on that world than scholars once hoped. A widely held older interpretation viewed the book as a prophetic survey of the history of the world, and especially the Christian church, in the centuries between John's time and our own. This view, known as the *church-historical* interpretation, proved itself bankrupt in the course of time as interpretations of specific passages had to be revised again and again in light of the rise and fall of an endless succession of new empires.

Another interpretation, the *futurist,* is that the book of Revelation has to do with the future of the world—not what was future to John and is now past or present to us, but what was future to John and is *still* future to us. It is as if time has stood still, as if the "prophetic clock" set to go off at the end of the world shut itself off right after John finished his book and is only now ready to start ticking again—after nineteen hundred years! Such an interpretation can never be proven wrong, for when events in the world do not match the scenario of John's visions, the answer is that the events John prophesied have not yet begun to happen.

The futurist view has its detractors, yet there is much to be said in its favor. Above all, it has the virtue of immediacy in confronting the modern reader with precisely the same promises, the same threats and the same choices that the book's original readers faced. Yet it shares a drawback (at least as sometimes presented) with the church-historical interpretation, in that both views regard John's visions as a literal timetable of events that will happen on earth sometime in John's future or ours.

Virtually all commentators recognize that this view is highly implausible in regard to certain passages of the book. Few would argue, for example, that Jesus Christ will be born into the world again as a baby at some future date (12:1-6) or that John himself will return to earth someday to take a scroll from the hand of an angel and eat it (10:8-10). But, in the case of the sequences of seven seals, trumpets and bowls, the tendency to take them as a chronological blueprint of the future is still widespread. The principal disagreement among such literal-minded interpreters is whether there will be a continuous fulfillment, first of the seals, then of the trumpets and then of the bowls (twenty-one judgments in all), or whether seals, trumpets and bowls are simply three ways of visualizing *the same* seven judgments over and over again (the so-called recapitulation or reiteration theory).

The seven messages to the churches (chaps. 2-3) are not normally incorporated into such schemes because it is quite clear that they are real messages to actual first-century congregations. To interpret them prophetically or symbolically would violate the literalism that these interpreters are trying to maintain. The only exception to this is found in certain early representatives of a school of thought known as dispensationalism. They saw the seven churches of chapters 2-3 as a bridge between John's time and our own. To them, the sequence of the churches was a prophetic representation of the Christian church at every stage of its history from the apostolic era (Ephesus) down to the present (Laodicea). In effect, these dispensationalists incorporated a church-historical interpretation into their own strongly futurist framework: chapters 2-3 spanned Christian history down to the present time, while chapters 4-22 unfolded to Christians today the eschatological future. This view has all but disappeared, even among dispensationalists, who now read chapters 2-3 as pastoral messages to actual first-century Asian congregations, with legitimate applications to churches in any time period and in any part of the world.

No similar development has taken place among traditional interpreters of chapters 4-22. They continue to read these chapters more or less chronologically as a scenario for the world's future. In places where the literal timetable seems implausible, they make adjustments by invoking the principle of "reiteration" or by assuming the existence of "interludes" in John's visions. Reiteration means that the chronology repeats itself two or three times (in the sequence of the seals, trumpets and bowls, and possibly in John's vision of a millennium followed by a great battle in chapter 20, echoing the earlier battle of Armageddon). Interludes interrupt the chronological sequence with visions related to, but not actually part of, the sequence itself: for example, an anticipatory glimpse of those who will be saved in chapter 7, and a renewal of John's prophetic call and a vision of two prophetic witnesses in chapters 10-11.

The difficulty is that the text does not actually signal any such reiteration or interludes. John never makes a statement such as, "I believe I've seen something like this before" or "I have the feeling I'm entering into some kind of an interlude" (see Michaels 1992:55). At most John identifies one voice heard on one occasion (4:1) as "the voice I had first heard speaking to me like a trumpet" (compare 1:10). Such interpretive categories as reiteration and interludes are often nothing more than creations of modern readers trying to make sense of John's visions as a kind of videotape of present and future events. This is not always the case (see, for example, Giblin 1994:94), but when the book of Revelation is read simply as a faithful record of *what John saw,* not as a taped preview of future events, such devices are of little help in outlining or structuring the visions.

In his first vision, John was told to write "the things you have seen, and what they are, and the things that are going to happen afterward" (1:19; for this translation, see discussion in the commentary). "The things you have seen" makes up most of the book, a series of visions introduced by "I saw" or "I heard." "What they are" refers to interpretive comments either by John himself or by certain heavenly voices explaining the meaning or significance of what he has seen. "The things that are going to happen afterward" are explicit predictions, in the future tense, woven into the fabric of the visions. These predictions are what should be taken "literally" in the book of Revelation. There are fewer of them than is usually assumed (see, for example, 5:10; 7:16-17; 11:3, 7-10; 12:5; 14:13; 21:3-8, 24-27; 22:3-5, etc.) and they consist of implications drawn from what John has seen, rather than visions that are complete in themselves. Surprisingly, they are just as common (if not more so) in the "present-oriented" messages to the churches in chapters 2-3 as in the more "future-oriented" chapters 4-22 (see, for example, 2:5, 7, 10, 11, 16, 17, 23, 26-27, 28; 3:3, 4, 5, 9, 10, 12, 16, 20, 21).

The qualified literalism that I am proposing requires that these explicit predictions of the future be taken as just that. It does not require that everything John saw or heard in his visions is similarly predictive. John's visions were his, not ours and not those of some future generation at the end of the world. Nothing in the book promises or threatens that all these visions are going to be reenacted some day on the earth. Rather, they are dramatic images whose purpose was to teach John how to counsel his readers in his day and to teach us how to face the power of evil in our world, whatever form it may take.

Just as chapters 2—3 are now read (much like Paul's letters) as pastoral messages to first-century congregations with implications for other churches in many different times and places, so chapters 4—22 should be read as a series of first-century visions containing promises and warnings to Christian believers always and everywhere. They remind us, for example, that the world we live in is a battleground between good and evil, that in heaven the battle is already won, and that Jesus Christ, the Lamb of God, is now in control (chap. 5). Troubles and disasters on earth are actually part of the divine plan, represented symbolically by the breaking of seven seals and the opening of a scroll (chap. 6). The devil is active on earth deceiving the nations because he was defeated and thrown out of heaven (chap. 12), not because he ever prevailed over God. Christians will confront the devil's futile anger in the form of an oppressive state that calls them to worship a human being rather than God (chap. 13). In John's situation the oppressive state was Rome. But even after Rome is destroyed, the devil deceives the nations again, as the conflict repeats itself (chap. 20).

Regardless of time and place, regardless of the order of events or the name of the oppressor, what is required of Christians is neither accommodation on the one hand nor armed resistance on the other, but patient endurance of suffering and faithfulness to Jesus Christ the Lamb, even to the point of death (2:10; 13:9-10). On these points most traditional interpretations of the prophecy are agreed. They part company and become problematic only when they try to move on from here to more sweeping and ambitious conclusions about the future of the world.

□ The Structure of the Visions

The notion that the book of Revelation is a blueprint of the world's future makes it seem presumptuous to offer any kind of definitive outline. But once we recognize that we are dealing simply with what John saw and not with the literal course of future events, we are more free to let the visions speak for themselves. Prophets in the New Testament customarily spoke and acted in, or with, the Spirit (1 Cor 12:3, 9; 14:2, 15, 16; Eph 3:5; 5:18). John mentions two occasions when he came to be in the Spirit (1:10; 4:2), and two more when he was taken away in the Spirit to see a particular vision (17:3; 21:10). These four uses of "in the Spirit" (Greek *en pneumati*) punctuate the book as a whole, dividing it into four main sections (1:9—3:22; 4:1—16:21; 17:1—21:8 and 21:9—22:15), preceded by an introduction (1:1-8) and followed by a conclusion (22:16-21).

After the title, or heading (1:1-3), and an epistolary introduction

(1:4-8), the first major section (1:9—3:22) consists of a vision on the island of Patmos "in the Spirit on the Lord's day" (1:10 NRSV), in which the risen Jesus appears to John in the form of an angel (1:9-20) and dictates to him a series of seven messages to congregations in Asia Minor (chaps. 2-3). In the second section, John is taken "in the Spirit" up to heaven and shown the heavenly temple and the throne room (4:1-11), where a slaughtered Lamb appears and takes a seven-sealed scroll from "the right hand of the one seated on the throne" (5:1-14 NRSV). The Lamb breaks open the seals one by one, and each time he breaks a seal something spectacular happens. The last three seals are set apart somewhat from the first four, which are grouped under the imagery of four horses and their riders speeding across the earth (6:1-8). The fifth, sixth and seventh seals introduce three distinctive, and progressively longer, segments of the vision: the fifth affords a glimpse of Christian martyrs on earth beneath the altar of God in heaven (6:9-11); the sixth reveals the end of the world as we know it amid earthquake, darkness, wind and falling stars (6:12—7:17); the seventh spells out these disasters at much greater length in the form of further sequences of judgments introduced by seven angels blowing trumpets and seven more pouring bowls of wrath on the earth (8:1—16:21).

The trumpet series, triggered by the breaking of the seventh seal, is itself part of the content of the seventh seal. There *is* reiteration or recapitulation of sorts in that the seventh seal does not represent a great advance beyond the sixth in finality or intensity. This seal, with the trumpet series it contains, is simply an elaboration or expansion of the sixth seal. But John's visions do not simply reenact the sequence of the seven seals from the beginning. Essentially the trumpets begin where the seals leave off. It is not what is normally meant by reiteration.

Like the seals, the seven trumpets can be divided between the first four and the last three. The first four (8:7-12) affect four distinct areas of the environment: the earth with its grass and trees, the sea with its sea creatures and ships, fresh water with the life it provides and the sun, moon and stars with the light they give off day and night. The last three (8:14—16:21) are introduced solemnly by an eagle (or vulture) overhead, crying "Woe! Woe! Woe to the inhabitants of the earth, because of the trumpet blasts about to be sounded by the other three angels!"

(8:13). Like the last three seals, the last three trumpets become progressively longer and more complex, as "the inhabitants of the earth" on the one hand, and Christian believers on the other, are increasingly affected. The fifth trumpet, or "first woe" (9:12), introduces a plague of locusts with the sting of scorpions over the earth (9:1-12).

The sixth trumpet, or "second woe" (9:13—11:14), introduces an even more fearful invasion, demonic horses with tails like serpents, which fails to bring people to repentance. It is followed by a renewal of John's prophetic call and the appearance of two prophetic witnesses whose martyrdom and resurrection finally impel the onlookers to repent and glorify God (see 11:13). Within the events signaled by the sixth trumpet, we are reminded that we are still within the trumpet series by an explicit anticipation of the seventh trumpet (10:7). We are reminded of the preceding series as well, for the scroll now stands open (10:2, 8-10), proving that the last of its seven seals has been broken.

The seventh trumpet, or "third woe" (11:15—16:21), encompasses yet a third series of judgments, "the seven last plagues" (15:1), or "the seven bowls of God's wrath" (16:1). The link between the trumpets and the bowls is less clear than the link between the seals and the trumpets, for the angels with the seven bowls do not appear immediately. The transition is marked by notices that a temple, or sanctuary *(naos),* was "opened" *(anoigē)* in heaven (11:19; 15:5). Between the opening of "God's temple in heaven" (11:19) and the opening of "the tabernacle of the Testimony" in heaven (15:5), the seventh trumpet introduces three great "signs" in heaven (*sēmeion,* 12:1, 3; 15:1): "a woman clothed with the sun" (12:1-2), "an enormous red dragon" that attacks the woman and her offspring (12:3—14:20), and "seven angels with the seven last plagues" (15:1—16:21). These three signs or portents within the seventh trumpet are the nearest thing to a true interlude to be found anywhere in the book. They, apparently, are what is meant by "the mystery of God" to be "fulfilled, as he announced to his servants the prophets" (10:7 NRSV), and by the notice that John himself "must prophesy again about many peoples, nations, languages and kings" (10:11).

The first two signs (12:1—14:20) encompass yet another series of angels harvesting the earth (14:6-20), while the third (15:1—16:21) corresponds roughly to the trumpet series out of which it comes. The main difference is that several of these "last plagues" build on some of the intervening material about the beast from the sea and its war against the people of God (chaps. 13-14). As the series draws to a close, John is indeed prophesying "about many peoples, nations, languages and kings," just as the angel who gave him the open scroll said he would (10:11; see, for example, 16:12-14).

In contrast to both the seal and the trumpet series, these last plagues do not get progressively longer. There is nothing even remotely resembling an interlude between the sixth bowl and the seventh, for the judgments of God are now hastening toward their conclusion. The seventh bowl, which completes the seventh seal and the seventh trumpet, introduces a loud voice from the temple in heaven shouting, "It is done!" (*gegonen,* 16:17). The accompanying "flashes of lightning, rumblings, peals of thunder and a severe earthquake" (v. 18), the disappearance of islands and mountains (v. 20), and "huge hailstones of about a hundred pounds each" (v. 21) recall similar phenomena in connection with both the seals and the trumpets (see 6:12-17; 8:5; 11:19). What is new is that the judgments, universal in scope and increasingly intense, now center on a particular place—"great Babylon," or "the great city" (v. 19). We have heard the name "Babylon" only once before, in the pronouncement of an angel in 14:8, "'Fallen! Fallen is Babylon the Great, which made all the nations drink the maddening wine of her adulteries.'" This Babylon now becomes the focus of God's wrath on the whole world and on all "the cities of the nations" (v. 19), and she has not even been formally introduced!

The third occasion on which John finds himself "in the Spirit" introduces the third major section of the prophecy (17:1—21:8). One of the angels in the preceding sequence of seven takes him "in the Spirit" to the desert, where he sees a vision of "Babylon the great" as a prostitute seated on a scarlet beast and then a vision of Babylon's destruction (17:1—19:10). The part of the vision mediated by the angel ends when John falls down to worship the angel and is told not to (19:10). But the vision itself continues with the defeat and judgment of Babylon's allies—first the beast and its cohort, the false prophet (19:11-21), then the dragon who deceived the nations (20:1-10) and finally death and Hades, with all the dead whose names were not written in the book of life (20:11-15). With the death of death, the way is open to eternal life, and an echo of the terrible words, "it is done" (*gegonen,* 16:17), is heard now in a context of life and salvation: "See, I am making all things new" (21:5 NRSV), and "it is done" (*gegonan,* 21:6). But because the vision has been from the start a vision of judgment, it ends with a grim reminder of the lake of fire and those who are in it (21:8).

The fourth and last main section of John's prophecy (21:9—22:15) is parallel in structure to the third. Again one of the angels who poured the seven bowls takes John away "in the Spirit," this time to a "mountain great and high," to show him "the Holy City, Jerusalem, coming down out of heaven from God" (21:10). The vision of the city ends with another attempt to worship the angel, who again warns John not to do so (22:8-9). The vision continues, this time more briefly, with the angel's few last words of exhortation about being within or outside the holy city (22:10-15). The conclusion consists of a final invitation and a warning attributed to Jesus (22:16-20), as well as an epistolary salutation (22:21).

Our discussion of structure yields the following outline, one of many that can help the reader understand the book of Revelation. While not identical with the simpler one that displays the contents in this commentary (pp. 42-44), it bears comparison with one I proposed earlier (Michaels 1992:69-71). The outline represents in some ways a more consistent development of the ideas embodied in that previous effort:

I. Heading or title (1:1-3)
II. Epistolary introduction (1:4-8)
III. John in the Spirit on the Lord's Day (1:9—3:22)
    A. John's call (1:9-20)
    B. The seven messages (2:1—3:22)
        1. Ephesus (2:1-7)
        2. Smyrna (2:8-11)
        3. Pergamum (2:12-17)
        4. Thyratira (2:18-29)
        5. Sardis (3:1-6)
        6. Philadelphia (3:7-13)
        7. Laodicea (3:14-22)
IV. John caught up in the Spirit to heaven (4:1—16:21)

- A. John's vision of heaven and the seven-sealed scroll (4:1—5:14)
- B. The seven seals (6:1—16:21)
    - 1. The first four seals: four riders (6:1-8)
    - 2. The fifth seal (6:9-11)
    - 3. The sixth seal (6:12-7:17)
        - a. Cosmic upheaval (6:12-17)
        - b. The 144,000 (7:1-8)
        - c. The unnumbered crowd (7:9-17)
    - 4. The seventh seal (8:1—16:21)
        - a. Silence, prayers and seven trumpets (8:1-5)
        - b. The trumpets (8:6—16:21)
            - (1) The first four trumpets (8:6-13)
            - (2) The fifth trumpet, or first woe (9:1-12)
            - (3) The sixth trumpet, or second woe (9:13—11:14)
                - (a) The angels at the Euphrates: no repentance (9:13-21)
                - (b) The renewal of John's call (10:1-13)
                - (c) The two witnesses: repentance (11:1-14)
            - (4) The seventh trumpet, or third woe (11:15—16:21)
                - (a) The open temple in heaven (11:15-19; compare 15:5)
                - (b) The three great signs in heaven (12:1—16:21)
                    - (i) The woman (12:1-2; compare vv. 4-6, 13-17)
                    - (ii) The dragon, his allies, and his opposition (12:3-14:20)
                        - The dragon (12:3-17)
                        - The beast from the sea (13:1-10)
                        - The beast from the earth (13:11-18)
                        - The lamb on Mount Zion (14:1-5)
                        - Seven angels and a harvest (14:6-20)
                    - (iii) The seven last plagues (15:1—16:21)

V. John taken in the Spirit to the desert (17:1—21:8)

- A. John and the angel (17:1—19:10)
    - 1. The woman and the beast (17:1-6)
    - 2. The angel's interpretation (17:7-18)
    - 3. The judgment of Babylon (18:1—19:9)

4. Conclusion (19:10)
B. The judgment of the two beasts and their armies (19:11-21)
C. The judgment of the dragon (20:1-10)
D. The judgment of the dead (20:11-15)
VI. John taken in the Spirit to a mountain (21:9—22:20)
A. John and the angel (21:9—22:9)
1. Description of Jerusalem (21:9-14)
2. Measurement of Jerusalem (21:15-21)
3. The city's light and life (21:22—22:5)
4. Conclusion (22:6-9)
B. Prophecies of the angel (22:10-15)
C. Jesus' final promises and warnings (22:16-20)
VII. Epistolary conclusion (22:21)

□ The Theology and the Ethics of Revelation

This book is among the most theological in the New Testament, yet its theology has been strangely neglected by most efforts to reconstruct a New Testament theology (Bauckham 1993 is a commendable exception). No New Testament writing emphasizes more strongly the sovereignty of God. None has a higher Christology, if by "high" we mean a Christology that places Jesus Christ on a level with God as the proper object of Christian worship.

Is it also trinitarian? Richard Bauckham argues that it is (1993:23-25), on the basis of the trinitarian form of John's epistolary greeting: "Grace and peace to you from him who is, and who was, and who is to come, and from the seven spirits before his throne, and from Jesus Christ" (1:4-5; contrast Paul's standard two-part formula, "Grace to you and peace from God our Father and the Lord Jesus Christ"). But it is hard to be sure. Later in John's visions these seven spirits of God are identified with seven lamps in front of the throne of God (4:5), and with the seven eyes of the Lamb. As the Lamb's eyes, they are "sent out into all the earth" (5:6). Jesus is the one who has the seven spirits (that is, who holds them in his hand, along with the seven stars, or angels of the seven congregations, 3:1).

Such imagery suggests (1) that the seven spirits, like the seven stars, are strictly subordinate to Jesus and are under his control and (2) that their proper sphere of activity is earth, not heaven. They are part of the heavenly throne scene, but only a minor part. If they represent the Holy Spirit, it is not as the third person of the Trinity defined by later Christian theology, but as the power and voice of Jesus *within* the Christian communities to which John wrote—presumably the prophetic spirit, or voice of the Christian prophets in the congregations. There are seven spirits, presumably, because there were seven congregations, yet in the seven messages to the congregations the Spirit repeatedly addresses all seven at once (see 2:7, 11, 17, 29; 3:6, 13, 22). The Spirit (singular) speaks twice more in the book of Revelation, both times from earth rather than heaven and from within rather than outside the congregations. The first is an affirmative response (like an "amen") to a voice from heaven (14:13). The second, and last (22:17), is also a response, this time to the voice of Jesus: the Spirit joins with the bride (that is, the people of God on earth) to invite the thirsty to "come" and receive the "water of life" that Jesus gives. In short, there is a strong emphasis on the Spirit in the book of Revelation that is compatible with later Christian trinitarianism, though not quite identical with it.

If there is some ambiguity about John's view of the Spirit, there surely is none about the centrality of Jesus Christ and of Christology. Revelation is the only book of the New Testament claiming to come directly from Jesus. If at one level it is a letter from John (1:4), ultimately it is a "revelation of Jesus Christ" (1:1), not in the sense that it is *about* Jesus (it is only partially so), but in the sense that it is a revelation *given by* Jesus. Its theology is the theology of Jesus himself, and its Christology is Jesus' own Christology.

Moreover, if we view the Bible as God's canonical self-revelation, and if we assign any significance to the canonical order of books, then the book of Revelation is God's *final* word of theology to God's church. After the title or heading (1:1-3), the full name "Jesus Christ" occurs only once more, three verses later, where "Jesus Christ" is further identified in a way that summarizes his entire redemptive ministry: "the faithful witness, the firstborn from the dead, and the ruler of the kings of the earth" (1:5). With these few words, John concisely reminds us of Jesus' life and death on earth, his resurrection and his universal lordship. From then on, he is always simply "Jesus" (1:9; 12:17; 14:12; 17:6; 19:10; 20:4;

22:16), except at the very end, where he is "Lord Jesus" (22:20, 21). Clearly the simple *Jesus* throughout the book does not refer just to Jesus' human life on earth, but presupposes the whole sweep of his redemptive work as set forth in 1:5. Actually it presupposes more, for it includes his preexistence as well (see 1:17; 2:8; 22:13; and probably 3:14).

The starting point for John's understanding of Jesus is the Jewish expectation of the Messiah, or Anointed One, from the line of David, king of Israel. This ancient hope is presupposed already in 1:5 (see note at 1:5 in commentary), where each phrase applied to Jesus is drawn from the messianic Psalm 89, about God's covenant with David. It is also presupposed in 5:5, where the only one who can open the seven-sealed scroll is said to be "the Lion of the tribe of Judah, the Root of David" (compare 22:16; also, perhaps, echoes of the messianic Psalm 2 in Rev 2:27-28; 12:5; 19:15).

But the ancient Jewish hope is transformed in characteristically Christian fashion: the "firstborn" of Ps 89:27 becomes "firstborn from the dead" (1:5), in light of Jesus' resurrection, while the messianic Lion becomes a "slaughtered" Lamb (5:6 NRSV) in light of Jesus' sacrificial death. The image of the Lamb serves to remind us that Jesus is not always named in the book of Revelation. He wears two "disguises," which long familiarity with the book has taught Christian readers to penetrate somewhat automatically: (1) an angelic figure who looks like a human being (1:13) and (2) the Lamb. The latter, like the traditional lamb of sacrifice (compare Is 53:7), is silent throughout the book. The former, like other interpreting angels in John's visions, speaks freely as God's messenger.

Although he is never called an "angel," Jesus first appears to John as one "like a son of man" (1:13), a phrase used elsewhere in the book to describe an angel (14:14; compare 21:17, where angels and humans are assumed to be of similar size and appearance). In John's opening vision, the one "like a son of man" identifies himself unmistakably as Jesus with the words, "Do not be afraid. I am the First and the Last. I am the Living One; I was dead, and behold, I am alive forever and ever! And I hold the keys of death and Hades" (1:17-18). Then he goes on to make the longest uninterrupted speech to be found anywhere in the book, dictating seven messages to Christian congregations in Asia Minor

(1:19—3:20).

When he appears again near the end of the book (19:11-16), he is recognizably the same figure, with the same two-edged sword coming out of his mouth, representing his power of speech (19:15; compare 1:16). Even his name bears out this impression: "the Word of God" (19:13). Unlike other angels in the book, he accepts John's worship (1:17), giving evidence that he is not simply John's "fellow servant" (contrast 19:10; 22:8-9), but is himself God. Clearly the repeated command, "Worship God!" (19:10; 22:9), is not meant to exclude the worship of Jesus (see commentary, note on 19:10). Jesus is the *one* "angel" (in the sense of divine messenger) who is worthy of Christian worship. Other angels are *his* messengers or surrogates in that what they say is what he says (see 22:10-15) and what they do is what he does: executing judgment (for example 14:6-20), or more specifically, coming on a cloud (14:14; compare 1:7) and treading the winepress of God's wrath (14:19-20; compare 19:15).

The same is true of Jesus as the Lamb. Just as God is "worthy *[axios]* . . . to receive glory and honor and power" (4:11), so too is the Lamb (5:12). Whether the two act together and are worshiped together (5:13; 6:16; 7:9-10; 14:4; 21:22-23) or whether the "Lord God the Almighty" is mentioned alone (as in 4:8; 11:17; 15:3; 16:7; 19:1-6), the effect is the same. In two instances (22:1, 3) they even occupy the same throne! Despite the obvious Jewishness of John's imagery, it is hard to imagine anything more offensive to Jewish monotheism than these visions of the sovereign God sharing honor, glory and a throne with an *animal,* a ritually clean animal with noble sacrificial associations, but an animal nonetheless.

The Lamb, of course, is a symbol, evoking the sacrificial death of Jesus on the cross and the distinctly Christian experience of cleansing from sin by his blood (see 1:5; 5:9; 7:14; 12:11; 22:14; compare 1 Jn 1:7). At the same time, by placing the Lamb alongside God on the throne, John's visions make the point that the sacrificial victim is none other than God himself. The victim is the victor. The Lion and the Lamb are one. The Jewish messianic hope is transformed into two seemingly contradictory assertions: the Messiah is a dying messiah, and yet the Messiah is God! Where in the New Testament, or anywhere else, do we come any closer than this to the heart of the Christian mystery? As Charles Wesley asked in wonder, "Amazing love! how can it be that Thou, my God, shouldst die for me?"

The book of Revelation shows this amazing love in action, but always behind the scenes. Love is not conspicuous in the visions themselves. While the book mentions Jesus' love for his people (3:9; 20:9) and attributes his redemptive death to that love (1:5), it does not dwell on love as the motivation for God's saving work in the same way or to the same extent that John's Gospel and 1 John do. Only twice does it mention mutual love as a Christian responsibility, and where it does (2:4, 19), this love is placed in the context of hard work, faithful service and patient endurance of suffering. Faithfulness or loyalty to God and the Lamb, even to the point of death (2:10), is the virtue dominating the ethical demand of the book of Revelation. The highest expression of love among Christian believers is that "they did not love their lives so much as to shrink from death" (12:11). To love is to "follow the Lamb wherever he goes" (14:4).

Love in the book of Revelation is a binding commitment between God and the people of God—not so much a romance as a marriage! Ethics is grounded in what theologians call "ecclesiology," the doctrine of the church, from *ekklēsia,* the Greek word for "church" or "congregation." When I was a small child, I asked my mother if Jesus was ever married. She answered that the bride of Christ was the church. Naturally I had a difficult time picturing the big stone cathedral on North Salina Street in Syracuse as a bride!

The notion of the church as the bride of Christ probably comes as much from Paul's letter to the Ephesians (5:25-27) as from the book of Revelation. While the word *bride* never occurs in the Ephesians passage, the Greek word *ekklēsia* in Revelation always refers to specific local congregations, never to the worldwide Christian community. Yet Jesus does have a bride, or wife, in this book, even though she is not explicitly called "the church." If anything, John's imagery is even more incongruous than the childish picture I had in my mind! For one thing, the bridegroom is a *lamb* (19:7-8) and for another, the bride is not a literal woman but a *city* (the new Jerusalem, 21:2, 9-10)! As Robert Gundry has pointed out (1987:254-64), "the holy city Jerusalem" is not a place, but a people—John's version of the universal church.

The marriage relationship between the Lamb and the bride comes to expression in the language of God's ancient covenant with Israel: "See, the home of God is among mortals. He will dwell with them as their God; they will be his peoples, and God himself will be with them" (21:3 NRSV; compare Lev 26:11-12; Ezek 37:27). That the early Christians applied such covenant language to Gentile as well as Jewish believers is clear from Paul's words to the congregation at Corinth: "For we are the temple of the living God. As God has said, 'I will live with them and walk among them, and I will be their God, and they will be my people'" (2 Cor 6:16). A distinctive touch in the book of Revelation is that the covenant promises are for his "peoples" (plural, as in the NRSV), not simply his "people" (as in the NIV). The language recalls 7:9, where John saw a multitude from "all tribes and peoples and languages, standing before the throne and before the Lamb" (NRSV; see commentary at 21:3).

For Paul, the inclusion of Gentile Christians in the covenant had implications for their relationship to the old vices of the Graeco-Roman world and, therefore, a negative as well as a positive side. "Do not be yoked together with unbelievers," he wrote, "for what do righteousness and wickedness have in common? Or what fellowship can light have with darkness? What harmony is there between Christ and Belial? What does a believer have in common with an unbeliever? What agreement is there between the temple of God and idols?" (2 Cor 6:14-16). After the positive recital of the covenant promises quoted above, Paul resumes the negative tone with a warning to "come out from them and be separate" and to "touch no unclean thing" (v. 17). But he ends with a promise, "I will receive you" and "I will be a Father to you, and you will be my sons and daughters" (6:18; compare Rev 21:7). He summarizes with an exhortation: "Since we have these promises, dear friends, let us purify ourselves from everything that contaminates body and spirit, perfecting holiness out of reverence for God" (2 Cor 7:1).

Students of Paul have wondered about this strange juxtaposition of the positive and negative implications of the new covenant, debating whether or not 2 Cor 6:14—7:1 is authentically Pauline and whether or not it belongs in its present place in 2 Corinthians. In any case, what is clear is that the same juxtaposition is found in the book of Revelation. Here too the implications of the profound covenant relationship between God and God's people are spelled out negatively as well as positively. Regarding evil Babylon, John hears a voice from heaven say, "Come out of her, my people, so that you will not share in her sins, so that you will not receive any of her plagues; for her sins are piled up to heaven, and God has remembered her crimes" (18:4). The lake of fire is full of "the cowardly, the unbelieving, the vile, the murderers, the sexually immoral, those who practice magic arts, the idolaters and all liars" (21:8; compare 22:15).

To a considerable degree, the ethical requirements of the book are negatives. Christians are *not* to "defile themselves with women" (14:4), *not* to practice sexual immorality or eat food sacrificed to idols (2:14, 20), and *not* to lie (see 14:5; compare 3:9; 21:8, 27; 22:15). But we should not conclude from this that the book of Revelation is only concerned with laws and prohibitions. From all these prohibitions we can infer two dominant positive counterparts: (1) sexual and ritual purity, both as virtues in themselves and as symbols of religious faithfulness, and (2) honesty or truthfulness. These twin virtues are the virtues of Jesus, whose very name is "Faithful and True" (19:11; compare 21:5; 22:6 KJV), and they are the heart and soul of the ethics of the book of Revelation. Faithfulness and honesty are the basis of every good marriage and every family. Here they are the basis of the covenant marriage of the Lamb and his bride—or if you will, of the covenant family consisting of God and all of God's sons and daughters (21:7; compare 2 Cor 6:18).

□ Preaching the Gospel from the Book of Revelation

There is every reason to preach from the book of Revelation as we approach the dawn of the third millennium. The first rule for preaching from this book is not to stop after the first three chapters. It is easy to confine our preaching to those chapters, using the messages to the seven congregations to browbeat our own congregations. It is just as easy to use chapters 4-22 to browbeat contemporary society. But the book is a unity, and it should be approached as such.

The seven congregations to which the book was written were not experiencing persecution, and neither is the church, for the most part, in America and Europe today. The greatest danger they faced was complacency, and the greatest danger we face is complacency. The whole book is for the world, and the whole book is for the church. As we have just seen, "the unbelieving, the vile, the murderers, the sexually immoral, those who practice magic arts, the idolaters" (21:8) are all thrown into the lake of fire, where Christians think they belong. But along with them, at the beginning and the end of the list, are "the cowardly" and "liars," which includes many inside as well as outside the church. I once read this verse to a class of seminarians, only to be caught up short by laughter at the phrase, "all liars," at the end of the verse. But then I realized how incongruous it must have sounded, after listing a motley crew of murderers, fornicators and idolaters. And yet it was true. There is no such thing as a "little white lie" in the book of Revelation. If we are liars, if we are not what we pretend to be, all the guns of the book of Revelation are aimed squarely at us, and it is the task of the preacher to point this out.

John wrote his visions and prophecies to be read aloud and consequently heard (1:3), not perused silently on a printed page. One major task of the preacher is to help recapture the book's *orality,* so that the church can share to some small extent in John's experience and in the experience of believers in the seven congregations, who heard it read aloud. At the very least, this means that the preacher should feel free at times to read extensively from the book without comment, letting John's words and the words he heard from heaven do their work. John was a prophet and a seer and a storyteller. The preacher today may not be a prophet or a seer, but can and should be a storyteller. The "story" the preacher should tell is John's story, consisting of *what John saw,* not what the preacher thinks is going to happen in the future. After all, the preacher knows what John saw, but does not know the precise circumstances of all that will happen in the future.

The one thing the preacher *does* know about the future, based on the book of Revelation, is that it brings good news. Whatever else it is, this book is *gospel,* and anyone who would preach the gospel must preach the book of Revelation. Most of us are accustomed to using the word *gospel* in relation to events that happened in the distant past—Christ died for our sins, was buried, and rose from the dead (1 Cor

15:3-4). The book of Revelation is gospel about the future. Catholic, Protestant and Orthodox all recognize that if the gospel is not about the future as well as the past, it is no gospel at all. Many a billboard on many a rural, fundamentalist church in America carries the inscription, "We preach Christ crucified, risen and coming again." Similarly, the Catholic liturgy includes the lines, "Christ has died. Christ is risen. Christ will come again." The future, no less than the past, is part of the Christian gospel, and has been from the very beginning of the Christian movement (see, for example, the accent on future hope in the earliest of all Christian writings, 1 Thessalonians).

But what about the present? A gospel about the past is no gospel unless if affects the present. That Christ died, even for our sins, is not good news unless Christ rose from the dead. And even the good news that Christ rose is no gospel unless we know that he rose never to die again and lives as sovereign Lord. We must be assured that the God who raised Jesus from the dead is *still* at work among us. Similarly, a gospel about the future is useless if the future does not impinge on the present in which we live. The future-oriented gospel in the book of Revelation passes this test. John's visions assure us that the God of the future is *already* at work among us. In chapters 5-6 the troubles on earth represented by the seven seals are evidence that God and the Lamb are at work breaking the seals and bringing the day of vindication closer. In chapters 12-13 the intensity of the devil's activity on earth is evidence that he has already been defeated in heaven. The triumphant future governs the present, not merely in the subjective sense of giving us hope but also in the sense that God is at work *now,* bringing the future to realization, even (and indeed especially) in events that seem to be the work of the enemy.

The clearest and most concise statement of this distinctive gospel, or good news, in the book of Revelation comes near the end of the book, where "the one seated on the throne" finally speaks directly and without symbolism: "I am making everything new" (21:5), and, "It is done" (21:6). The gospel contained in John's visions is itself a kind of vision that the preacher must try to communicate to those who read or hear the book today. It is akin to Paul's vision in 2 Corinthians 5:17: "So if anyone is in Christ, there is a new creation: everything old has passed away; see, everything has become new" (NRSV). John, like Paul, knows that this vision has not literally come to pass. The risen Jesus who speaks to John knows exactly where we live, "where Satan has his throne" (2:13). But the preacher's task, like John's and like Paul's, is to help us look *through* present circumstances to see "a new heaven and a new earth" and "the Holy City, the new Jerusalem, coming down out of heaven from God, prepared as a bride beautifully dressed for her husband" (21:1-2). This is the gospel of the book of Revelation—or as John would put it, "This is the word of God and the testimony of Jesus."

Outline of Revelation

1:1-3	**The Title**
1:4-8	**The Greeting**
1:9-20	**The Opening Vision**
2:1—3:22	**The Seven Messages**
2:1-7	The Message to Ephesus
2:8-11	The Message to Smyrna
2:12-17	The Message to Pergamum
2:18-29	The Message to Thyatira
3:1-6	The Message to Sardis
3:7-13	The Message to Philadelphia
3:14-22	The Message to Laodicea
4:1—5:14	**The Throne Scene in Heaven**
4:1-11	The Throne and Its Surroundings
5:1-14	The Seven-Sealed Scroll and the Lamb
6:1—8:5	**The Seven Seals**
6:1-8	The Opening of the First Four Seals
6:9-11	The Opening of the Fifth Seal
6:12—7:17	The Opening of the Sixth Seal

8:1-5 ______ The Opening of the Seventh Seal

8:6—11:19 ____ The Seven Trumpets
8:6-13 _____ The First Four Trumpets
9:1-12 _____ The Fifth Trumpet, or First Woe
9:13—11:14__ The Sixth Trumpet, or Second Woe
11:15-19 ____ The Seventh Trumpet, or Third Woe

12:1-17 ______ Two Great Signs and Their Interpretation
12:1-6 _____ The Two Signs
12:7-17 _____ The Interpretation of the Signs

13:1-18 ______ The Two Beasts and Their Deception
13:1-10 _____ The Beast from the Sea
13:11-18 ____ The Beast from the Earth

14:1-20 ______ The Firstfruits and the Harvest
14:1-5 _____ The Redeemed of the Earth
14:6-20 _____ The Harvest

15:1—16:21 ___ The Seven Last Plagues
15:1-8 _____ The Third Great Sign in Heaven
16:1-7 _____ The First Three Bowls of Wrath
16:8-9 _____ The Fourth Bowl
16:10-11 ____ The Fifth Bowl
16:12-16 ____ The Sixth Bowl
16:17-21 ____ The Seventh Bowl

17:1—19:10 ___ Babylon and Her Destiny
17:1-7 _____ The Vision of the Woman and the Scarlet Beast
17:8-18 _____ The Angel's Interpretation
18:1-3 _____ The Bright Angel's Announcement
18:4-20 _____ The Voice from Heaven
18:21-24 ____ The Angel with the Millstone
19:1-8 _____ The Rejoicing of Heaven and Earth
19:9-10 _____ John and the Angel

19:11-21 _____ The Battle
19:11-16 ____ The Mounted General

19:17-21 ____ The Grim Invitation and Its Outcome

20:1-10 ______ The Millennium

20:1-3 ______ The Imprisonment of the Dragon, or Satan
20:4-6 ______ The Reign of the Martyrs
20:7-10 _____ The Release of Satan

20:11—21:8 ___ From the Old Creation to the New

20:11 _______ The Judgment of the Old Creation
20:12-15 ____ The Judgment of the Dead
21:1-8 ______ The New Creation

21:9—22:15 ___ Jerusalem and Her Destiny

21:9-21 _____ The Vision of the City
21:22-27 ____ John's Interpretation of the Vision
22:1-5 ______ The Vision of the River of Life and Its Interpretation
22:6-15 _____ John and the Angel

22:16-21 ______ Conclusion

COMMENTARY

□ The Title (1:1-3)

We expect books, stories, articles and poems to have titles. A title is a kind of invitation to read, and publishers try to help their authors think up catchy titles that will sell their books. Bible readers take it for granted that the books of the Bible have titles too—not catchy, but informative. The title is supposed to tell us what the work is (for example, a Gospel, as the early Christians called their accounts of Jesus' life and teaching, or a letter or sometimes just a book) and often who wrote it (for example, the Gospel of Mark or the letter of Paul to the Romans). The last book of the Bible is known simply as the book of Revelation, or the Revelation of John, or sometimes the Apocalypse, or the Apocalypse of John (*apocalypsis* being the Greek word for "revelation"). No one expects it to be called "The Late Great Planet Earth" or "God's Great Tomorrow"!

Few Bible readers are aware that most biblical books did not originally have titles at all. They simply began, said what they had to say, and ended. The titles were added in very early manuscripts, but the authors themselves did not bother to attach them. There are a few possible exceptions, depending on how the opening words are interpreted. Some have argued, for example, that "The beginning of the gospel about Jesus Christ" in Mark 1:1, and "The book of the generation of Jesus Christ" in Matthew 1:1 (KJV) are titles. Revelation is probably the clearest New Testament example of a work that does give itself a title. Its title is not "The Revelation of John," for these words were supplied by later scribes who copied the manuscript. The real title is very long, like some obscure eighteenth-century religious tract. It is emphatically *not* a catchy title. In fact, it comprises all of the first three verses of chapter 1! If there is a short title, it has to be the simple phrase with which the longer one begins, "the revelation of Jesus Christ."

This revelation has the form of a letter, the longest letter in the New Testament (1:4—22:21). But the title, or heading prefixed to the letter, makes it clear from the start that this is no ordinary letter from a Christian leader to a group of churches. It is a letter from heaven, a prophetic revelation from Almighty God! While the voice that speaks in the letter is John's voice, the voice that speaks in the long title is anonymous. It could be John. But if so, John is distancing himself from his own persona by referring to himself in the third person as his servant John. It could also be an individual Christian or a Christian community that is "publishing" John's long letter after the fact for a wider audience. Quite simply, there is no way to be certain. As far as we know, the voice that speaks in the extended title is not heard again, for the rest of the book (1:4—22:21) stands complete as a letter. It has the customary beginning (1:4-6) and ending (22:21) of early Christian letters, like Paul's or Peter's.

The Revelation of Jesus Christ (1:1) The word *revelation* never occurs again in the book that has come to bear that name. Every other time the book refers to itself, it is as a *prophecy* (v. 3; compare 22:7, 10, 18) or a "book of prophecy" (22:19). *Revelation* should therefore be understood in much the same sense as in 1 Corinthians 14:6, 26, where Paul lists "a revelation" among the things prophets in early Christian congregations received from God in the Spirit—along with knowledge, prophecy, teaching (v. 6), a psalm, a teaching, a tongue, an interpretation (v. 26).

Paul uses the phrase "revelation of Jesus Christ" in Galatians 1:12

Notes 1:1 The Greek word for "revelation" is often transliterated into English as "Apocalypse." As G. E. Ladd points out (1972:20), "This word 'apocalypse' has been taken from John's revelation by modern scholarship and applied to the genre of Jewish-Christian literature called 'apocalyptic.'" But there is no evidence that this author was consciously

(NRSV) to refer to the divine message he had received, and by virtue of which he became apostle to the Gentiles. Both in Galatians and here in Revelation the phrase "revelation of Jesus Christ" tells us primarily where the revelation comes from, not what it is about. It is a revelation given by Jesus Christ from heaven, now that God has raised him from the dead. Much of it, of course, will also be about Jesus, but above all the title is saying that the book is from Jesus.

If Jesus is the immediate source of the revelation, God is its ultimate source. God gave the revelation to Jesus Christ to show it in turn to *his servants.* The point is much the same as in John's Gospel, where Jesus insists again and again that the words he speaks are not his own words, but the words of "him who sent me" (for example, Jn 7:16-17, 28; 8:28; 12:49-50). The decisive fact that Jesus has been raised from the dead does not mean that his role as God's Agent or Revealer is over. Quite the contrary! He has a great deal more to say to his followers (compare Jn 16:12), but now he will say it through *his servants,* and in particular through *his servant John.*

The Nearness of the End (1:1) If Jesus Christ is the giver of the revelation, its content is summed up in the phrase *what must soon take place* (compare 4:1; 22:6). It is a message about the future, and everyone is curious about the future. This is the fascination and the appeal of the book of Revelation. The phrase, "what will happen," or take place, is found in another biblical book concerned with the future, the book of Daniel (see 2:28-29), where it refers to the sovereign plan of God. But now it is a matter of *what must soon take place.* One little word makes a big difference! *Soon* anticipates the announcement to follow that *the time is near* (v. 3; compare 22:10). In Daniel it was a matter of what must happen "in days to come," while here the momentous events are *soon* (as in Christ's repeated promise that "I am coming soon" in Rev 2:16; 3:11; 22:7, 12, 20).

Much of the flavor and excitement of the book of Revelation is traceable to this fervent conviction that the end of the world is near.

---

attempting to write "apocalyptic literature" according to established models (his only real models seem to have been the biblical prophecies of Daniel and Ezekiel). It is preferable not to carry the Greek word over into English as "apocalypse," but to translate it as "revelation" (see introduction).

Many Christian readers and preachers today downplay that conviction in light of the fact that nineteen hundred years have passed, and the expected end has not come. Christians tend to get nervous about any implication that the Bible might be mistaken. Yet a great deal is lost when the striking words *soon* and *the time is near* are not given their proper force. The conviction that the end of the world is near is what makes the book of Revelation larger than life.

Anyone who has faced the prospect of imminent death, whether from illness or accident, and then recovered knows how precious life then seems. The colors of the world are brighter and its contrasts sharper. Everything around us is etched more deeply than before in our senses and in our memories. When we assume that life will go on forever, one day often blurs into another, but when we are reminded that it has an end, every moment and every perception can come alive. Samuel Johnson once said that the prospect of one's own imminent death "wonderfully concentrates the mind," while the verdict of one character on the murdered grandmother in Flannery O'Connor's well-known story, "A Good Man Is Hard to Find," is that "she would of been a good woman . . . if it had been somebody there to shoot her every minute of her life" (O'Connor 1988:153).

Such is the eschatological perspective of the book of Revelation: living every moment as though it were our last. This perspective pervades the entire New Testament, beginning with John the Baptist (Mt 3:2, 7-10) and continuing with Jesus (Mk 1:15 par. Mt 4:17), Paul (Rom 13:11-12), James (5:8), Peter (1 Pet 4:7) and John (1 Jn 2:18). But nowhere is it so consistently in evidence as in this last New Testament book. Far from covering life with a shroud of gloom, the intense awareness of the end of all things infuses the book's imagery with sharpness and rich color. The announcement that "the time is near" provokes not resignation or a feeling that nothing matters, but on the contrary a kind of jubilation at the preciousness of life and at the world God created and will create anew in the events that *must soon take place*. For the writer of this book and for his readers, the time of the end will be a time of new beginning.

The Visions and the Angel (1:1) The revelation will be given in pictures as well as words, for Jesus will *show his servants* what is going to happen. Again we are reminded of the Gospel of John, where Jesus "shows," or makes visible in the world, that which the Father has shown him (compare Jn 5:20; 10:32; 14:8). But there are differences. In John's Gospel the "servants"of Jesus become his "friends" by virtue of the revelation they receive (Jn 15:15), while in the book of Revelation they will remain "servants" to the end, even in the new Jerusalem (22:3). Another difference is that in the book of Revelation an angel is introduced as an additional link in the chain. The revelation proceeds from God to Jesus Christ through the angel to one servant in particular, named John. The long letter of "John" comprises the remainder of the book.

Who is this angel and, more importantly, who is "John"? The two are seen together near the end of the book. At the end of John's final vision of the new Jerusalem (21:9—22:5), the angel who "showed" him the vision in all its detail (21:9, 10; 22:1) concludes with the solemn assurance, "These words are trustworthy and true" (22:6). This angel is "one of the seven angels who had the seven bowls full of the seven last plagues" (21:9; compare 15:1, 6), which one we are not told. When the angel has finished speaking, another voice adds by way of summary, "'The Lord, the God of the spirits of the prophets, sent his angel to show his servants the things that must soon take place'" (22:6). An angel identified in a similar way (17:1) plays much the same role in a preceding vision of God's judgment on "Babylon the prostitute" (17:1—19:10), concluding with a similar assurance from the angel that "these are the true words of God" (19:9).

Here at the beginning of the book the angel is still unidentified, and he will play no recognizable role in John's early visions. Only in the two later visions will the reader come to know the angel by what he does for John as revealer and interpreter. Yet so important is the angel in John's experience that John twice falls down to worship him (19:10; 22:8) and has to be reminded that the angel is merely a "fellow servant with you and with your brothers the prophets and of all who keep the words of this book. Worship God!" (22:9; compare 19:10). If we are reading the book for the second time, we may sense that the closing scenes of John's visionary experience are still fresh in his mind as he begins to write. He has learned not to confuse the messenger of God with God himself, yet he cannot forget the messenger.

Most of us are not that perceptive in our reading, however, and many of us (like the original readers) may be reading the book of Revelation for the first time. To us the angel is simply an angel, lending to these opening lines a touch of mystery and anticipation. Angels are not a familiar part of our world today, even among devout Christians. When I was in college, a friend from high school then studying for the Russian Orthodox priesthood asked me if I believed in angels. Being a new Christian, I said I did, not because I had given the matter much thought but because I felt this was the proper answer. My friend was surprised at my reply, telling me he that had never before met a Protestant who believed in angels. The fact is, however, that we cannot make much sense of the book of Revelation without believing in angels, or, if we cannot quite bring ourselves to believe, we must at least make a conscious effort to suspend our disbelief in order to participate fully in the story.

The Testimony of John (1:2) "John" is identified only as one who *testifies to everything he saw.* The title makes no claim that John was a creative writer or a literary or religious genius. He simply transcribed a vision. What John saw is summed up in the twin phrases, *the word of God and the testimony of Jesus Christ.* These phrases reiterate the assertion in verse 1 that God is the ultimate source and Jesus is the immediate source of all that is going to be revealed. The *word of God* and the *testimony of Jesus Christ* are not two messages, but one. *Word of God* recalls the message of the biblical prophets (compare "word of the Lord" in Jer 1:2, 4; Ezek 1:3; Hos 1:1; Joel 1:1; Jon 1:1; Mic 1:1; Zeph 1:1; Hag 1:1; Zech 1:1; Mal 1:1). Like many of those oracles, it is based on what someone "saw" (Is 1:1; Ezek 1:1; Amos 1:1; Obad 1:1, Mic 1:1, Nahum 1:1). Now, however, the *word of God* is identified with the *testimony of Jesus Christ* because it is by virtue of Jesus' resurrection from the dead that John will be called and commissioned to write (compare vv. 12-18). The prophets' "word of the Lord" becomes in this last book of the Bible the word of the risen Jesus.

1:2 According to the NIV, John *testifies,* but the Greek verb is aorist, or past tense: he "testified." The heading looks back on John's completed letter (1:4—22:21) after the fact.

The Beatitude (1:3) The title concludes with the first of seven beatitudes to be found in the book (the other six occurring in 14:13; 16:15; 19:9; 20:6; 22:7, 14). The fact that there are precisely seven of these pronouncements is probably coincidental, not stemming from John's fascination with the number seven. John's use of the beatitude form shows familiarity with the written or oral traditions behind the Gospels, if not with the Gospels themselves (see, for example, Mt 5:3-12; Lk 6:20-23). The beatitude found here corresponds to one attributed to the risen Jesus in Revelation 22:7: "Blessed is he who keeps the words of the prophecy in this book." Both recall the saying of Jesus found in Lk 11:28: " 'Blessed rather are those who hear the word of God and obey it.' " The difference is that in Revelation the beatitude refers to a written document. The blessing, therefore, is first on *the one who reads the words of this prophecy* (that is, aloud to a Christian congregation), and second on *those who hear it and take to heart what is written in it* (that is, the congregation to whom the letter is read).

It is easy to forget that among the early Christians almost no one owned any portion of what is now considered Scripture. Even whole congregations were fortunate if they owned more than one of the Gospels. The only access that ordinary Christians had to the Gospels and letters that now make up the New Testament was public reading in worship services. The public reader therefore performed a ministry to the congregation far beyond what is normally the case today (compare 1 Thess 5:27; Col 4:16). The beatitude here is the author's way of saying, "Make sure you have this prophecy read in your worship assemblies! Make sure you listen and pay attention to your reader! And above all, make sure you act on what you have heard!"

The urgency of the implied command is accented by the decisive statement that *the time is near.* Almost at the end of the book, the same phrase points up the contrast between this prophecy and the book of Daniel: the words given to Daniel were "closed up and sealed until the time of the end" (Dan 12:9), while the words given to John are not to be sealed "because the time is near" (Rev 22:10). For John and his readers

John "testified" by writing this letter, and his testimony is now complete. A more accurate translation would be "who testified to everything he had seen."

the lateness of the hour demanded that his letter not be a closed book but a disclosure, an actual revelation open for all to read, understand and obey. With the passage of nineteen hundred years, it is tempting to assume that the time came and went long ago and nothing happened, or that the time is far off and the book is sealed up again, like Daniel, until some distant "last day." In either case, the book of Revelation becomes irrelevant and, like most irrelevant things, is left to "experts," whether we define them as professional biblical scholars preoccupied with a distant past or as confident television preachers preoccupied with an imminent, yet somehow theoretical, future. It is time to reclaim the book of Revelation for those who read it and for those who hear it read in church, and above all for those prepared to take its message to heart. Only in the conviction that somehow "the time" is as near as ever can John's letter still be read as larger than life and vivid in its sights and sounds.

□ The Greeting (1:4-8)

We all like to get letters, preferably letters addressed to us personally, not simply to "Occupant." Anyone who has lived away from home for even a short time knows that there is no substitute for a personal letter from home and loved ones. On the other hand, we have all experienced the annoyance of receiving letters that bear our name, yet come from people or corporations that know nothing about us. In the age of the laser printer, such deceptions are common, and we no longer give them a thought.

John's letter is a form letter of sorts too, but with no such deception. In verses 4-6, John follows the precedent of virtually every one of the letters of Paul (he will end like Paul too; see 22:21). First is the author's self-identification (*John*); second, an identification of those to whom the letter is written (*the seven churches in the province of Asia*); third, a formula introduced by the words *grace and peace;* and finally an expression of praise to God, in Paul's case a thanksgiving or a blessing, in John's a doxology: *To him who loves us and has freed us from our sins by his blood . . . to him be glory and power forever and ever! Amen.* John differs from Paul only in appending to his doxology two prophetic pronouncements (vv. 7-8) identifying the letter as a work of prophecy and introducing its major themes.

The Sender and the Recipients (1:4) *John* needs no introduction beyond what is given in verses 1-2 (as Jesus' "servant," who "testified to everything he saw"), and beyond what he will give in verse 9 ("your brother and companion"). "The seven churches of Asia" are not just any seven, but a distinct group that will be enumerated in verse 11 and addressed individually in chapters 2-3. John makes no pretense of addressing every individual in "the seven churches of Asia" personally. As far as we know, he did not even go to the trouble of making a copy for each of the seven churches. He expected the churches to share the letter by having it read in each congregation and then passing it on to the next.

The letter includes one brief section specifically aimed at each congregation, so that in effect John is allowing—even compelling—the seven churches of Asia to read each other's mail! Unlike form letters today, which look personal but are not, this form letter will turn out to be far more personal than its introductory greeting promises—uncomfortably so, in fact! Years ago there was a *Peanuts* cartoon in which Lucy asked Charlie Brown what he was reading. He said he was reading the Bible, the letters of Paul, and Lucy replied that she made it a habit never to read other people's mail. If these seven ancient churches were in some sense reading each other's mail in chapters 2-3, are we not reading someone else's mail throughout the entire book? Do these extraordinary prophecies really have anything to do with us?

This is a legitimate question, and the church began to ask it almost from the time the book of Revelation was written. One ancient Christian source appealed to the fact that both John and Paul wrote to seven churches (in Paul's case Corinthians, Ephesians, Philippians, Colossians, Galatians, Thessalonians and Romans) and cited this as evidence that both were, in effect, addressing the whole church "diffused throughout the whole globe of the earth" (*The Muratorian Canon;* Theron 1957:111). We may question the logic of this, especially when the writer claims that Paul got the idea from John. Still, the church's acceptance of the book of Revelation at the very end of its Bible—with solemn warnings in 22:18-19 against adding to or taking away from what had been written—stands as powerful testimony that John's words to "the seven churches in Asia" indeed became words to all Christian churches, always and everywhere. This development is anticipated already in the long title (vv. 1-3) prefixed to the letter proper. Certainly the beatitude on the one who reads and on those who hear and obey (v. 3) knows no limitation of time or place.

Grace and Peace, Glory and Power (1:4-8) John's *grace and peace* formula has sometimes been described as trinitarian, centering on Father, Son and Holy Spirit. This is possible if "the seven spirits of God that are before his throne" (compare 4:5) are understood as a peculiar way of referring to "the Spirit of God in the fulness of his activity and power" (Caird 1966:15). Yet John is quite capable of referring to "the Spirit" in the singular when he wishes to do so (2:7, 11, 17, 29; 3:6, 13, 22; 14:13; 22:17). Referring to the *seven spirits* is probably a way of underscoring the majesty of God, as in 4:5, where they stand as John's explanation of "seven lamps" of fire blazing before the throne, or in 5:6, where they are identified with the seven eyes of the Lamb (Jesus Christ), and are said to be "sent out into all the earth" (see also 3:2). These texts suggest that the *seven spirits* have no identity distinct from God or Christ, whether as a source of prophecy or a means of worship. John's greeting, therefore, is more like Paul's customary greeting, "from God our Father and the Lord Jesus Christ" (without explicit mention of the Spirit), than it may seem at first (compare, for example, Rom 1:7; 1 Cor 1:3; 2 Cor 1:2; Gal 1:3; Eph 1:2; Phil 1:2; 2 Thess 1:2; Philem 3). The greeting begins and ends with God, *who is, and who was, and who is to come* (vv. 4, 8), but in between focuses its attention on Jesus (vv. 5-7).

Something is missing, however, in John's formula. Unlike Paul, John accents God's power and majesty so strongly that he never calls God "our Father," only the Father of Jesus (that is, "his Father," v. 6; compare 2:28; 3:5, 21; 14:1). To know God as Father is at most a promise in the book of Revelation, even for victorious Christians (see 21:7), not a

---

1:4 It is impossible to show in English translation the oddity of John's grammar in his greeting from the one *who is, and who was, and who is to come.* The pronoun *from* (Greek *apo*) would ordinarily take the genitive case (as it does with "the seven spirits" and with "Jesus Christ"), but when the eternal God is the object, John uses a participle in the nominative case (Greek *ho ōn,* "the one who is") to show that God is unchanging. God is always the Subject, the one who acts, never one who is acted upon. Because Greek has no past participle for the verb "to be," John uses a different construction with the finite verb "was" (*ho ēn,* literally "that which was," as in 1 Jn 1:1, but here because of its use as

present reality. In this respect, Revelation is more Jewish in its perspective than most of the New Testament. Jewish piety was reluctant to approach its sovereign, transcendent God as "Father." Christians, by contrast, pray the "Our Father" almost routinely, and they are glad to claim Paul's words about praying "Abba," or "Father," in the Spirit (Rom 8:15; Gal 4:6). Yet few Christians realize the bold step they are taking in addressing the eternal God so intimately, a step they would never have taken had Jesus not taken it first and invited them to follow (compare Mk 14:36; Lk 11:2).

Some modern readers of the Bible are no more ready than John was to call God "Father." They include feminists for whom the term carries too many implications of male domination, as well as numberless men and women for whom the notion that God resembles their human fathers destroys all possibility of trusting God. The horror of child abuse and the void created by hundreds of thousands of absent or unknown fathers in our society has made the very term *father* problematic for many, both inside and outside the church. For them, the fatherhood of God belongs not to the present but to a future they are not ready even to imagine (see 21:7). If they are Christians, their God is not yet the "Abba" of Paul's letters, but "the Lord God" of the book of Revelation, *the Alpha and the Omega . . . who is, and who was, and who is to come, the Almighty* (*pantocrator,* v. 8; cf. 4:8; 11:17; 15:3; 16:7, 14; 19:6, 15; 21:22). It is fair to say that the eternal, sovereign God keeps his distance throughout the book of Revelation. But Jesus and his angels draw near on almost every page, in judgment or in love.

Jesus Christ, named in verse 5, is given three titles (*the faithful witness, the firstborn from the dead, and the ruler of the kings of the earth*), accenting each stage of Jesus' saving work, from his obedience and death on the cross to his resurrection to his final victory over human

a participle "the one who was"). Although John, in keeping with Jewish and Christian tradition, consistently uses male imagery for God ("King," "Lord," etc.), it is impossible to attribute gender to God. The eternal God of this book is far above all human distinctions, including male and female.

1:5 The three designations for Jesus Christ in verse 5 are taken from Psalm 89, where God says of "David my servant" (89:20) that "I will also appoint him my firstborn, the most exalted of the kings of the earth" (89:27) and "I will establish his line forever, his throne as long as the heavens endure" (89:29). John applies this Jewish promise of a messianic

powers and hostile armies. The first two are the presupposition of the entire book of Revelation, while the third will come to full realization in John's visions as the book draws to a close. The full name, *Jesus Christ,* occurs in verse 5 for the third and last time in the book of Revelation (compare vv. 1, 2). From here on, starting at 1:9, John will always use the simple human name, "Jesus," reserving "Christ" (in good Jewish fashion) for use as a title: "the Christ" or "the Messiah" (11:15; 12:10; 20:4, 6).

In the middle of verse 5 John abruptly breaks into song. There will be many songs and hymns in the book of Revelation, including more elaborate ones that are sung later on by the angels in heaven (see, for example, 4:8-11; 5:9-14; 7:11-12; 11:15-18; 12:10-12; 15:3-4; 16:5-7; 18:2-8; 18:21-14; 19:1-8). This, however, is a song to be sung on earth, one that the public readers of John's letter can lead their congregations in singing. Jesus remains the center of attention in this song, for it is Jesus *who loves us and has freed us from our sins by his blood* (v. 5), and *has made us to be a kingdom and priests to serve his God and Father* (v. 6). The repetition of "us" and "our" draws John and his readers together as a confessing community of faith, beneficiaries in common of Jesus Christ's death on the cross. All that Jesus has done is "for us." Christians collectively are *a kingdom and priests,* like ancient Israel (compare Ex 19:6). They are a people belonging to God, acknowledging Jesus as King, and destined to reign with him (compare 5:10; 20:4, 6; 22:5).

John's song has the form of a doxology (from the Greek word *doxa,* "glory" [*to him be glory and power forever and ever! Amen,* v. 6]). In Paul's letters a thanksgiving (for example, Rom 1:8; 1 Cor 1:4; Phil 1:3; Col 1:3; 1 Thess 1:2) or blessing (2 Cor 1:3; Eph 1:3) customarily followed the "grace and peace" formula. Only in Galatians, where there was no thanksgiving, did Paul introduce a doxology between an opening greeting and the body of the letter (Gal 1:5; most other New Testament

king from David's line to Jesus Christ (see Rev 5:5; 22:16) by interpreting "firstborn" as *firstborn from the dead.* John's first phrase, *the faithful witness,* echoes Psalm 89:37, where the moon is "the faithful witness in the sky" to which the line of David is compared. Psalm 89 may be in mind even in verse 6, where the phrase, "his God and Father," recalls 89:26: "He will call out to me 'You are my Father, my God, the Rock my Savior.'"

1:8 *Alpha and Omega* were the first and last letters of the Greek alphabet (like *A* and *Z* in English). The expression *I am the Alpha and the Omega* is explained by "I am the First and

doxologies conclude either a letter or one of its major sections). True doxologies normally end with "amen" (for example, Gal 1:5; Rom 11:36; Eph 3:21; Phil 4:20), but in this case John has used the "amen" to link the doxology to a prophetic pronouncement that follows (v. 7). The "Yes, Amen" at the end of verse 7 echoes the simple *Amen* at the end of verse 6 (so that v. 7 serves as a prophetic response to John's song), while at the same time introducing a final pronouncement in verse 8 by the one *who is, and who was, and who is to come.*

The subject in verse 7 is still Jesus Christ, but the accent has now shifted from past to future. Drawing loosely on two biblical texts, Daniel 7:13 and Zechariah 12:10, John dramatically announces the one event above all others that "must soon take place" (1:1), that is, the "coming" of Jesus. Like the eternal God on his throne, Jesus Christ *is to come* (vv. 4, 8). John announces it here in the third person as if he were a prophet watching it happen ("Look, he is coming"). Jesus himself will repeat it several times in the course of John's visions ("I am coming" or "I will come"), more as a warning or a threat than a promise (for example, 2:5, 16; 3:3, 11; 16:15; 22:7, 12). At the end of the book, however, John has made his peace with the sobering prospect of that coming, as Jesus says, "Yes, I am coming soon" and John answers, "Amen. Come, Lord Jesus" (22:20). Here at the outset John sees that coming in his mind's eye, and he hints at its implications for a guilty world. It will be visible to all, *even those who pierced him,* and an occasion of mourning for *all the peoples of the earth* (v. 7).

John says nothing of what that coming will mean for his Christian readers. Their hope is based rather on verse 8, where *the Lord God* becomes the Speaker: *I am the Alpha and the Omega . . . who is, and who was, and who is to come*—echoing and affirming the letter's opening words, *Grace and peace to you from him who is, and who was, and who is to come* (v. 4). Only twice in the entire book of Revelation does God

---

the Last" (22:13; compare 1:17; 2:8) or "the Beginning and the End" (21:6; 22:13), referring to God's eternal existence and preexistence (compare Is 44:6). The discovery of a "magic square" (the so-called Rotas-Sator Square) at Pompeii (destroyed in A.D. 79) suggests that "Alpha and Omega" (in its Latinized form as "A and O") was already a popular designation for God among Jews or Christians before the book of Revelation was written (see Beasley-Murray 1974:60-63).

speak directly (the other time being 21:5-8), and each time it is with the self-identification "I am the Alpha and the Omega" (see Aune 1983:280).

□ The Opening Vision (1:9-20)

Humility, or "the common touch," is a great asset for anyone aspiring to public life or a position of leadership, on two conditions. First, people must be convinced that the potential leader is not patronizing them by merely pretending to come down to their level. More is needed than empty phrases like "fellow citizens," or "my fellow taxpayers." Second, no one wants a leader who is actually, and in every respect, "just like the rest of us." The rhetoric of the common touch has its limitations.

John now provides the self-introduction he omitted at the opening of his letter. Here at the beginning of his series of visions (and once more at the end, 22:8) he refers to himself emphatically and by name as *I, John*. And he has the common touch. Instead of making a direct claim to personal authority comparable to Paul's (or Peter's) "apostle of Jesus Christ," he identifies himself to his readers simply as *your brother and companion in the suffering and kingdom and patient endurance that are ours in Jesus* (v. 9). Yet even Peter, who called himself "an apostle of Jesus Christ" (1 Pet 1:1), could appeal in the same letter to church elders as their "fellow elder, a witness of Christ's sufferings and one who also will share in the glory to be revealed" (1 Pet 5:1). To him, the warm collegiality of "fellow elder" was by no means incompatible with the authority implied by the term *apostle*.

In a similar way, John is not presenting himself simply as his readers' equal. His stance is much like that of the angel at the end of his own series of visions who revealed so much to him. When John tried to worship the angel, the angel refused worship, identifying himself as a "fellow servant" with John and his brothers the prophets, and with all

---

1:9 John uses the word *kingdom* differently here than in verse 6, where it refers to a community of people destined to reign with Jesus. Here it refers to God's dominion or rule that will one day supersede "the kingdom of the world" (11:15), but is evident already among God's people, even in their experiences of oppression and persecution (compare 12:10-12).

1:10 *The Lord's Day* (literally the "lordly," or "dominical" day; Greek *kyriakē;* compare "Lord's Supper" in 1 Cor 11:20) probably means Sunday. Ignatius, writing to the same geographical area as the book of Revelation less than two decades later, uses the word in

Christians (22:9; compare 19:10). The self-identification was necessary precisely because the angel was for John an authority figure, the reliable interpreter of everything John was shown. Similarly, John is an authority figure for his readers, one who needs no introduction (v. 4), but wants to reassure them that he is on their side and shares in their struggles. There is nothing to identify him as an apostle, but much to suggest that he is a Christian prophet. The prophets, after all, are his "brothers" (22:9), and what he writes is called a "prophecy" (1:3; 22:7, 10, 18-19).

The Voice (1:9-11) As a prophet, John immediately recounts for his readers a prophetic experience, which he is careful to locate as to place and time. The place was *the island of Patmos,* and John was there *because of the word of God and the testimony of Jesus* (v. 9; compare v. 2). The time was *the Lord's Day,* and John had gone into a prophetic trance (*I was in the Spirit,* v. 10). It is important to understand that John is not necessarily giving his present location. He is consistent with Paul and other New Testament letter writers in not furnishing a "return address" (the only possible exception is "Babylon" in 1 Pet 5:13). We cannot assume John is *still* on the island of Patmos any more than we can assume it is still "the Lord's Day" (see note at v. 10) as he writes, or that he is still in the same prophetic trance. He never mentions "the Lord's Day" again, and when he is "in the Spirit" he says so explicitly (4:2; 17:3; 21:10).

A tradition as old as Tertullian (third century) interprets the phrase *because of the word of God and the testimony of Jesus* to mean that John was temporarily banished to Patmos, possibly by a Roman provincial governor, because of his proclamation of the Christian message (Tertullian, *Prescription Against Heretics* 36; see Caird 1966:21-22). This may well be true, yet John places no emphasis on his own unique predicament and makes no appeal for sympathy or support. On the contrary,

---

this way in *Magnesians* 9.1: "No longer living for the Sabbath, but for the Lord's Day, on which also our life sprang up through him" (compare *Didache* 14.1: "on the Lord's Day of the Lord, come together, break bread, and give thanks," and the apocryphal Gospel of Peter 35 and 50, with reference to the first day of the week, when Jesus rose from the dead). Some commentators (for example, Beasley-Murray 1974:64-65) find in John's language an intentional contrast to the Roman custom of setting aside one day a month as an "imperial" or "emperor's" day, but such a motive is not explicit either in this verse or in its Christian parallels.

he calls attention to the common lot of all Christians: *in the suffering and kingdom and patient endurance that are ours in Jesus* (compare Acts 14:22; 2 Thess 1:4-5). This is understandable if his exile on Patmos is over by the time he writes (Michaels 1992:16-17).

Every other time John is said to be "in the Spirit," he is taken somewhere, whether to God's throne in heaven (4:2) or to a desert (17:3) or to a very high mountain (21:10), and is shown a vision. Here he stays where he is, on Patmos. At first he sees nothing, only hearing a voice behind him. It is *a loud voice like a trumpet* (v. 10), yet recognizably a real voice with real words, not just any sound. The voice tells him to *write on a scroll what you see and send it to the seven churches: to Ephesus, Smyrna, Pergamum, Thyatira, Sardis, Philadelphia and Laodicea* (v. 11).

Just as John's self-introduction in verse 9 supplemented his letter's opening greeting from "John" (v. 4), so his account of the voice in verse 11 spells out precisely what churches were included in the letter's address to "the seven churches in the province of Asia." The language in both places ("the seven churches") gives the impression that these seven were the only Christian congregations in the province of Asia, but this was not the case. Two others are mentioned in the New Testament (Colossae and Hierapolis, Col 1:2; 4:13), while two more (Tralles and Magnesia) are addressed, along with Ephesus, Smyrna and Philadelphia, in early second-century letters from Ignatius of Antioch. In view of the symbolic importance of the number seven throughout the book of Revelation, it is likely that these seven were intended to represent all of the Asian congregations, and perhaps all Christian congregations everywhere.

The Vision (1:12-16) When John turns and looks behind him *to see the voice* (that is, to see where it was coming from), he sees *seven golden lampstands* (v. 12) and an extraordinary figure, apparently human, which he describes in considerable detail (vv. 13-16). The figure recalls more than anything else the "man dressed in linen" seen by Daniel "on

---

1:13 The phrase "like a son of man" should not be linked to Jesus' self-designation "the Son of Man" in the Gospels (as in the NRSV, "one like the Son of Man") nor viewed as an intentional allusion to Daniel 7:13 (by the use of quotation marks, as in the NIV's *someone "like a son of man"*). The RSV is preferable to both. In Hebrew and Aramaic "a son of man"

the bank of the great river, the Tigris" according to Daniel 10:4-6. John's vision, like Daniel's, is given a precise geographical location, and the two figures have in common a golden belt or sash, a shining face, eyes like fire, feet of burnished bronze and an overwhelming voice. There are echoes of other biblical visions as well: Ezekiel's "man clothed in linen" in the Jerusalem temple (Ezek 9:2, 3, 11), Daniel's "Ancient of Days" whose "clothing was as white as snow" and "the hair of his head . . . white like wool" (Dan 7:9), and Daniel's "one like a son of man, coming with the clouds of heaven" who "approached the Ancient of Days and was led into his presence" (Dan 7:13). All of these were either representatives or representations of the God of Israel.

Despite this rich background, nothing in John's account suggests that he recognized the figure that stood before him or that he identified it with any of these figures out of Daniel or Ezekiel. None of them had been holding *seven stars,* and none had *a sharp double-edged sword* sticking out of its mouth (v. 16). Nor did John at once identify the figure with Jesus, who united him with all Christians and for whose testimony he found himself on Patmos. All he could have said was that this figure, despite its human appearance, bore with it both the majesty and the terror of Almighty God. (The pronoun *it* is appropriate because as yet the figure has no personality for John, and no definite gender. It is for him nothing more—and nothing less—than a glorious, terrifying divine Presence). Such a figure in Jewish or Christian tradition is commonly called an angel (as, for example, in Rev 10:1), and it is a fair conjecture that an angel is what John would have called it too if words had not failed him. The reader's natural (though incorrect) assumption is that this is the "angel" mentioned in the title ("He made it known by sending his angel," 1:1).

The Explanation (1:17-20) Like Daniel, John fell at the angel's feet *as though dead* (v. 17; compare Dan 10:8-9). The same right hand that held *the seven stars* (v. 16) touched him as if bringing him back to life (compare Dan 10:10). At once the angelic figure identifies itself,

is simply a man or a human being, and here the phrase is simply John's Semitic way of saying that the figure before him, in spite of its strangeness and splendor, looked human (compare 14:14). Nowhere in Revelation does John show any awareness of the Gospels' use of "the Son of Man" (with the article) as a title for Jesus Christ.

confirming the impression that John is facing a representative of "the Lord God" who had spoken in 1:8 ("I am the Alpha and the Omega . . . who is, and who was, and who is to come, the Almighty"). Echoing the words in verse 8, the angels says, *Do not be afraid* [compare Dan 10:12]. *I am the First and the Last. I am the Living One* (v. 17).

These words do not quite prepare us, however, for what follows: *I was dead, and behold I am alive for ever and ever! And I hold the keys of death and Hades* (v. 18). It is as if "the Almighty" and he who was "pierced" (1:7) and "freed us from our sins in his blood" (1:5) have merged into one. The mighty angel turns out to be Jesus himself—Jesus raised from the dead and clothed in divine splendor—but John cannot know this and we do not know it, until he so identifies himself. John had fallen to the ground *as though dead* (v. 17), but here was one who had actually been dead and had come back to life again (v. 18; compare "firstborn from the dead" in 1:5), and who consequently held *the keys of death and Hades,* the power to give life or take it away.

The self-identification, though not by name, is unmistakable. John has not only "seen" the voice (compare v. 12), but found it to be the voice of Jesus. There is no explicit acknowledgment of this on his part—no moment of recognition like Mary Magdalene's "Rabboni" (Jn 20:16) or Thomas's "My Lord and my God" (Jn 20:28)—yet the reader now knows, and John knows, that Jesus is indeed the Speaker. The angelic figure of verses 12-16 is only one of his many disguises in the book of Revelation. The whole section from verse 17 to the end of chapter 3 is one long, uninterrupted speech of Jesus, the risen Lord. Jesus takes over from John as the narrator—the "I"—from this point on until John's voice breaks in again at 4:1. Throughout chapters 2-3 John is out of the picture, listening and (presumably) writing.

Jesus repeats in verse 19 the command, "Write on a scroll what you see" (v. 11). He elaborates the command into a threefold expression understood by many translations as a reference to present and future (as NIV, *Write, therefore, what you have seen, what is now and what will take place later*). More likely, Jesus is telling John to write not only the visions he will see but whatever explanations may accompany them so as to shed light on the future: "Write, therefore, *the things you have seen,* and *what they are,* and [consequently] *the things that are going to take place after this"* (italics mine; see Introduction; also Michaels 1991:604-8; 1992:98; Stuart 1845:2.54). As if to illustrate this, Jesus immediately provides just such an explanation of two details in John's first vision: the seven stars in his right hand and the seven golden lampstands that first caught John's eye when he turned around. The *mystery* (that is, the explanation; compare 17:7) is that *the seven stars are the angels of the seven churches, and the seven lampstands are the seven churches* (v. 20). The explanatory "are" of these identifications echoes the phrase "what they are" in the preceding verse. John's responsibility is to record not only his visions but something of their meaning as well. This he has done, both here and throughout the book (see, for example, 4:5; 5:6, 8; 7:14; 14:4-5; 16:14; 17:9-18; Michaels 1991:608-20; also 1992:99-104).

A problem most of us have with the book of Revelation today is that the explanations provided within the text are often as difficult to understand as the images they are supposed to explain. For example, it is not much help to know that the seven stars in Jesus' right hand are the "angels" of the seven churches unless we know what role angels have in relation to churches. The word *angel* means messenger, and some (for example, Tenney 1957:55) have theorized that these "angels" were actually human messengers of God, either the minister or the pastor of each church—assuming churches had a single leader by this time—or a prophet, or perhaps the public reader of John's letter to the assembled congregation (see 1:3).

Everywhere else in the book of Revelation, angels are supernatural messengers, and there is no reason to make an exception here. When angels in this book are identified, it is always either in relation to whomever they serve (for example, God's angel, or Christ's, in 1:1; 3:5; 22:6, 16; "Michael and his angels" in 12:7; "the dragon and his angels" in 12:7, 9), or in relation to the realm over which they rule (for example, "the angel of the Abyss" in 9:11 or the angel "who had charge of the fire" in 14:18 or "the angel in charge of the waters" in 16:5). "Angels of the seven churches" belong to the latter group. They rule or preside over the churches just as an angel presides over the sources of fresh water or over fire or over the realm of death and destruction (compare the four angels in control of the winds "who had been given power to harm the land and the sea" in 7:2). Like these angels over various spheres of existence, the angels of the seven churches are not easily characterized as either good or evil. They share in the moral ambiguity of the congregations over which they preside, as well as in the praise and the blame that those congregations deserve (see Beckwith 1922:445).

Today, because of our love for abstraction, we find John's distinction between the angels and their respective congregations—between the stars and the lampstands—rather confusing. Many of us would be more comfortable speaking of the ethos, the atmosphere or even the spirit (in a rather secular sense) of a congregation or a community than of its "angel." Yet to John they are, quite literally, angels whom God holds responsible for the life and well-being of the congregations. Paul had referred to speaking "in the tongues . . . of angels" (1 Cor 13:1) and had urged proper conduct in worship at Corinth "because of the angels" (1 Cor 11:10). They seem to have had their greatest importance in Paul's Asian congregations (Colossae and Laodicea), and Paul is careful to point out the danger of esteeming them too highly or putting them at the center of Christian worship or religious experience (see Col 2:18). Perhaps because of such tendencies in Asia, they are not pictured here in Revelation as dwelling "in the heavenly world" (Boring 1989:86) or as the churches' "spiritual counterparts" in heaven (Caird 1966:25). They are as much a part of this world as the churches for which they are responsible. "I know where you live," says Jesus to the angel of Pergamum, "where Satan has his throne" (2:13).

□ The Seven Messages (2:1—3:22)

The seven communications to the angels (2:1—3:22) are commonly known as the seven letters of Revelation, or the letters to the seven churches. They are not letters, however, in any sense of the word. The whole book of Revelation presents itself as one long letter, as we have seen. The communications in chapters 2-3 have none of the formal characteristics of early Christian letters—no self-identification by name followed by an identification of the recipients and a "grace and peace" formula. There is no evidence that any of them ever circulated separately. Rather, they are the oracles of a prophet, given in the name of the divine Being who speaks through them (compare the eight oracles of the prophet Amos in Amos 1:2—2:16). The recurring expression "these are the words of . . ." (literally "thus says . . .") is the common Old Testament formula for introducing a prophet's message from the God of Israel: "Thus says the LORD." In the New Testament, the oracle of the prophet Agabus in Acts 21:11 is introduced by the words "thus says the Holy Spirit." Instead of "the seven letters," chapters 2-3 of Revelation should be called "the seven messages."

The messages themselves mix encouragement with threat, and scolding with praise. Nowhere is the old saying, "If the shoe fits, wear it," better demonstrated than here. Once the values presupposed by the messages are clear, each reader will know whether to find in them praise or blame. The effect of directing each message to "the angel" rather than to the church at large is that "the members of John's churches only indirectly 'overhear' the message to the church's 'angel'"(Boring 1989:87). The angel is a kind of buffer between the Speaker and the actual individuals or groups that make up each congregation. When the risen Jesus wants to single out individuals or groups, he does so in words that are either indefinite ("some of you," 2:10; "a few people in Sardis," 3:4) or in some way conditional (see, for example, the double refrain at the end of each message, "let anyone who has an ear listen" and "everyone who conquers" NRSV; such phrases as "unless they repent," 2:22, and "if anyone hears my voice and opens the door," 3:20). No individual's fate is determined by the "angel" of the church to which he or she belongs. Everyone is free to choose, there is still time to choose, and there are "overcomers" or "conquerors" in every congregation.

To this extent the situations addressed in these seven messages are interchangeable. Much that is said to any one congregation is said to all. At or near the end of each message comes the appeal to listen to "what the Spirit says to the churches" (not just this church in particular). At one point in the message to Thyatira comes a promise that "all the churches will know that I am he who searches hearts and minds, and I will repay each of you according to your deeds" (2:23). The language recalls expressions of Jesus in the Gospels, such as "let anyone with ears to hear listen" (eight occurrences) or "what I say to you I say to everyone: 'Watch!'" (Mk 13:37).

One interchangeable feature of the seven messages is the self-introduction of the divine Speaker at the beginning of each message. By this time we know that the Speaker is Jesus, but he introduces himself with a different designation each time: (1) *him who holds the seven stars in his right hand and walks among the seven golden lampstands* (2:1); (2) *him who is the First and the Last, who died and came to life again* (2:8); (3) *him who has the sharp, double-edged sword* (2:12); (4) *the Son of God, whose eyes are like blazing fire and whose feet are like burnished bronze* (2:18); (5) *him who holds the seven spirits of God and the seven stars* (3:1); (6) *him who is holy and true, who holds the key of David. What he opens no one can shut, and what he shuts no one can open* (3:7); (7) *the Amen, the faithful and true witness, the ruler of God's creation* (3:14).

There are occasional small connections between the titles Jesus gives himself at the beginning of each message and the messages themselves. In one instance he who has *the sharp, double-edged sword* in his mouth (2:12) threatens to use it (2:16); in another, he who *died and came to life again* (2:8) promises *the crown of life* as a reward for being faithful *to the point of death* (2:10); in still another, he who has *the key of David* so that *what he opens no one can shut* (3:7) immediately promises *an open door that no one can shut* to the congregation in question (3:8). These, however, are exceptions. For the most part, any of the seven self-designations of Jesus could have been used to introduce any of the seven messages. They are not based primarily on the message that each introduces, or the local situation to which that message is directed, but on John's preceding vision on Patmos and the material leading up to it.

To a point at least, these seven self-designations present a rerun, in reverse order, of certain details from John's vision. The first (2:1) recalls 1:20, the explanation of the "seven stars" and the "seven lampstands." The second (2:8) echoes 1:17-18, "I am the First and the Last. . . . I was dead, and behold I am alive for ever and ever." The third (2:12) echoes 1:16, "out of his mouth came a sharp, double-edged sword." The fourth (2:18) echoes the description in 1:14-15 of eyes "like blazing fire" and feet "like bronze glowing in a furnace," but prefaces it with a familiar title for Jesus, "the Son of God," which is not taken from John's vision—unless it is intended as the interpretation of "one like a son of man" in 1:14. The fifth (3:1) draws together "the seven spirits" of 1:4 and "the seven stars" of 1:16 and 20. The sixth (3:7) is unparalleled in John's introductory vision: while *the key of David* is vaguely reminiscent of "the keys of death and Hades" mentioned in 1:18, "the holy one, the true one" has no equivalent at all in the preceding vision. The seventh (3:14) enlarges "the faithful witness" of 1:5 into *the faithful and true witness,* but combines it with two other terms (*the Amen* and *the ruler of God's creation*), which were not found in chapter 1.

The cumulative effect of these self-designations is to reinforce the identification of the angelic figure on Patmos with Jesus Christ. Some of the titles not drawn from chapter 1 are paralleled in John's subsequent visions (see, for example, "Sovereign Lord, holy and true," 6:10; "Faithful and True," 19:11). Yet none of these later parallels are of any help on a first reading or hearing of the seven messages. They are of interest only to the bookish modern reader or scholar who pores over the book of Revelation again and again, making minute comparisons among its various passages. The same is true of the promises near the end of each of the messages to everyone who "overcomes": for example, 2:7, *the right to eat from the tree of life, which is in the paradise of God* (compare 22:2, 14, 19); 2:11, *will not be hurt at all by the second death* (compare 20:6, 14); 2:28, *the morning star* (compare 22:16); 3:5, *I will not blot your name out of the book of life* (compare 20:12, 15; 21:27); 3:12, *I will write on you . . . the name of the city of my God, the new Jerusalem that comes down from my God out of heaven* (compare 21:2, 10). Here again, scholarly readers who systematically study the book of Revelation will easily discover these parallels between the promises to the "overcomers" in chapters 2-3 and the concluding visions of chapters 20-22. They will even find it explicitly stated that the one "who overcomes will inherit these things, and I will be his God and he will be my son" (21:7).

The problem is that the scholarly reader is not the typical reader of the Revelation—or the one for whom the work was intended. As we have seen, the first readers were the few individuals who read "the words of this prophecy" aloud to their congregations. The rest of the book's recipients were only hearing what was read to them (compare 1:3). A hearer cannot know the end from the beginning, any more than John knew what was coming later in his visions. Consequently, even the modern reader must learn to read the book of Revelation as if for the first time, taking things as they come and not interpreting them in light of something remembered from a previous reading of the text. Not all the promises to the "conquerors" in the seven messages anticipate John's concluding visions in chapters 20-22. Some call forth other associations, whether from Scripture (for example, 2:28, *authority over the nations,* with a citation from Ps 2:9; 2:17; *a new name,* compare Is 62:2), Jewish traditions (*the hidden manna,* 2:17), or the customs of the Hellenistic world (*a white stone,* 2:17) or even the Gospel tradition (3:5, *I will . . . acknowledge your name before my Father and his angels;* compare Mt 10:32; Lk 12:8). Some have only very general associations in biblical literature or the book of Revelation itself (for example, 3:5, being *dressed in white;* 3:12, being *a pillar in the temple of my God;* 3:21, *having the right to sit with me on my throne*).

It is not necessary to disentangle and catalogue all these possible allusions to other texts and traditions in order to understand the varied promises to those who "overcome" in the seven messages. They all have in common the assurance of divine approval or vindication of some kind, and consequently the assurance of eternal life. They are, like the self-designations of the Speaker, basically interchangeable and by no means linked to the varying circumstances of the seven congregations. At the same time, there are things in each of the seven messages that do speak to the particular social setting of the congregation to which that message is primarily directed. These settings, and these aspects of the seven messages, must now be looked at one by one. Here the moral and religious values governing the book of Revelation are most clearly seen.

The Message to Ephesus (2:1-7) Many Americans who favor a strong work ethic are suspicious of people who sit and read the book of Revelation too much, or go on and on about the "battle of Armageddon" or the "second coming of Christ" or the "rapture of the church," as those who actually believe in such things. Such believers are often perceived, even in "Christian" America, as religious fanatics—unpredictable, unstable and not to be trusted. Even President Reagan was widely criticized

2:7 If the promise that *I will give the right to eat from the tree of life, which is in the paradise of God* anticipates the three later references to "the tree of life" in 22:2, 14, 19, then *the paradise of God* is actually the holy city of chapters 21-22, and *the tree of life* is not a single tree but a kind of tree lining either side of the river of life in that city (22:2; Kennicott

some years ago for referring to Armageddon and the coming of Christ, not because he was being too openly Christian in a public pronouncement, but because it was suggested that he might recklessly plunge the country into nuclear war. Americans, for all their religiosity, are suspicious of those who seem "so heavenly minded that they are no earthly good," since they have traditionally valued consistency, stability and hard work. And yet these values are the first ones to emerge in the book of Revelation, specifically in the message to Ephesus!

Besides being the capital of the province of Asia, Ephesus was, from a New Testament standpoint, the most important of the cities to which John wrote. The apostle Paul found there a group that had already believed in Jesus but knew only John the Baptist's baptism (Acts 19:1-7). For three years Paul made Ephesus his home (Acts 20:31), as well as his base for evangelizing the entire Asian province (Acts 19:10). Paul wrote a letter designated in some ancient manuscripts as a letter to "the saints in Ephesus" (Eph 1:2) and in others without reference to a specific location (Eph 1:2, NIV margin). Possibly this letter, called "Ephesians," was actually a circular letter to several of the same congregations that were recipients of the book of Revelation. In any event, Ephesus was also the sphere of Timothy's ministry, according to 1 Timothy (1:3; compare 2 Tim 1:18), and the sphere of the apostle John's ministry, according to later Christian tradition (for example, Irenaeus, *Against Heresies* 3.22.5; Eusebius, *Ecclesiastical History* 3.31.3; 3.39.1-7).

Whether the "John" of Revelation is the "apostle John" remembered by later writers or not, his vision places Ephesus at the head of the list of congregations to which his letter is addressed. The dominant values in the message to Ephesus are the same as those recognized and praised by Paul and others in their congregations. *I know,* says the risen Jesus, *your deeds, your hard work, and your perseverance. . . . You have persevered and have endured hardships for my name, and have not grown weary* (vv. 2-3). That the *deeds* of the Ephesian congregation were works of love is clear from what follows: *Yet I hold this against*

1747:243-45 argued that Ezek 47:8-12 is determinative for John's meaning in both passages). The reader, however, would not have grasped these subtleties at this early point in the book.

you: You have forsaken your first love. Remember the height from which you have fallen! Repent and do the things you did at first (vv. 4-5).

Such language recalls Paul's words to the Thessalonians ("We continually remember . . . your work produced by faith, your labor prompted by love, and your endurance inspired by hope," 1 Thess 1:3), as well as those of another New Testament letter possibly sent to Christians at Rome ("God . . . will not forget your work and the love you have shown him as you have helped his people and continue to help them" Heb 6:10; compare 10:32-36). The values accented in such texts are not so different from the values Americans like to claim as their own—love, generosity, hard work, courage and persistence. Despite its apocalyptic character, so foreign to our achievement-oriented society, the book of Revelation highlights these same values. Its work ethic is alive and well, even as the end of the world draws near.

Another value Americans respect, even when they do not practice it, is the ability to distinguish between a phoney and the real thing. The message to Ephesus acknowledges that the congregation has this ability: *I know,* says Jesus, *that you . . . have tested those who claim to be apostles but are not, and have found them false* (v. 2), adding that *you hate the practices of the Nicolaitans, which I also hate* (v. 6). The one sin in the book of Revelation that stands out above all others is lying, after the manner of those who pretend to be something they are not (compare, for example, 2:9; 3:9; 14:5; 21:8; 22:15). It is unclear in the present instance who the "false apostles" were and what their message was (compare Paul's opponents in 2 Cor 11:13), but in any case the Ephesians were not deceived. A decade or two later, Ignatius of Antioch would write to them that their bishop, Onesimus, had praised them because "you all live according to truth, and no heresy dwells among you; in fact you will not even listen to anyone who does not speak about Jesus Christ in truth" (Ignatius, *To the Ephesians* 6.2). "I have learned," Ignatius added, "that some from elsewhere who have evil teaching stayed with you, but you did not allow them to sow it among you, and stopped your ears, so that you might not receive what they sow" (*To the Ephesians* 9.1).

There is no way to be certain whether or not the "false apostles" at Ephesus were the same as the *Nicolaitans* (v. 6), about whom we will learn more in the message to Pergamum (2:14-15). The claim to be apostles may suggest a group sent "from elsewhere" (as Ignatius put it); the word *apostle* (Greek *apostolos*) means literally "someone sent"—a missionary or a messenger. In the case of the Nicolaitans, nothing is said as to whether they were traveling messengers or a faction within the congregation itself. There is in fact no evidence that the Nicolaitans were even present in Ephesus. The reference here could simply mean that the Ephesians frowned on their activities at Pergamum (compare 2:15).

Clearly, there was much to praise at Ephesus. The view that this congregation (perhaps along with Laodicea) is the most severely condemned of the seven (Wall 1991:69) is an exaggeration. The persistence and courage of the Ephesians in the face of outside threats had not lapsed (v. 3), and their attitude toward false teaching was exemplary. The same could not be said, however, of their love toward God and their generosity toward each other (v. 4). In Matthew, Jesus had predicted that "many false prophets will appear and deceive many people" and that "the love of most will grow cold" (Mt 24:11-12). The message to Ephesus was that it was no good to avoid the first of these warnings only to fall victim to the second. Loss of *your first love* is not primarily the death of passion, as in a stale marriage, but the failure to maintain the commitment once made to help and serve one another. Here as everywhere in the Bible, love for God and love for one another are inseparable.

For this alone the *angel* at Ephesus is criticized and is told, *Repent and do the things you did at first,* with the stern warning, *If you do not repent, I will come to you and remove your lampstand from its place* (v. 5). The lesson for all who value a work ethic is that such an ethic must be motivated by generosity, love and compassion, or it is worthless. The message to Ephesus is a message to Christians today as well. It is doubtful that the threat of the risen Jesus to *come to you and remove your lampstand from its place* was directed only to the Ephesian angel. More likely it is implicit in all seven messages, if those who "have ears" in all the churches fail to listen to what is said (v. 7). Quite simply, if they—if we—do not pay attention, we will lose our identity and cease to exist.

The Message to Smyrna (2:8-11) Smyrna was a port city with a good harbor about thirty-five miles northwest of Ephesus. The seven cities formed a natural postal route from Ephesus up the coast to Smyrna and Pergamum, and from there inland by the imperial road to Thyatira, Sardis, Philadelphia and Laodicea (Ramsay 1904:186). This is the route contemplated in John's vision, even though it is impossible to prove that the book of Revelation actually circulated in this fashion. The vision, after all, took place on the island of Patmos (1:9), and a messenger traveling by boat from Patmos would normally land either at Miletus, where Paul in his day met the Ephesian elders (Acts 20:17), or at Ephesus itself (see Acts 20:16). Ephesus is therefore the natural starting place from a literary standpoint. Yet because the actual place of writing of the book of Revelation is unknown, it is impossible to say historically which city in Asia it reached first or in what direction it circulated from there.

In any case, the first three cities (Ephesus, Smyrna and Pergamum) were rivals for power and prestige. Smyrna (the modern Izmir) laid claim on its coins to being the "first city of Asia in size and beauty" (Ramsay 1904:255), and it was indeed a city of great natural beauty. Well over a century after Revelation was written, the traveler Apollonius of Tyana urged the Smyrneans "to take pride rather in themselves than in the beauty of their city; for although they had the most beautiful of cities under the sun, and although they had a friendly sea at their doors, which held the springs of the zephyr, nevertheless, it was more pleasing for the city to be crowned with men than with porticoes and pictures, or even with gold in excess of what they needed" (Philostratus, Life of Apollonius 4.7; translation from Loeb Classical Library edition, 1.357). Smyrna had also a long history of loyalty to Rome, having dedicated a temple to the goddess Roma as early as 195 B.C. (Tacitus Annals 4.56).

There is no record of how Christianity came to Smyrna. Like the other Asian cities, Smyrna was probably reached as a result of Paul's ministry in Ephesus (compare Acts 19:10). The message to Smyrna accents the contrast between the Roman city and the congregation of Christians who

2:10 *Ten days.* For the number ten in connection with suffering or testing in Jewish tradition, see *Pirqe Aboth* 5.1-6, especially 5.3: "With ten temptations was Abraham our father tempted, and he stood steadfast in them all, to show how great was the love of Abraham

lived there. If the city was rich (as Apollonius implies), the Christian community was poor, yet had its own kind of riches (v. 9). If the city was crowned "with porticoes and pictures, or even with gold in excess of what they needed," the angel of the church in Smyrna was promised *the crown of life* (v. 10), or (in the words of another New Testament writer) the crown consisting of the "life that God has promised to those who love him" (Jas 1:12). By the early second century (a decade or two after John's visions), the congregation at Smyrna had a pastor or bishop named Polycarp. Ignatius of Antioch wrote letters, which still exist, to both Polycarp and his congregation. Polycarp himself wrote a letter to the Philippian Christians in Macedonia and (according to an account in the *Martyrdom of Polycarp*) was martyred in Smyrna in the year 156. Nowhere were the words *be faithful, even to the point of death, and I will give you the crown of life,* more aptly fulfilled than in the life and death of Polycarp.

When we were children, most of our mothers taught us not to call names. In recent years the academy, the media and the church have taken our mothers' places by urging us to be always polite and politically correct in language we use about various religious or ethnic groups. Yet the Bible is sometimes far from politically correct! There is a considerable amount of name calling, or labeling, in Jesus' teaching and in early Christianity. Nowhere is this more evident than in the book of Revelation. The message to Smyrna assumes that the congregation will soon face an outbreak of persecution, linked to a group labeled *a synagogue of Satan* (v. 9) and composed of *those who say they are Jews and are not.* Like the "false apostles" who had come to Ephesus, these bogus *Jews* are liars (compare 3:9) in claiming to be something other than what they are. Most commentators (for example, Beasley-Murray 1974:82; Wall 1991:73) identify this group as actual Jews in Smyrna who refused to accept Jesus as Messiah (compare Paul's distinction between those who are Jews "outwardly" and those who are Jews "inwardly . . . by the Spirit, not by the written code," Rom 2:28-29). The assumption is that Christians, even Gentile Christians, by the end of the first century were

our father" (Danby 1933:455). The *ten days* in the message to Smyrna may be an echo of Dan 1:12, 14, where Daniel and his companions were "put to the test" for exactly that length of time.

regarding themselves as the true "Jews," and the actual ethnic Jews as no Jews at all.

It is true that many Jews in Smyrna were deeply hostile to Christianity, at least by the mid-second century, and eagerly joined with the Romans in consigning Polycarp to the flames (*Martyrdom of Polycarp* 11.2; 12.1). Still, when the message to Smyrna speaks of *those who say they are Jews and are not* (v. 9), it is safer to take the words literally. Do we really want to put John (much less the risen Jesus) in the position of claiming that when a Jew calls himself a Jew, he is lying? Even the fine art of name calling requires fair play!

A better interpretation is that the *synagogue of Satan* consisted of Gentile Christians who had "Judaized," that is, who adopted Jewish ways or even converted to Judaism, perhaps in order to avoid persecution by the Romans (Wilson 1992:613-15). Judaism was an ancient religion, largely tolerated in Roman Asia, while Christianity, being relatively new, was regarded with suspicion by many Asians as an erratic and possibly subversive cult. Judaism may have seemed to some Christians in Smyrna a tempting haven of safety. Ignatius commented in the second century that "it is absurd to talk of Jesus Christ and practice Judaism, for Christianity did not develop into faith in Judaism, but Judaism into faith in Christianity, in which people of every language who believed in God were brought together" (*To the Magnesians* 10.3; Grant 1966:64). He also warned that "if anyone interprets Judaism to you, do not listen to him. For it is better to hear Christianity from a man who has received circumcision than Judaism from one who has not" (*To the Philadelphians* 6.1; Grant 1966:103). Such parallels from the Asian cities support the view that the label *synagogue of Satan* was directed not at Jews, but at Judaizing Gentiles. Some in the Jewish community may even have agreed with this judgment!

Possibly these Judaizing Gentiles are the "cowardly" (21:8), who at the end of John's visions find their place in the lake of fire along with other liars, as well as murderers, the immoral, sorcerers and idol worshipers. The message to Smyrna, however, focuses less on the group's cowardice or avoidance of persecution than on their *slander* (literally "blasphemy," v. 9) against Christians in that city. Like the Jews of Smyrna in Polycarp's day, they may have actually fomented persecution against others to divert attention from themselves. Whatever the range of reasons, the message to Smyrna views the *synagogue of Satan* as enemies of the Christian community in that city. The very name "Satan" meant the "Enemy" or "Adversary," as it still did after nineteen centuries (when the Ayatollah Khomeini stirred up the people of Iran by calling America "the great Satan"). The corresponding label, *the devil* (v. 10), meant the Accuser (compare 12:10), the ultimate source of all false charges against Christians before the Roman authorities.

The congregation at Smyrna, unlike the one at Ephesus, was facing persecution, imprisonment for some, even death. The heart of the message was not "repent," but *be faithful, even to the point of death,* and the command was reinforced not by a threat (as in 2:5), but by a promise: *I will give you the crown of life* (v. 10), matching the promises to those who "overcome" in all seven messages (compare v. 11). In the message to Smyrna, the *angel* is a "conquering" angel, and the Christians there a whole assembly of "conquerors."

The Message to Pergamum (2:12-17) The name calling continues in the next message. The city itself, Pergamum, once the center of a small kingdom, is here labeled a place *where Satan has his throne,* or *where Satan lives* (v. 13). One reason often suggested for this statement is that Pergamum housed a famous temple to Asklepius, the Greek god of healing, symbolized by the figure of a snake (Finegan 1981:173). An evil dragon in one of John's later visions is labeled "that ancient serpent called the devil, or Satan, who leads the whole world astray" (12:9; compare 20:2). Another possible reason for placing Satan in Pergamum is that Antipas, possibly the first Christian martyr in Asia, was killed there (v. 13), and "Satan" is simply the label attached to his persecutors (like "Satan" or "the devil" at Smyrna).

Other "bad names" are drawn from the Old Testament: *Balaam* in this message (v. 14) and "Jezebel" in the message to Thyatira (2:20). Both were foreigners linked to false prophecy in Israel. In these messages both are linked to certain prophetic groups in the congregations. Balaam in Numbers 22—24 appeared to be a true prophet who refused to utter a curse against Israel, but in Numbers 31:16, and consequently in later Jewish and Christian tradition, he was blamed for

Israel's idolatry and immorality as described in Numbers 25 (see Philo, *Life of Moses* 1.48-55; Josephus, *Antiquities* 4.126; 2 Pet 2:15-16; Jude 11). The "Balaamites" and the "Nicolaitans" at Pergamum are almost certainly not two groups but one, "Nicolaitans" being a coined nickname based on what some believed to be the Greek equivalent of "Balaam." The latter, in Hebrew, could be read as "master of the people" (*ba'al 'am*), while "Nicolaitan" in Greek could be read as "conqueror of the people."

The point at issue was not so much the conduct of the Nicolaitans as their teaching. Like Balaam of old, they were urging believers to sin *by eating food sacrificed to idols and by committing sexual immorality* (v. 14). This was a problem that had plagued the Christian movement almost from the beginning. In the book of Acts, the Jerusalem Council decided not to force circumcision on Gentile converts, provided they agreed to "abstain from food polluted by idols, from sexual immorality, from the meat of strangled animals and from blood" (Acts 15:20; also v. 29). In 1 Corinthians Paul struggled with the issue of sexual immorality (chaps. 5-7) and food offered to idols (chaps. 8-10). His letter, like Revelation, cites as examples Israel's conduct in the desert: "Do not be idolaters, as some of them were . . . We should not commit sexual immorality, as some of them did" (1 Cor 10:7, 8). Paul's argument in Romans traces all human sin back to idolatry (Rom 1:20-23, 25) and sexual immorality (1:24, 26-27). Yet Paul seems to have distinguished idolatry, in the sense of actual participation in pagan feasts (1 Cor 10:19-22), from the mere eating of food that had been consecrated for such feasts (1 Cor 8:1-6; 10:25-30).

No such distinction is evident in the decree of the Jerusalem Council in the book of Acts, nor in the seven messages of the book of Revelation. Probably the "Nicolaitans" were prophet-teachers who were urging compromise with Roman values and Roman religion in order to gain social acceptance (and avert economic disaster) in the Asian cities.

2:13 The phrase *your faith in me* is literally "my faith" or "my faithfulness" (like "my name" in the preceding clause). The point is not that Christians at Pergamum have maintained their faith in Christ as an admirable quality in themselves, but that they did not renounce Jesus and his faithful ministry toward them. "My faithfulness" is echoed in the reference to "Antipas, my faithful witness." Those faithful to the point of death, as Jesus was, are those

Probably their arguments were similar to arguments Paul encountered at Corinth: "everything is permissible" (1 Cor 6:12; 10:23); "food for the stomach and the stomach for food" (1 Cor 6:13); "we know that an idol is nothing at all in the world and that there is no God but one" (1 Cor 8:4). Paul accepted such arguments in principle, but then qualified them in such a way as to negate the conclusions his opponents had drawn from them, for example, "but not everything is beneficial" (1 Cor 6:12; 10:23); "but God will destroy them both" (1 Cor 6:13); "but not everyone knows this" (1 Cor 8:7).

The book of Revelation, by contrast, does not even give such arguments the time of day. The Nicolaitans are idolaters and immoral. It is as simple as that. The message could have stated that they would have their part in the lake of fire (both "the sexually immoral" and "idolaters" are mentioned in 21:8 and 22:15), but contents itself with Christ's threat that *I will soon come to you and will fight against them with the sword of my mouth* (v. 16; compare v. 12; 1:16). Notice that the threat is *against them,* not "against you." The angel, and presumably therefore the congregation as a whole, is not implicated in the sins of the Nicolaitans—yet! There is still time to repent. But as for the Nicolaitans, they will find themselves allied not with Christ but with his enemies in the great battle at the end of the book, and they will perish at the hand of the one with the sharp sword coming out of this mouth (19:15).

Not everything is bad in Pergamum, and not all the labels are negative. The message acknowledges that *you remain true to my name and did not renounce your faith in me* (literally "my faith"), *even in the days of Antipas, my faithful witness, who was put to death in your city* (v. 13). Antipas is otherwise unknown, but the fact that one martyr can be singled out indicates that martyrdom was not yet a common experience in the cities of Asia. The first identifiable martyr in Pergamum, possibly in all the Asian provinces, is labeled here with a term ("faithful

who are truly his (compare "those who remain faithful to Jesus" in 14:12).

2:17 The promise of *hidden manna* is based on both the Hebrew Bible and Jewish traditions. According to Exodus 16:32-34, a pot of the manna that sustained the Israelites in the desert was stored in the ark of the covenant (compare Heb 9:4). In later tradition the ark was rescued when the temple was destroyed in 586 B.C. (2 Macc 2:4-8) and hidden

witness") reserved elsewhere for Jesus (1:5; 3:14)— because he followed in Jesus' footsteps. If there is one value that emerges from the message to Pergamum, it is this "faithfulness," or firm commitment to what is right, coupled with a stubborn refusal to compromise in order to achieve respectability and status in Roman society or any other society.

The Message to Thyatira (2:18-29) For some people today tolerance is the only real virtue and intolerance the only vice. The message to Thyatira goes against the grain of modernity by setting limits to tolerance. The main criticism of the *angel* of Thyatira is that he has tolerated something—and someone—that should not be tolerated (v. 20).

Thyatira was a smaller city located further inland in the fertile Lycus River valley. Little is known of its history beyond the fact that it once belonged to the kingdom of Pergamum, and few archaeological remains have been found. Yet the message to Thyatira is the longest of the seven messages. According to Acts 16:14, Thyatira was the home of Lydia, a "dealer in purple cloth" and a "worshiper of God" whom Paul encountered at Philippi in Macedonia. The reference suggests the city's significance in connection with the dye industry, and perhaps also the relative freedom and mobility of at least some of its women in pursuing careers.

The situation at Thyatira was similar to that at Pergamum, except that the false teaching (and consequently the name calling) centers on a single individual. This is unique in the seven messages. Antipas, the only other named individual (2:13), was singled out for praise rather than scorn or condemnation. *That woman Jezebel,* by contrast (v. 20), is given not her real name but a nickname, after Israel's idolatrous queen (1 Kings 16:31; 21:25) whose terrible fate at the hands of Jehu was prophesied by Elijah (1 Kings 21:23; 2 Kings 9:30-37). The power and influence of this *Jezebel,* a self-styled *prophetess* at Thyatira, must be

---

in the earth "until God gathers his people together again and shows his mercy" (2 Macc 2:7; compare the later apocalyptic work, *2 Baruch* 6.5-10 and 29.8). The meaning of the *white stone* (or pebble) is less clear; the color white is conspicuous in the Revelation as a symbol of purity or righteousness (see, for example 3:4-5; 6:11; 7:9, 13-14). The stone is a kind of amulet, with a *new name written on it, known only to him who receives it.* It is natural to ask whether the unknown new name is that of Christ (19:12) or the believer who receives it, but to John the two amount to the same thing (see 3:12).

2:20 A few manuscripts (including Codex Alexandrinus, the single most important manuscript of the book of Revelation) add "your" to the phrase *that woman,* yielding the

viewed in light of three facts: (1) women prophesied freely in early Christianity (see, for example, Acts 2:17; 21:9; 1 Cor 11:5); (2) women often played major roles as priestesses in contemporary Roman and Eastern cults in Asia Minor; (3) the Christian Montanist movement in the same region a century later assigned conspicuous leadership roles to two prophetesses—Priscilla and Maximilla (Eusebius, *Ecclesiastical History* 5.14-19).

Clearly, Jezebel is not a true prophetess in the eyes of the risen Jesus. There is no reason to think that the book of Revelation has anything against "prophetesses," any more than against "apostles" or "Jews." But as with those who claimed to be apostles at Ephesus (2:2) or Jews at Smyrna (2:9), the implication is that Jezebel is a liar. Like the Nicolaitans at Pergamum, she was urging *sexual immorality and the eating of foods sacrificed to idols* (v. 20; compare 2:14), in other words, the violation of the decree of the Jerusalem Council. A possible further reference to that decree appears in words directed *to the rest of you in Thyatira, to you who do not hold to her teaching,* when Jesus says, *I will not impose any other burden on you* (v. 24; compare Acts 15:28, "not to burden you with anything beyond the following requirements").

The risen Jesus makes no distinction between prophets who condone idolatry and immorality and those who practice such things. He compares Jezebel to a prostitute, like the prostitute "Babylon" in chapters 17-18. She has had time to repent, but has not done so. Her punishment is to be put to bed (v. 22), "a bed of sickness in contrast with the bed of adultery" (Beckwith 1922:467). Her followers at Thyatira (*those who commit adultery with her*) still have time to repent, but are similarly in danger of intense, though unspecified, sufferings (v. 22). As for her *children,* that is, anyone who perpetuates her teaching, they will be struck dead by a plague (v. 23). Like Jezebel of old, her name and her

meaning "your wife" (with the implication that the "angel" of the congregation is its pastor or leader, and Jezebel is his wife). But as we have seen, it is unlikely that the "angels" of these congregations are human beings. Also, the four other instances of "you" and "your" (singular) in verses 19-20 would have made it natural for a scribe to slip in one more by mistake. On Jezebel as *prophetess,* it is worth noting that one ancient source from Asia Minor refers sarcastically to a male Montanist prophet living with another male as "the prophetess" (Eusebius, *Ecclesiastical History* 5.18.6). But in Jezebel's case, "prophetess" was a title she claimed for herself, not part of the name calling. It is unlikely, therefore, that *Jezebel* was male.

influence will disappear from the earth (compare 2 Kings 10:1-28).

Jezebel seems to have justified her freedom from traditional restraints by appealing to the spiritual maturity of herself and her followers. She may even have quoted Paul to the effect that "God has revealed it to us by his Spirit" and "the Spirit searches all things, even the deep things of God" (1 Cor 2:10). Possibly with Paul's statement in view, the risen Jesus announces, not just to Thyatira but to *all the churches* (v. 23), that *I am he who searches hearts and minds, and I will repay each of you according to your deeds,* adding that the "deep things" of such groups as this are not the profound truths of God, but the *deep secrets* of Satan himself (v. 24).

The angel at Thyatira is, if anything, even less implicated with the false prophets than was the angel at Pergamum. He is not charged with any of Jezebel's crimes, only with excessive tolerance of her and her partisans. In contrast to the angel at Ephesus (2:4-5), he is commended for *doing more than you did at first* (v. 19). He is not, like the angel at Pergamum, told to "repent," but simply to *hold on to what you have until I come* (v. 25). Consequently, the "coming" of the risen one is not a threat (as in 2:16), but a hope. This suggests that Jezebel and her clan may not have been an actual part of the congregation, but a separate community trying to entice away its members. As for the angel, the words of praise at the beginning of the message (*I know your deeds, your love and faith, your service and perseverance,* v. 19) are still in effect.

The Message to Sardis (3:1-6) "We have met the enemy," Walt Kelly announced a generation ago in his comic strip *Pogo,* "and he is us!" The message to Sardis lists no specific enemies, internal or external. There is no name calling—no liars, no Balaam or Jezebel, no deep secrets of

---

2:23 *I will strike . . . dead* is literally "I will kill . . . with death," but the expression is not as redundant as it sounds. "Death" is probably used here in the sense of "disease" or "the plague." The reference is not to sexually transmitted diseases, but is simply a traditional way of listing divine judgments on the world (as in 6:8, "sword, famine and plague," where again the word "plague" is literally "death").

2:26-27 The military tone of the promises at Thyatira echoes the warnings at Pergamum ("I will fight against them with the sword of my mouth," 2:16). "The Son of God" (v. 18) promises *authority over the nations*—authority the Son received from his Father—to *rule*

Satan, no synagogue of Satan, no throne of Satan. Consequently, of all the congregations in Asia, we know least about Sardis and its problems. Yet no other message is more damaging or more urgent than this one. Walt Kelly was right. Too often, when we encounter no spiritual adversaries, it is because *we* are the enemy. The only enemy named at Sardis is the angel to whom the message is addressed.

Sardis was situated almost directly south of Thyatira, in the direction of Smyrna and the sea. Its greatest days were behind it, but this once proud capital of the ancient kingdom of Lydia (later the western capital of the Persian Empire) was still, under Roman rule, an important center of the woolen industry. Abundant archaeological remains include a temple to Artemis, a huge gymnasium and the largest synagogue yet found in the ancient world, suggesting a Jewish community numbering in the thousands (Finegan 1981:177-78). A sermon of Melito, a Christian bishop at Sardis, entitled *On the Passover* (see Hawthorne 1975:147-75), testifies to a spirited, sometimes bitter, debate with this Jewish community in the second century. Yet as far as we are told, the problem of the congregation in John's time was not with the Jews, nor with the Roman Empire, nor with false prophecy, but solely with itself.

The Speaker's grim indictment of the angel at Sardis swings between overstatement (3:1) and understatement (v. 2). *You are dead* (v. 1) is a dramatic way of saying "you are spiritually asleep" (compare Eph 5:14), for the angel is then told, *Wake up! Strengthen what remains and is about to die* (v. 2). The call to awake, and to *remember, obey* and *repent* (v. 3) assumes the real possibility of change. Yet the milder-sounding words that follow, *I have not found your deeds complete in the sight of my God* (v. 2), are deliberately understated, implying that the angel's works are unacceptable to God, and therefore a failure (Beckwith 1922: 474; compare Dan 5:27, "You have been weighed

---

them with an iron scepter (vv. 26-27; compare Ps 2:7-9; Rev 12:5; 19:15). These "overcomers" are conquerors in a military sense, for they will stand alongside the risen Jesus in battle and participate fully in the victory yet to be won (see 17:14; 19:11-21). Whether the military imagery is literal or metaphorical remains to be seen.

3:2 Although the phrase *what remains* is neuter, as the translation suggests, the reference is not to things but to people. Possibly the neuter is used in anticipation of the word in verse 4 translated as "people" (Greek *onomata,* literally "names"). The Greek word for "names" is neuter, but refers there to persons (compare Acts 1:15).

on the scales and found wanting").

This message makes it clear that the angel, like any human leader, is deeply involved in the life of the congregation. The message recalls Jesus' words to the faltering Simon Peter in Luke 22:32, "I have prayed for you, Simon, that your faith may not fail. And when you have turned back, strengthen your brothers." This angel, *dead* or not, has the responsibility to *strengthen what remains and is about to die* (v. 2). He functions much like a human pastor, except that what is said to him is actually said to the congregation as a whole.

Sardis faces a threat: *if you do not wake up, I will come like a thief, and you will not know at what time I will come to you* (v. 3). Many (for example, Ramsay 1904:377-78; Mounce 1977:110-11) have tried to link this pronouncement to certain incidents in the history of Sardis, when the city was taken unawares by hostile armies. This is unlikely because (1) these incidents were centuries earlier; (2) the message is to the Christian congregation, not the city of Sardis; (3) the image of the thief in connection with a command to "watch" or "stay awake" was common in early Christianity, based on well-known sayings of Jesus (see Mt 24:43-44 par. Lk 12:39-40; 1 Thess 5:1). The warning could as easily have been directed to Ephesus or Laodicea, or to the unfaithful in any congregation.

The message to Sardis reveals nothing definite about the church's predicament beyond the fact that it is *about to die*. Only the metaphorical reference to those *few people in Sardis who have not soiled their clothes* (v. 4) offers a possible clue. They are promised that *they will walk with me, dressed in white, for they are worthy* (v. 4), a promise immediately reinforced by a word to those who "overcome," who *will, like them, be dressed in white,* whose names will not be blotted from the book of life, but rather acknowledged *before my Father and his angels* (v. 5; compare Mt 10:32-33 par. Lk 12:8-9). At Sardis, clearly, the few who had not soiled their garments were the "overcomers."

Clean, white clothing in the book of Revelation is consistently a symbol of religious and moral purity, especially in the face of persecution (see 3:18; 4:4; 6:11; 7:9, 13), while soiled or disheveled clothing, or no clothing at all, is a symbol of religious and moral impurity and shame (see 3:17-18; 16:15). It is likely that the problem at Sardis was a strong tendency to compromise Christian faith for the sake of conformity to social and cultural standards set by Asian society and the Roman Empire. This spirit of compromise was linked not to one particular faction in the Christian community (as at Pergamum and Thyatira) but to the majority. The ones who had *not soiled their clothes* had become marginalized. *They* were the small faction. This explains the severe tone of the message, but it is impossible to be more specific as to the exact nature of the compromises made at Sardis.

The Message to Philadelphia (3:7-13) In 1681, a London widow named Jane Lead took over the Philadelphian Society, a mystical, millenarian group that regarded itself as "the Germ of the commencement of the sole true Church, Virgin Bride of Jesus Christ, whose members, dispersed among the diverse Religions of the World, are soon to appear and unite with them, in order to form this pure and holy Church, such as the church of Philadelphia was at the birth of Christianity" (Schwartz 1980:4648). Even today there are preachers who regard the seven churches in Revelation as a kind of chronological portrait of the Christian church through the centuries. They seize upon the church at Philadelphia as a model for the true church—usually their own small but faithful congregation, in contrast to the mainstream but apostate "church at Laodicea"!

Philadelphia was a city of some importance founded in the second century B.C. by Attalus, king of Pergamum, in honor of his predecessor, Eumenes Philadelphus. The city was strategically situated in a fertile river valley on the main road from Sardis to Laodicea, directly east of Smyrna. The message to Philadelphia has captured the imagination of Christians through the centuries because no other message (not even the one to Smyrna) is so rich in promises. The Speaker's self-identification (v. 7) sets the stage for the first promise (v. 8), which is given unconditionally to the angel at Philadelphia and thus to the whole congregation. Like Eliakim, gatekeeper of the king's palace in Jerusalem (Is 22:20-22), he holds *the key of David,* so that *what he opens no one can shut, and what he shuts no one can open* (v. 7). Consequently, he places before the angel *an open door* (v. 8).

Preachers who claim this promise for their congregations tend to interpret the *open door* as a door to mission or evangelism, as in Acts 14:27. W. M. Ramsay (1904:391-400) called Philadelphia a "missionary city" because of its strategic location for the spread of Greek culture eastward into Lydia and Phrygia. Yet the open door in the message to Philadelphia is more likely a door into heaven (see 4:1) or into the temple of God or into the new Jerusalem (see v. 12) than a door for evangelism. The open door is simply a guarantee of salvation or eternal life, like the promises to the "overcomers" in all seven messages. Another way of saying it is that *I will also keep you from the hour of trial that is going to come upon the whole world to test those who live on the earth* (v. 10). Like the "two witnesses" in 11:12 or the child born of the woman in 12:5, they will be "raptured," or taken up to God in heaven, before the wrath of God is poured out on the earth.

The problem here, as at Smyrna, is the presence of a *synagogue of Satan,* probably a group of Judaizing Gentiles who *claim to be Jews though they are not, but are liars* (v. 9; compare 2:9). Ignatius, as we have seen, mentioned Judaizing Gentiles in Philadelphia a few decades later (*To the Philadelphians* 6.1), and John's vision here is that Christ *will make them come and fall down at your feet and acknowledge that I have loved you* (v. 9). The promise echoes such biblical passages as Isaiah 45:14, 49:23 and 60:14, in which Gentile nations come to pay homage to Israel and Israel's God. The message is a reminder that *the synagogue of Satan* are Gentiles after all, and that their present allegiance to Judaism is no more than a lie and a pretense to avoid persecution. In the end, the angel and his congregation will be vindicated against these bogus Jews, for even with *little strength* they *have kept my word and have not denied my name* (v. 8).

There are echoes here not only of Isaiah but also of Jesus' prayer for his disciples in the Gospel of John, for example (italics mine), "I have made *your name* known to those whom you gave me from the world. They were yours, and you gave them to me, and they have *kept your*

3:10 *The hour of trial* is not simply a period of persecution (as in 1:9; 2:9-10, 22), but the actual "hour" or moment in which God brings judgment on the world (compare the uses of "hour" in 3:3; 9:15; 11:13; 14:7, 15; 17:12; 18:10, 17, 19). Persecution, even "the great tribulation," at the hands of their enemies is something Christians must endure (see 7:14), but they are spared *the hour of trial* because the latter's purpose is *to test those who live on*

word" (Jn 17:6 NRSV). "Holy Father, protect them *by the power of your name*—the name you gave me. . . . While I was with them, I protected them and *kept them safe by that name* you gave me" (17:11-12). "I pray not that thou shouldest take them out of the world, but that thou shouldest *keep them from the evil"* (17:15 KJV). "May they be brought to complete unity to let the world know that you sent me *and have loved them* even as you have loved me" (17:23). The italicized words in these several quotations point to parallels in the message to Philadelphia in the book of Revelation: not only *kept my word* and *not denied my name* (v. 8), but *acknowledge that I have loved you* (v. 9) and *keep you from the hour of trial* (v. 10).

The parallels by themselves do not prove common authorship of John and Revelation, nor are they close enough to suggest that either one is using the other as a source. They may be coincidental or traceable to terminology common to early Christian prayer and preaching. They do underscore the significance of the "name" of God or Jesus in affording protection and assurance to God's people. Actually, the message to Philadelphia mentions three names, *the name of my God and the name of the city of my God, the new Jerusalem* and *my new name* (v. 12). There is probably no fixity to these names, nor any meaningful distinction among them. Later we will learn that Christ's name can be one "that no one knows but he himself" (19:12) or it can be "the Word of God" (19:13) or "King of Kings and Lord of Lords" (19:16). The redeemed bear on their foreheads "his name" (22:4) or, alternatively, "his name and his Father's name" (14:1). The effect is the same. Whether the city of God has a special name other than "the new Jerusalem" we are not told (see, however, Ezek 48:35, "and the name of the city from that time on will be: THE LORD IS THERE").

Whatever the names may be, they represent to the angel at Philadelphia security, stability and divine protection. John may have remembered Eliakim again, who was "like a peg into a firm place," and a "seat

the earth, a group clearly distinguished from the Christian community (see 6:10; 8:13; 11:10; 13:8, 12, 14; 17:2, 8). Students of the Bible who hold to what they call a "pretribulation rapture" are on good ground if they define "the tribulation" specifically as *the hour of trial* mentioned in this verse.

of honor for the house of his father" (Is 22:23), but Eliakim turned out to be a peg that would not hold (Is 22:25). Instead, the risen Jesus extends to whoever "overcomes" at Philadelphia the hope of becoming *a pillar in the temple of my God. Never again will he leave it* (v. 12). God's *temple,* or sanctuary, must be the temple in heaven, for there is no temple in the new Jerusalem (21:22). The image of being fixed as a *pillar* in the heavenly temple will come to life later in a graphic description of those "before the throne of God" who "serve him day and night in his temple" (7:15-17). In both passages, living in the temple of God becomes a metaphor for eternal salvation in the same way in which Christians have always understood the closing words of Psalm 23: "and I will dwell in the house of the LORD forever."

The Message to Laodicea (3:14-22) In Amos Niven Wilder's haunting poem, "Alien: A Period Piece" (Wilder 1972:28), a wounded stranger wanders outside a beautiful place of joy and celebration. A gentle, homeless pilgrim, he hears the music within and knows he cannot enter, but he holds no bitterness toward those who are gathered there. Wilder leaves it to us to identify the stranger, but there is no denying that the poem's imagery evokes the message of Christ to Laodicea. If the angel at Philadelphia was given an "open door" (3:8), individuals at Laodicea are told of another door, one that *they* must open: *Here I am! I stand at the door and knock. If anyone hears my voice and opens the door, I will come in and eat with him, and he with me* (v. 20). These words have often been romanticized in popular religious art, in pictures of Jesus "knocking at the heart's door." What is wrong is that Jesus is standing *outside* the door, excluded from the banquet like the homeless stranger in Amos Wilder's poem. The poignant plea, though directed first to the church at Laodicea, is strategically placed near the end of the series of messages as Christ's last appeal to *any* congregation that has shut him

3:14 Although *the Amen* as a title for Jesus is not based in any obvious way on John's opening vision in chapter 1, it could be a personalization of the "Amen" of 1:6 and the "Yes, amen" of 1:7 (compare 2 Cor 1:19-20). It is linked here to the term *the faithful and true witness* (compare "the faithful witness" in 1:5) because of the root meaning of the Hebrew verb *'man,* to "be faithful" or "remain true." Again, the last title, *the ruler* [Greek *archē,* literally "beginning"] *of God's creation,* is not taken directly from chapter 1, yet vaguely recalls two designations of Jesus in 1:5, "the firstborn from the dead" and "the ruler

out. The beautiful "invitation" is at the same time a severe indictment of a church that is self-sufficient, complacent and only marginally Christian.

Laodicea was situated southeast of Philadelphia in the Lycus River valley. Its congregation was the only one of the seven, with the possible exception of Ephesus, to receive communications both from the apostle Paul and from John of Patmos. This congregation formed a cluster with two others (mentioned by Paul, but not by the book of Revelation) at Colossae and Hierapolis, and possibly with certain other house churches in the same general area. Paul in Colossians speaks of his strenuous efforts "for you and for those at Laodicea, and for all who have not met me personally" (Col 2:1). He mentions his coworker Epaphras, who had brought the Christian message to the region (1:7) and was still "working hard for you and for those at Laodicea and Hierapolis" (4:13). He sends greetings "to the brothers at Laodicea, and to Nympha and the church in her house" (4:15), requesting that "after this letter has been read to you, see that it is also read in the church of the Laodiceans and that you in turn read the letter from Laodicea" (4:16).

From this we learn that the letter to the Colossians was intended for Laodicea as well (including a house church there in the home of a woman called Nympha) and that Paul sent yet another letter to Laodicea, possibly a letter now lost, possibly the one known as "Ephesians" or possibly "Philemon," which was addressed to a house church in the same general area in the home of a certain Philemon, Apphia and Archippus (Philem 1-2). If Revelation, like Paul's letters, was meant to be shared with other congregations beyond the seven named, the message to Laodicea may have included congregations at Colossae and Hierapolis as well (Papias, for example, bishop of Hierapolis in the second century, was apparently quite familiar with the book of Revelation; see Eusebius, *Ecclesiastical History* 3.39.12).

[*archōn*] of the kings of the earth." More clearly, it echoes two phrases from Paul's letter a generation earlier to neighboring Colossae, phrases that may still have been read and remembered in Laodicea: "He is . . . the firstborn over all creation" (Col 1:15) and "he is the beginning [*archē*] and the firstborn from among the dead" (Col 1:18). "Beginning" (KJV) or "origin" (NRSV) is a better translation than "ruler" for *archē*, but whether the expression has in view the original creation of the world or the new creation to come (compare 21:5, "I am making everything new") is uncertain. It is probably intended to evoke both ideas.

By the time Revelation was written, the Christian community in Laodicea and vicinity seems to have prospered. The angel at Laodicea is described as boasting, *I am rich; I have acquired wealth and do not need a thing* (v. 17; compare "Babylon the Great" according to 18:7). But in contrast to the angel at Smyrna, who was materially poor but rich in God's sight (2:9), this angel is *wretched, pitiful, poor, blind and naked* (v. 17; compare 18:8). His works are compared to tepid water, *neither cold nor hot. I wish you were either one or the other! So, because you are lukewarm—neither hot nor cold—I am about to spit you out of my mouth* (vv. 15-16).

The site where Laodicea once stood includes an elaborate fountain and a water tower supplied by an aqueduct from hot springs at the site of modern Denizli, four miles south. Not surprisingly, many have suggested a possible local reference here, "a play on words, contrasting what may have been the tepid water of the aqueduct at Laodicea with the possibly fresher and colder water at Colossae and with the very hot water of the cascades at Hierapolis" (Finegan 1981:182). Yet readers in any of the Asian cities, no matter how close or how far away their water supply, would have understood the metaphor. Either cold or hot water is good for something, but lukewarm water is not. The point of the rebuke is not lack of zeal or enthusiasm. If it were, "lukewarm" would at least have been better than "cold"! The point is rather the utter worthlessness of what the congregation has done and is doing. The metaphor is a more blunt and colorful way of saying what was said to the angel at Sardis: "I have not found your deeds complete [that is, acceptable] in the sight of my God" (3:2).

What must the angel do? The answer (v. 18) echoes the last three characteristics mentioned in verse 17—*poor, blind and naked.* The angel must *buy* three things. Because he is poor, *gold refined in the fire, so you can become rich;* because he is naked, *white clothes to wear, so you can cover your shameful nakedness;* because he is blind, *salve to put on your eyes, so you can see* (v. 18). The imagery of "buying" (strange to those who are poor!) recalls the great invitation in Isaiah 55:1, "Come, all you who are thirsty, come to the waters; and you who have no money, come, buy and eat! Come, buy wine and milk without money and without cost"—an invitation with which John seems thoroughly familiar (see 21:6; 22:17).

Those at Laodicea, however, are not "thirsty," but are themselves like useless water that quenches no one's thirst! They must "buy" from Jesus other things—pure gold, white clothing and eye salve. Probably *gold refined in the fire* had already come to suggest to the early Christians faith tested by persecution (compare 1 Pet 1:7), while white clothing calls to mind here, as at Sardis, the purity of those who pass the test and "overcome" (compare 3:4-5; also 6:11; 7:9, 13-14). The message to Laodicea is that the congregation needs, for its own sake, to face persecution so as to shatter its complacency and test and shape its faith. Behind this need is the principle, rooted in the experience of Jew and Christian alike, that "those whom I love I rebuke and discipline" (v. 19; compare Prov 3:12; Heb 12:6).

Before this can happen, the angel at Laodicea, like those at Ephesus, Pergamum and Sardis, must *be earnest, and repent* (v. 19). To do this, he must change his perception of what is real, and above all his perception of himself—hence the *salve to put on your eyes, so you can see* (v. 18). If he sees himself as rich and in need of nothing when in fact he is desperately poor and miserable, there is indeed something terribly wrong with his eyes! The image of eye salve is unusual, and here again many have suggested a local reference. Because Strabo (*Geography* 12.20) mentions a school of medicine near Laodicea in the first century, some have tried to link the production of a famous eye medicine known as "Phrygian powder" to Laodicea in particular (Ramsay 1904:419), but there is no conclusive evidence of this. It is doubtful that the reference is more meaningful here than it would have been in any of the seven messages.

The promise to the "overcomer" at Laodicea reveals the hidden presupposition of all the similar promises in every one of the seven messages, that is, that Jesus is himself the model for what it means to "overcome," or "conquer." The promise is, "To him [that is, to anyone] who overcomes, I will give the right to sit with me on my throne, just as I overcame and sat down with my Father on his throne" (v. 21). Those who "overcome" (or "conquer" or "triumph") in every congregation will do so in the same way Jesus did. Thus the conclusion to the seven messages sets the stage for John's subsequent visions of the triumph of

Jesus and his people over the powers of evil (compare 5:5-6).

□ The Throne Scene in Heaven (4:1—5:14)

John McPhee, in his 1965 biography of basketball great (later Senator) Bill Bradley, explains the book's title, *A Sense of Where You Are.* When McPhee asked Bradley about the mechanics of his spectacular no-look, over-the-shoulder shot, Bradley replied, "When you have played basketball for a while, you don't need to look at the basket when you are in close like this. . . . You develop a sense of where you are" (Bantam Pathfinder Edition [1967], 13). In its own way, reading the New Testament is just as demanding as playing basketball. Here too we try to develop a sense of where we are. At the end of the seven messages, it was easy to forget that we were still with John on the island of Patmos on the "Lord's Day" (1:9-10) because the risen Jesus had been speaking continuously since commanding John not to "be afraid" (1:17). Presumably John was busy writing down what he was told to write, but otherwise he had faded out of the story. He reasserts himself with the words *after this I looked* (4:1). How long *after this?* We are not told. Are we still on the island of Patmos? Is it still the "Lord's Day"? The text does not say. All we know is that a new vision is under way, introduced with the verb *I looked,* or "I saw" (Greek *eidon;* compare "I heard," 1:10, and "I saw," 1:12).

The Throne and Its Surroundings (4:1-11) As he looks up into the sky, John sees *there before me . . . a door standing open in heaven* (v. 1). If the sky was like an open window to Jesus at his baptism (Mk 1:10-11), it is like an open door to John, for a voice, the same trumpetlike voice he heard once before, beckons him to pass through the door: *Come up here, and I will show you what must take place after this* (v. 1). John stops short of narrating a full-blown heavenly journey like the journeys of such characters as Enoch in Jewish literature (see, for example, 1 Enoch 14:8-25) or even like the journey of Paul, who was

---

4:1 John's *door standing open in heaven* recalls the "open door" promised shortly before to the congregation at Philadelphia (3:8), except that the door is now open for John to ascend to heaven and receive revelation as a prophet, not to gain salvation or deliverance. This is also the purpose of the command *"Come up here"* (in contrast to 11:12, where the

"caught up to the third heaven" and "heard inexpressible things, things that man is not permitted to tell" (2 Cor 12:2, 4). All John will say is, *At once I was in the Spirit* (v. 2), just as in the introductory vision on Patmos (1:10). There he was "in the Spirit" first and then heard the voice; here it is the other way around. Nowhere have we been told when or under what circumstances John stopped being "in the Spirit," but now we are told that he is *in the Spirit* once more. This time he is indeed caught up to heaven, for he sees before him *a throne in heaven with someone sitting on it* (v. 2). But in this chapter and in those to follow we will again look in vain for any clear signal as to when John stops being "in the Spirit" or when he "comes down" from heaven. Only to a limited degree can we attain in our reading of the Revelation "a sense of where we are."

John's description of what he saw in heaven is, like the rest of the New Testament, true to the classic Jewish principle that "no one has ever seen God" (Jn 1:18; 1 Jn 4:12; compare Ex 33:20). In many ways it recalls Ezekiel's introductory vision (Ezek 1:4-28), except that John is, if anything, even more reticent than Ezekiel about naming or describing God directly. What John sees is both a throne room and at the same time (because it is *God's* throne room) a place of worship, specifically a temple. Ezekiel in his day saw "a throne of sapphire" and on it "a figure like that of a man" (Ezek 1:26), which he identified as "the appearance of the likeness of the glory of the Lord" (1:28). John, by contrast, speaks only of *a throne in heaven* and *someone* seated on the throne (v. 2). This *someone* has no name or title, but for the moment at least is simply *the one who sat there,* with *the appearance of jasper and carnelian* (v. 3).

To John the *throne* represents the power and majesty of the one sitting on it, and everything else he sees is described in relation to this central throne. Encircling it he saw *a rainbow, resembling an emerald.* Surrounding it in a wider circle were *twenty-four other thrones,* on which were seated *twenty-four elders* in white, wearing gold crowns (v. 4).

same words signal deliverance, or vindication against one's enemies).

4:3 The *rainbow* around the throne recalls Ezekiel's vision of divine radiance "like the appearance of a rainbow in the clouds on a rainy day" (Ezek 1:28). Some see it also as a reminder of God's mercy, like the rainbow that served as a covenant sign to Noah that God

From it came *flashes of lightning, rumblings and peals of thunder* (v. 5). Before, or in front of it, *seven lamps were blazing,* which John identifies for us as *the seven spirits of God* (v. 5). In front of it too he saw *what looked like a sea of glass, clear as crystal* (v. 6). Finally, *in the center, around the throne* John saw *four living creatures,* with eyes on every side and six wings, who continually said, *"Holy, holy, holy is the Lord God Almighty, who was, and is, and is to come"* (v. 8).

What started as a heavenly tableau unfolding step by step before John's eyes now becomes a scene of active worship and proclamation. The use of verbs in the present tense, beginning in verse 5, and the phrase *day and night* in verse 8 give the impression that this is no longer something John saw once in a vision, but a ritual in heaven repeating

---

would never again destroy the earth and its creatures with a flood (Gen 9:16). But if it is such a reminder, it carries with it a certain irony: although the earth is not struck with a flood in the book of Revelation, it is struck and damaged in almost every other way (8:6-13, 16:1-21). Although a well-known African-American spiritual captures the irony quite well—"God gave Noah the rainbow sign, no more water but fire next time!"—it is doubtful that John's vision contains any conscious allusion to the Noah story.

4:3-4 The same Greek word *kyklothen* is translated as *encircled* in verse 3 and *surrounding* in verse 4. The implication is that the rainbow encircled the throne in an arc overhead, while the thrones of the twenty-four elders were set in a circle around the central throne in John's vision.

4:4 Because there were elders in Israel and because many early Christian congregations were ruled by "elders" (Greek *presbyteroi;* Acts 14:23; 1 Tim 5:17; Jas 5:14; 1 Pet 5:1), it is commonly assumed that the *twenty-four elders* in some way represent the people of God (with twenty-four often explained as the sum of the twelve tribes of Israel and the twelve apostles). But there is no reason to assume that the elders represent anyone but themselves. In John's vision they are simply heavenly beings of some sort, and it is best to leave it at that. Not surprisingly, the number twenty-four in this heavenly "temple" corresponds to the twenty-four divisions of priests and Levitical singers in the earthly temple at Jerusalem, according to 1 Chronicles 24—25.

4:5, 8 There are certain details in this vision that John does not literally see. For example, he states that the seven blazing lamps he saw *are the seven spirits of God* (v. 5; compare 1:4). This is something he could not have seen, yet knows somehow as a prophet. In a similar way, he knows that the four living creatures sing their song *day and night* without stopping (v. 8), even though we are not intended to assume the passage of any extended period of time. John also knows that each of the living creatures is *covered with eyes all around* (v. 8), *even under his wings,* or "inside" (NRSV), beyond John's range of vision. There is more to what is described than meets the eye, even the eye of a seer. But John, because he is prophet as well as seer, is at times able to look beneath the surface of what he sees to its deeper significance.

4:6 The *sea of glass* (both here and in 15:2) recalls the giant bronze basin of water, called a "sea," in the temple at Jerusalem (1 Kings 7:23-26; 2 Chron 4:4-6). Its presence suggests that this heavenly throne room is also the heavenly temple. G. B. Caird (1966:65) has argued that the "sea," whether in the earthly or heavenly temple, is "a reservoir of evil" and "the

itself over and over again without rest or interruption. The throne is suddenly alive with living creatures hailing the anonymous *someone* seated on it as *the Lord God Almighty* (compare 1:8). In reply, the twenty-four elders continually fall down to worship this one *who lives for ever and ever* (v. 9), laying their crowns in front of the throne (v. 10) and saying, *"You are worthy, our Lord and God, to receive glory and honor and power, for you created all things, and by your will they were created and have their being"* (v. 11). The elders' song celebrates creation and God the creator, probably as a reference point for the new creation to come. Although John in his vision does not claim to experience the passage of time, he manages to convey a sense that what he saw is something still going on in heaven even as we read his prophecy today.

---

one discordant note" in John's vision, a symbol of "everything that is recalcitrant to the will of God." It is true that the evil beast that dominates the latter chapters of the book will arise from the sea (13:1), that the sea is a place of death (20:13), and that in John's concluding vision of the new heaven and earth "there was no longer any sea" (21:1). But this sea is different, for it is *of glass,* and *clear as crystal,* like the new Jerusalem, John's "holy city" (compare 21:11, 18, 21). Such language implies that this sea is by no means a symbol of evil, but on the contrary radiates the glory of God. It is one of several common features in biblical visions of heaven, corresponding to the crystal expanse Ezekiel saw (Ezek 1:22) or to the pavement of clear sapphire in the vision of Moses and the elders of Israel (Ex 24:9-10).

4:6 *In the center,* around the throne (literally "in the center of the throne and around the throne") is a highly unusual expression. *Around* (Greek *kyklō*) implies here a tighter ring than the "encircling" rainbow or the "surrounding" twenty-four thrones (vv. 3-4; Greek *kyklothen*). R. G. Hall (1990:609-13) argues persuasively that the living creatures are actually seen as part of the throne, in keeping with biblical descriptions of winged cherubim as part of the decoration of the ark of the covenant (Ex 25:17-22; 37:6-9). He cites a comment by Josephus about these cherubim that "Moses says that he saw them sculpted upon the throne of God" *(Antiquities* 3.137), and concludes that John's living creatures are " 'within the space taken up by the throne,' as the back, arms, and legs of a chair are within the space taken up by the chair. They are around the throne . . . as the legs, arms, and back surround a chair. Though part of the throne, they are not static but living creatures . . . hence they can fall down before the Lamb" (612). In this sense the throne is a living entity.

4:7 The description of the living creatures as *like a lion, like an ox,* with *a face like a man,* and *like a flying eagle,* respectively, corresponds to Ezekiel's vision (Ezek 1:10), except that each of Ezekiel's four living creatures had all four faces (though listed in a different order: the human, the lion, the ox, the eagle). Some have inferred from these designations that the living creatures are "angelic representatives, perhaps 'celestial doubles,' of God's animate creation" (Wall 1991:94), but as in the case of the twenty-four elders, it is wiser just to let angels be angels.

4:8 Contrary to the popular hymn, "Holy, Holy, Holy," the thrice-repeated *holy* is probably not intended to hint at "God in three persons, blessed Trinity," but rather at the explicit point that the Holy One is an eternal God "who was, and is, and is to come."

The Seven-Sealed Scroll and the Lamb (5:1-14) There is a story about a mother who noticed that her six-year-old son was deeply engrossed in trying to draw and color an elaborate picture. "What are you drawing, dear?" she asked. "I'm drawing a picture of God," he answered. "That's very nice, dear," she said, "but you know, no one really knows what God looks like." "They will now," was the triumphant reply. John, as we have seen, started out with characteristically Jewish restraint in describing the one seated on the throne in his vision. Yet as the plot of his vision unfolds, the scene will end in a way that must have been truly disturbing to any Jewish reader—with the worship of an animal, a Lamb, as God!

Whether there is a pause in the ceaseless worship described in 4:8-11, or whether the scenario played out in chapter 5 is also assumed to go on "day and night" forever (4:8), we are not told. In any event, for the first time since 4:1 John uses the words *I saw* (5:1), indicating that a new vision, or at least a new phase of the vision in the throne room, is under way. His attention is fastened on *a scroll with writing on both sides and sealed with seven seals,* held *in the right hand of him who sat on the throne* (5:1). *A mighty angel,* not introduced before, asks, *"Who is worthy to break the seals and open the scroll?"* (v. 2), but no one was found worthy to open it or to look inside. John, caught up emotionally in the scene, *wept and wept* at this (v. 4). One of the elders told him not to weep because *the Lion of the tribe of Judah, the Root of David, has triumphed. He is able to open the scroll and its seven seals* (v. 5). We are not told why it was so important that someone be found to look inside the scroll. Despite his tears, even John may not have known, and if he knows, he is not telling.

The one announced by the elder's authoritative voice is the Jewish Messiah as traditionally understood, descended from the line of David,

5:1 Once again John seems to describe something he could not literally see; that is, the scroll had writing *on both sides,* or "on the inside and on the back" (NRSV). John's terminology is different from that of Ezekiel, who saw a scroll with writing on the front and on the back, and even that much only because the scroll was spread open before him (Ezek 2:9). Possibly John could see the back of the scroll in his vision, and he may have assumed it had writing inside because if it did not there would be no reason to seal it. More likely this is the same phenomenon we encountered in 4:5, 8, where John was granted prophetic insight into details not actually visible to him.

yet the one who promptly appears is the Christian Messiah, pictured here as *a Lamb, looking as if it had been slain,* having *seven horns and seven eyes* (v. 6). John intuitively knows that the seven eyes, like the seven lamps blazing before the throne (4:5), are actually *the seven spirits of God sent out into all the earth* (v. 6; compare 1:4, "the seven spirits before his throne"). The Lamb is clearly no stranger to the heavenly throne room, but an integral part of the scene. Like the living creatures, he stands *in the center of the throne,* but unlike them he is not said to be "around the throne" (4:6) He is not part of the throne, as they are, but an occupant of it, as much an occupant as the divine one seated there, and every bit as much an object of worship.

The discrepancy between what is announced (*the Lion of the tribe of Judah, the Root of David,* v. 5) and what actually appears (*a Lamb, looking as if it had been slain,* v. 6) is not the kind of discrepancy that compels the reader to make a choice. Rather, each designation interprets and clarifies the other: the Jewish Messiah *is* the Christian Messiah; the triumphant Lion *is* the slaughtered Lamb; the mighty King *is* the crucified divine Savior. He has indeed *triumphed* (v. 5) or "conquered" (NRSV), not by the sword but by his death (compare 3:20). In this respect, Revelation is no different from Matthew's Gospel, which identifies "Jesus Christ the son of David, the son of Abraham" (Mt 1:1) as "'Immanuel'—which means, 'God with us'" (1:23), nor is it different from Paul in Romans, who identifies Jesus the "descendant of David" as one "declared with power to be Son of God by his resurrection from the dead" (Rom 1:3-4). The old Jewish messianic expectation is transformed in light of the ministry, death and resurrection of Jesus.

As soon as the Lamb takes the scroll *from the right hand of him who sat on the throne* (v. 7), he becomes the object of worship. Living creatures and elders alike fall down before him, each with a harp and

---

5:2 The word order of the mighty angel's question, *"Who is worthy to break the seals and open the scroll?"* is the reverse of the original Greek. The NRSV has it correctly: "Who is worthy to open the scroll and break its seals?" To the NIV translators this must have seemed illogical: How can anyone open the scroll without first breaking its seals? But John seems to regard the opening of the scroll and the breaking of its seals as virtually the same act (see v. 5, "He is able to open the scroll and its seven seals"). This process will be described in chapters 6-8.

golden bowls full of incense, which John (without being told) is able to identify as *the prayers of the saints* (v. 8; compare Ps 141:2, "May my prayer be set before you like incense; may the lifting up of my hands be like the evening sacrifice"). This is the first of only three references to petitionary prayers in the book of Revelation (compare 6:10; 8:3-4), and the reader cannot help but wonder whether John has in mind the routine daily prayers of God's people or specific prayers about some urgent need. The answer is not given here, but will become clear in connection with the other two references.

For the moment, the accent is on praise and worship rather than petitionary prayer, as the living creatures and elders sing a "new song":

"You are *worthy* to take [that is, *receive*] the scroll
  and to open its seals,
for you were slaughtered and by your blood you ransomed for God
  saints from every tribe and language and people and nation;
you have made them to be a kingdom and priests serving our God,
  and they will reign on earth" (vv. 9-10 NRSV; the NIV identifies the redeemed as "men").

The italicized words, *worthy . . . to receive. . . for,* serve to accent the similarity in form between this *new song* and the previous song of the elders before the throne in 4:11. The first was directed to "him who sits on the throne," or "our Lord and God," in praise for the work of creation. The second is now directed to the Lamb in praise for the work of redemption. The popularity of hymns to creation and redemption in first-century Asia Minor

---

5:5 *Lion of the tribe of Judah* recalls Jacob's blessing on Judah in Genesis 49:9-10, "You are a lion's cub, O Judah; you return from the prey, my son. Like a lion he crouches and lies down, like a lioness—who dares to rouse him? The scepter will not depart from Judah, nor the ruler's staff from between his feet, until he comes to whom it belongs and the obedience of the nations is his." *The Root of David* echoes "the Root of Jesse" (David's father) in Isaiah 11:10 and anticipates Jesus' pronouncement, "I am the Root and the Offspring of David" near the end of Revelation (22:16).

5:6 The NRSV translation "slaughtered" is more accurate than the NIV *slain* in the description of the Lamb, and is more appropriate to the traditional idea of the lamb as sacrificial victim. As to the positioning of the Lamb, however, the NIV rendering *standing in the center of the throne, encircled by the four living creatures and the elders* is preferable to the NRSV "between the throne and the four living creatures and among the elders." The phrase *in the center of the throne* is the same phrase used of the living creatures themselves (4:6), and the point is that the Lamb is at the very center of the whole scene (literally, "in the center of the throne and of the four living creatures and in the center of the elders"). The

can be seen in a pair of hymns in Paul's letter to the Colossians about Christ's work both of creating all things (Col 1:15-17) and reconciling all things to God (1:18-20; compare also Jn 1:1-18).

The *new song* of redemption is echoed in another song of *many angels, numbering thousands upon thousands, and ten thousand times ten thousand* (v. 11):

"*Worthy* is the Lamb that was slaughtered
to receive power and wealth and wisdom and might
and honor and glory and blessing!" (v. 12 NRSV)

Again the italicized words echo 4:11 ("worthy . . . to receive"), but this time what the Lamb "receives" is not simply the scroll, but "power and wealth and wisdom and might," corresponding generally to the "glory and honor and power" that the Lord God was worthy to receive according to 4:11. The Lamb and the One seated on the throne are worthy of the same ascriptions of praise. This is made explicit in the final hymn, emanating from beyond the immediate scene John sees in heaven, from *every creature in heaven and on earth and under the earth and in the sea, and all that is in them* (v. 13):

"To the one seated on the throne and to the Lamb
be blessing and honor and glory and might
forever and ever!" (v. 13 NRSV).

What was implicit now becomes explicit: God on the throne and the Lamb *in the center of the throne* are inextricably joined together as objects of Christian worship. Again and again throughout John's visions

---

Lamb is actually "in" or "on" the throne, no less than the one seated there, not somewhere "between" the throne and the other participants in the drama (compare 7:17). It is no more possible to visualize the exact relationship between someone "sitting" on a throne and someone *standing in the center* of that same throne than it is to explain the precise relationship between God the Father and God the Son in Christian theology.

5:9-10 The persistent view that the elders and living creatures are representative of the church and of creation respectively comes to expression in the words of the KJV, based on late and unreliable Greek manuscripts: "for thou . . . hast redeemed *us* by thy blood . . . And has made *us* unto our God kings and priests: and *we* shall reign on the earth" (italics mine). On this understanding, the elders and living creatures are celebrating their own redemption, while in the NIV, NRSV, and all modern versions a clear distinction is made between these angelic beings who sing in heaven, and the redeemed people of God on earth (for fuller discussion of the manuscript evidence, see Stonehouse 1957:88-108 and Michaels 1992:77-81).

they will be seen together as equals sharing the same throne, both as objects of fear or worship and as the decisive actors in the drama of salvation. Examples include 6:16, "hide us from the face of him who sits on the throne and from the wrath of the Lamb"; 7:9, "standing before the throne and in front of the Lamb"; 7:10, "Salvation belongs to our God, who sits on the throne, and to the Lamb"; 14:4, "firstfruits to God and the Lamb"; 21:22, "the Lord God Almighty and the Lamb are its temple;" 21:23, "the glory of God gives its light, and the Lamb is its lamp;" 22:1, "flowing from the throne of God and of the Lamb"; 22:3, "the throne of God and of the Lamb will be in the city." In John's visionary context, it appears that the whole universe is worshiping an animal, but as it turns out, the "Lamb" (like the awe-inspiring angel of chap. 1) is merely one of several disguises worn by the risen Jesus. In this, the first of John's visions of heaven, the traditional Jewish Messiah has been transformed into the divine and sovereign Christ of Christian theology. The liturgy of the heavenly throne room concludes with the "amen" of the four living creatures, as the twenty-four elders *fell down and worshiped* (v. 14).

□ The Seven Seals (6:1—8:5)

Some years ago, a young man named Vernon Howell, a.k.a. David Koresh, together with over a hundred followers, held police and federal agents at bay outside a heavily armed compound near Waco, Texas. The story had a tragic ending. Koresh believed he was Christ, the Lamb of God and the only one able to open the seven seals and bring about the end of the world. Clearly, the ancient images of Revelation command people's attention today. Yet they are disturbingly subject to the uses and abuses of the human imagination. To the would-be interpreter, whether scholarly, pastoral or prophetic, these images should carry a warning label: Danger. Handle with care.

5:10 The announcement that the redeemed are ***a kingdom and priests*** echoes 1:5. The image of ***priests to serve our God*** has helped shape the classic Protestant notion of the priesthood of all believers, but in this context it follows naturally on the comparison of "the prayers of the saints" to incense in verse 8. The saints are "priests" in that their prayers are like incense, but in verse 8 the actual priestly work is done by heavenly beings (the twenty-four elders; compare the angel with the golden censer in 8:5). The earlier characterization of believers as "a kingdom" (1:6) is here explained by the promise that

The Opening of the First Four Seals (6:1-8) In John's vision the Lamb, who is Jesus of Nazareth and no one else, has been holding the seven-sealed scroll from the moment he took it from the hand of the one seated on the throne (5:7). Now he begins to open its seals. If the scroll is sealed in normal fashion, it obviously cannot be opened and read until all seven of its seals are broken. This prompts a question that John does not ask, but we cannot help asking, When in the book of Revelation is the scroll itself actually opened? We never see this happening, unless the scroll is the same as "the book of life" opened at the last judgment (20:12, 15; "scroll" and "book" are the same word in Greek). This "book of life," twice identified as belonging to the slain Lamb (13:8; 21:27), is said to contain a list of the names of all who would be redeemed (compare 3:5 and 17:8). But this scroll is simply one of many "books" or scrolls opened at the last judgment (20:12), while the scroll in chapter 5 is never explicitly described as a scroll "of life."

A more likely possibility is that the scroll taken by the Lamb in chapter 5 is the same one John will later see lying open in the hand of a mighty angel (10:2, 8-10). If so, the opening of the seventh and last seal (8:1) implies the opening of the scroll itself, or the opening of the scroll is visualized as a process taking place as the seals are broken, not afterward. As we have seen, the Greek word order in 5:2 and 5:5 (see NRSV) suggests that the scroll was to be opened first, and then its seals were to be opened, which makes no sense if taken literally. To John, opening the scroll and breaking the seals amount to the same thing, but even the opening of the scroll is not quite the same thing as looking into it (5:4) or examining its contents. The latter is what must wait until chapter 10 or beyond. Only in chapter 10 is the scroll actually said to be "open" (10:2, 8), and only then are its contents revealed. Even in the framework of a very literal interpretation of John's visions, the placement

---

they will reign on the earth (v. 10). John is not told when this will happen, but see 20:4, 6; 22:5.

6:1-7 Nothing is gained by linking the reference to *one of the four living creatures* (v. 1), and *the second* (v. 3), *third* (v. 5) and *fourth* (v. 7) living creature to the description of them in 4:7 as like a lion, an ox, a human being and an eagle, respectively (Farrer 1964:98-99 tried unsuccessfully to make a connection). The distinct identities of the four living creatures in chapter 4 seem to be forgotten in chapter 6.

of the seven seals this early in the prophecy suggests that the end of the world was by no means so near as David Koresh believed.

The First Seal (6:1-2) The opening of the first four seals is the work of the Lamb and the four living creatures together. As the Lamb opens each of the seals, one of the living creatures gives the command, *"Come!"* A horse and rider go forth, apparently on earth. Actions in heaven are determining events on earth. The series recalls similar groups of four horsemen or chariots sent throughout the earth according to Zechariah 1:8-11 and 6:1-7. The first horse is *white,* with a rider carrying a bow and wearing a crown riding out *as a conqueror bent on conquest* (v. 2). Herman Melville, in the chapter entitled "The Whiteness of the Whale" in his novel *Moby Dick,* wrote that

> in the Vision of St. John, white robes are given to the redeemed, and the four-and-twenty elders stand clothed in white before the great white throne, and the Holy One that sitteth there white like wool; yet for all these accumulated associations with whatever is sweet, and honorable, and sublime, there yet lurks an elusive something in the innermost idea of this hue, which strikes more of panic to the soul than that redness which affrights in blood. This elusive quality it is, which causes the thought of whiteness, when divorced from more kindly associations, and coupled with any object terrible in itself, to heighten that terror to the farthest bounds. (Melville 1931:873)

The biblical perspective on the color white, in connection with the opening of the first seal, is more ambiguous than Melville assumed. If we recall the white stone promised to the angel at Pergamum (2:17) or the white garments mentioned in the letters to Sardis (3:4-5) and Laodicea (3:18), we might agree that the white horse was (in Melville's words) something "sweet, and honorable, and sublime." Reading the book for a second time, we would have this impression confirmed by recalling the figure on a white horse in 19:11-16, who bears such names as "Faithful and True" (19:11) and "the Word of God" (19:13). It is no surprise, therefore, that many have identified the rider on the *white horse* in chapter 6 either as Jesus himself or as the Christian message being

6:6 The voice *among* (literally, "in the center of") the four living creatures could be the voice of the Lamb, or it could be the voice of God himself, with whom the Lamb shares

proclaimed throughout the world (see Ladd 1972:99).

But the second, third and fourth riders are bearers of judgment, not salvation, and it is natural to wonder if the same is not true of the first. Because an antichrist figure is by definition a counterfeit of Jesus Christ, any characteristic that identifies this first rider as the one serves equally well to identify him as the other. The phrase *as a conqueror bent on conquest* (v. 2) could point to Christ (3:20; 5:5), but it could just as easily point to the antichrist (Rissi 1966:73), who also "overpowers" or "conquers" (11:7; 13:7). Although the term *antichrist* (1 Jn 2:18; 4:3; 2 Jn 7) never occurs in the book of Revelation, the idea is conspicuous in chapters 13-20. More broadly, the rider on the white horse could represent false prophets or false messiahs (for example, Vos 1965:181-92) or even the god Apollo, who in Hellenistic mythology was linked to prophecy and was often depicted as carrying a bow (Kerkeslager 1993:116-21). Other interpretations are that he represents military conquest as a kind of abstraction (Wall 1991:110) or the dreaded Parthian empire beyond the eastern borders of Rome's dominion (for example, Boring 1989:122, "the only mounted archers in the first century; white horses were their trademark").

Although there will never be total agreement in regard to the first rider's identity, the concern over false prophets in chapters 2-3 suggests false prophecy as the most likely interpretation. This would parallel Jesus' last discourse in Mark, where false prophets are one of the signs, indeed the *first* sign, of the end of the age (Mk 13:5, 22). And to the degree that the antichrist figure in the book of Revelation is associated with false prophecy (see 13:11-17, as well as the pairing of "the beast and the false prophet" in 16:13; 19:20; 20:10), the first rider is "antichrist" as well.

The Second, Third and Fourth Seals (6:3-8) Clearly the first rider cannot be understood apart from the three that follow. The rider on the second, *fiery red,* horse (vv. 3-4) is given authority *to take peace from the earth* so that people would kill one another. He receives *a large sword.* The rider on the third, *black,* horse (vv. 5-6) is *holding a pair of scales in his hand,* while *what sounded like a voice among the four living*

---

the throne. The voice announces a level of inflation tantamount to famine, in which a day's wages (literally 'a denarius,' a Roman unit of currency) will buy only *a quart of wheat* or

creatures said, *"A quart of wheat for a day's wages, and three quarts of barley for a day's wages, and do not damage the oil and the wine!"* (vv. 5-6). The rider on the fourth, *pale,* horse (vv. 7-8) has a name *(Death)* and a companion *(Hades),* and John adds that *they were given power over a fourth of the earth, to kill by sword, famine and plague, and by the wild beasts of the earth.*

The question is whether *they* refers specifically to *Death* and *Hades* or to the whole series of four now being concluded. Clearly the *sword* is an apt characterization of the second rider (see v. 4) as *famine* is of the third. What then is the new terror brought by the fourth rider? Not killing as such, for that was intimated already in connection with the second (v. 4). Rather, *Death* is linked to *plague* (or "pestilence," NRSV), just as in the message to Thyatira (see note above on 2:23). So close is the connection that within one verse (v. 8) the same Greek word (*thanatos*) is translated both as *Death* and as *plague.* The fourth rider adds to the first three the awful prospect of disease, as well as the bearers of disease and desolation, *the wild beasts of the earth.* In effect, the statement that *they were given power over a fourth of the earth to kill by sword, famine and plague* summarizes the activities of the second, third and fourth riders, not merely the fourth.

Listing calamities to come was common in Jewish and Christian prophecy, not least in prophecies attributed to Jesus, for example, "wars and rumors of wars" (Mk 13:7), "wars and revolutions" (Lk 21:9), "great earthquakes, famines and pestilences in various places" (Lk 21:11), "nation . . . against nation, and kingdom against kingdom" with "earthquakes in various places" (Mt 24:7). Jesus said that such disasters were "the beginning of birth pains" (Mk 13:8). They "must happen, but the end is still to come" (Mk 13:7). Similarly in John's vision, the things described under the first four seals are harbingers of more terrible judgments to come.

But if *sword, famine and plague* at the end of the fourth seal

---

three quarts of barley. The added statement, *do not damage the oil and the wine,* implies that only the poor were affected by the high prices. The necessities of life (wheat and barley) went up in price, while luxury items the poor could not afford anyway (oil and wine) stayed the same. To remedy such a situation, the emperor Domitian in A.D. 92 passed a law against new vineyards in order to use the land for grain, but the vineyard keepers lobbied successfully for "a repeal of the law which ordered the earth to be laid waste and

summarize the effects of the second, third and fourth riders, respectively, how do they affect our identification of the first rider as false prophecy, which was also mentioned in the Gospels (Mk 13:5, 21-22; Lk 21:8)? Why, for example, does this rider carry a bow? The background of such imagery is that the God of Israel sends his "arrows" of judgment against the nations (Ps 45:5) and in two notable passages, Deuteronomy 32:23-25 and Ezekiel 5:16-17, even against *his own* people (see Feuillet 1966):

> I will heap calamities upon them and spend my *arrows* against them. I will send wasting *famine* against them, consuming *pestilence and deadly plague;* I will send against them the fangs of *wild beasts,* the venom of vipers that glide in the dust. In the street the *sword* will make them childless; in their homes terror will reign. (Deut 32:23-25)
>
> When I shoot at you with my deadly and destructive *arrows of famine,* I will shoot to destroy you. . . . I will send *famine* and *wild beasts* against you, and they will leave you childless. *Plague* and bloodshed will sweep through you, and I will bring the *sword* against you. I the LORD have spoken. (Ezek 5:16-17; see also Jer 15:2-3; Ezek 5:12; 14:12-21).

The italicized expressions suggest a causal relation of some kind between the first rider with his bow and the three terrible riders that follow. If the fourth rider summarizes the last three, the first rider anticipates them and speeds them on their way. They are like arrows from his bow. If he represents false prophets and false prophecy, the vision confirms John's view that false prophets like the Nicolaitans at Pergamum and "Jezebel" at Thyatira, urging compromise with the values of the Roman Empire, are responsible for all the other troubles to come.

At the same time, it is clear that these four terrible horsemen all stand under the sovereignty of God and the Lamb, who opens the seals. They all ride out at the bidding of the four living creatures who worship at God's throne. Whatever dreadful things may happen on earth, they are

---

not planted" (see Philostratus, *Life of Apollonius of Tyana* 6.42; for more references and discussion, see Court 1979:59-60).

6:8 *Hades,* used in Revelation only in the company of *Death* (see 1:18; 20:13-14), refers to death's immediate consequence, the grave (see 20:13). Here death and the grave are personified as a rider followed by his servant or squire (in real life, the squire would have his own horse, but this 'fifth' horse is not counted as part of John's vision).

all within God's plan and under God's sovereign control. God in effect is the one who draws the bow and sends out the arrows of misfortune, here no less than in Deuteronomy or Ezekiel. Both the first and the second riders (vv. 2, 4), and then all four (v. 8), are said to have been *given* (Greek *edothē*) the authority to do what they do. The first is *given a crown,* or garland of victory (see Farrer 1964:100), the second *a large sword,* and all four *power over a fourth of the earth*. The true giver of such things can only be God or the Lamb. The terms of the famine introduced by the third rider are announced from the very throne of God. Perhaps the whiteness of the white horse is less a counterfeit of the purity of God and the Lamb and more a signal to John and to us that these horsemen are riding out as agents of God, even though the tasks they perform are destructive.

We moderns are reluctant to blame God for the evil in the world. John, however, intends it as encouragement, reminding us that no matter what happens, God and the Lamb are on the throne, setting limits to evil and bringing their own wise purposes to realization. To be sure, there *are* enemies in the book of Revelation—evil forces arrayed against the power of God. These forces have been hinted at in chapters 2-3, as well as in the allusion to false prophecy here, but they are not formally introduced until the latter half of the book, most notably in chapters 12-13. The dualism of Revelation, in the sense of a great conflict between good and evil, does not truly begin until chapter 11 at the very earliest. For the moment, God's sovereignty is unchallenged.

The Opening of the Fifth Seal (6:9-11) Nowhere in the series is it more important to maintain "a sense of where we are" than in connection with the fifth seal. John is still in heaven, while the visions under the first four seals are calamities happening on earth (v. 4, "to take peace from the earth," and v. 8, "over a fourth of the earth"). But does the fifth

6:10 *Sovereign Lord* (Greek *despotēs*) was used of slave owners (1 Tim 6:1; Tit 2:9; 1 Pet 2:18), but without the negative connotation of the English word "despot." It is also used of God (2 Tim 2:21; 2 Pet 2:1; Jude 4) and specifically in prayer with the implication that those praying are God's "servants" or "slaves" (Greek *douloi,* Lk 2:29; Acts 4:24, 29). Here the martyrs are told to wait for the full number of their "fellow servants" (Greek *syndouloi,* v. 11). The phrase *holy and true,* recalling the self-introduction of the risen Jesus in the message to Philadelphia (3:7), could suggest that the martyrs' prayer is addressed to Jesus

seal present a vision of earth or a vision of heaven?

The Souls and the Altar (6:9) It is commonly assumed that the *souls* John sees *under the altar* (v. 9) are in heaven because the altar is assumed to be the altar in God's heavenly temple. When we read on in the book, we discover that this assumption is reasonable, since "the altar" in heaven is mentioned again in 8:3 (twice), 8:5, 9:13, 14:18 and 16:7. What is odd is that in describing the fifth seal John speaks of *the altar* (with a definite article) as if it is well-known to his readers, even though he now introduces it for the first time. No altar was included in his detailed description of the heavenly throne room scene in chapters 4-5. The closest he came to mentioning an "altar" (Greek *thysiastērion*) was his reference to "golden bowls of incense" (Greek *thymiamata*), representing as he said "the prayers of the saints" (5:8). Another odd thing is the phrase itself: *under the altar.* Who are these *souls of those who had been slain because of the word of God and the testimony they had maintained* (v. 9), and why are they *under* the heavenly altar? There is general agreement that they are martyrs. Even though no specific enemies or forces of evil have been named in chapters 4-6, the stubborn fact of martyrdom proves that such enemies do exist and sooner or later must be faced.

Elsewhere in the book of Revelation the testimony associated with martyrs is called "the testimony of Jesus" (1:9; compare 12:17; 17:6; 19:10; 20:4), but here it is more general: *the testimony they had maintained.* Because martyrdom was not yet a widespread experience in the Christian movement, this first vision of martyrs is probably meant to include Old Testament and Jewish, as well as Christian, martyrs (for example, those put to death in the time of the Maccabees; see 2 Macc 6:7—7:42; 4 Macc 5:1—6:30; 8:3—12:19; Heb 11:32-38). The assumption behind the visions is that those *who were to be killed as they had been* (v. 11), or (as stated in 14:13) "the dead who die in the Lord from now

---

rather than God the Father, but it is difficult to be sure because the two function almost interchangeably throughout the book.

The inhabitants of the earth, or "those who live on the earth," are always sharply distinguished in the book of Revelation from Christian believers. This was true in the message to Philadelphia (3:10) and continues to be true throughout (8:13; 11:10; 13:8, 12, 14; 17:2, 8). Here they are responsible for the deaths of the martyrs, and consequently the martyrs are crying out against them.

on," would be Christians martyred specifically for "the testimony of Jesus."

Many commentators find in the fifth seal an allusion to Leviticus, where the blood of a sacrificed bull was poured out "at the base of the altar of burnt offering" (Lev 4:7), with the understanding that "Since life was thought to be in the blood of the animals, and of humans (Lev 17:11, 14), and since 'life,' 'soul,' 'self,' were interchangeable terms, the lives or selves of sacrificed victims could be thought of as being at the base of or 'under' the altar" (Boring 1989:125). But would John have said *under the altar* when he meant "at the base of the altar"? If he did not want to use the exact words of Leviticus, why would he not have written "before" or "in front" of the altar (Greek *enōpion*) in the same way he described earlier what was "before" the throne (4:5-6)?

The preposition translated *under* (Greek *hypokatō*) is a strong one, meaning "below" or "beneath" (compare the phrase "under the earth," in distinction from "in heaven" or "on earth," in 5:3, 13). John's choice of words raises the distinct possibility that the souls he saw *under the altar* were not in heaven at all, but far below it on earth—the same earth that had just been scarred by the disasters of the first four seals. John could have written "under heaven" (in the sense of "on earth," as in Gen 6:17; 7:19) or "under the throne." Instead he wrote *under the altar,* probably because the vision centered on what he calls elsewhere "the prayers of the saints" (5:8; 8:3-4). Not the *souls* themselves but their prayers are the sacrifices that ascend like incense from earth to heaven—from "under the altar" to the altar itself.

These *souls* are not disembodied spirits. They are, after all, visible to John. Nor are they the "lives" or "selves" of slaughtered victims as a kind of abstraction, nor are they typical of what theologians like to call "the intermediate state" (the interval between a believer's physical death and the final resurrection). Rather, at least within the horizons of John's vision, these *souls* are people with voices and real bodies, like the "beheaded" souls of 20:4. They are martyrs, not just in the sense of bearing *testimony* (Greek *martyria,* v. 9), but in the sense of having been "killed" (v. 11) for their testimony. Like Abel, the first martyr, who "still speaks, even though he is dead" (Heb 11:4; compare Gen 4:10), they cry out for justice to be done. Their prayer (v. 10) is the heart of the fifth seal. It is the prime example of what was meant by the "prayers of the saints" (5:8; compare 8:3-4).

The Prayer and Its Answer (6:10-11) The prayer of these "souls" is like an accusing question (*How long . . . until you judge the inhabitants of the earth and avenge our blood?*), tempered by a reverent address to God as *Sovereign Lord, holy and true*. It is a prayer for justice or vindication that borders on vengeance and echoes such biblical prayers as Psalm 79:5-7 ("How long, O LORD? Will you be angry forever? How long will your jealousy burn like fire? Pour out your wrath on the nations that do not acknowledge you, on the kingdoms that do not call on your name; for they have devoured Jacob and destroyed his homeland") or 79:10 ("Why should the nations say, 'Where is their God?' Before our eyes, make known among the nations that you avenge the outpoured blood of your servants").

This anguished plea for justice is sometimes compared unfavorably with the prayer of Jesus on the cross (Lk 23:34) or the prayer of Stephen at his martyrdom (Acts 7:60), both for the forgiveness of their tormentors. Kiddle (1940:119) states that "the modern conscience is shocked at the passionate longing for vengeance breathed out by the martyrs, and, indeed, it is beyond doubt lower in tone than the lofty spirit of forbearance which distinguished the Christian church in its earliest days." R. H. Charles (1920:1.176) places the prayer in a long tradition of apocalyptic Jewish prayers of vindictive martyrs, with the cautionary note that the offending call for vengeance is "made here once and for all and not uninterruptedly pressed as in Judaism."

Such comments, aside from their not-so-subtle anti-Semitism (as if Judaism taught vengeance while Christianity always urged unlimited forgiveness), presuppose a rather one-sided understanding of the ethics of both Jesus and Paul. Jesus asked in connection with one of his parables, "And will not God bring about justice [literally "retribution"] for his chosen ones, who cry out to him day and night?" (Lk 18:7). When he blessed "those who hunger and thirst for righteousness" (Mt 5:6), his words could as easily be translated, "those who hunger and thirst for justice." As for Paul, he urged kindness toward our enemy in order to "heap burning coals on his head" (Rom 12:20). If liberation theology has taught us nothing else, it has taught us that God's love and forgiveness can never be divorced from God's justice, or judgment on evil. The words of the ancient prophet, "let justice roll on like a river, righteousness like a never-failing stream" (Amos 5:24), are nowhere countermanded in the New Testament. The prayer of the martyrs in Revelation is not a cry for personal vengeance, but an appeal to a "Sovereign Lord, holy and true" to bring about justice in the world by destroying the powers of evil. It is an eschatological prayer, no different in its import from "your kingdom come" (Mt 6:10), "deliver us from the evil one" (Mt 6:13), "come, O Lord" (Aramaic *marana tha*) with its accompanying curse on anyone who "does not love the Lord" (1 Cor 16:22) or even "come, Lord Jesus" at the end of Revelation itself (22:20), just after a pair of solemn warnings to those who add to or take away from what is written.

In the context of the opening of the seals, the martyrs' prayer is simply a prayer for the series to continue to its appointed end. It has the same function as the four living creatures' repeated summons to the four horsemen to "Come!" (vv. 1, 3, 5, 7). The series will indeed continue, but the immediate answer to the prayer is a kind of stopgap measure. Each of the martyrs is given *a white robe* and is told to *wait a little longer, until the number of their fellow servants and brothers who were to be killed as they had been was completed* (v. 11). Their number will be complete when the sixth seal is opened, and the white robes will enable John—and us—to recognize these martyrs when we see them again (7:9, 13-14).

The Opening of the Sixth Seal (6:12—7:17) It has become almost a commonplace to view chapter 7 as an "interlude" or "parenthesis" in the progressive opening of the seals (for example, Wall 1991:115), as if John were able to step out of the sequence after 6:17 and back into it again

---

6:11 The NRSV translates the Greek *adelphoi* (literally, "brothers") as "brothers and sisters," in keeping with its policy of inclusive language. This generally sound principle is doubtful in this instance because in a later vision (14:4) John identifies the martyrs as distinctly male in his statement that they "did not defile themselves with women."

The notion of a "number" of martyrs (or more generally of the righteous) that must be *completed* before the end can come is found in a Jewish apocalypse written not long after the book of Revelation: "Did not the souls of the righteous in their chambers ask about these matters, saying, 'How long must we remain here? And when will come the harvest

in 8:1, when the seventh seal is opened. Perhaps the traditional chapter divisions have contributed to the popularity of this theory. But there is no evidence at all for such an interlude, nor even a hint of what an "interlude" might mean. Are we to imagine that the Lamb says to John, "Time out! I have something else to show you over here before we proceed"? The phrase *after this* in 7:1 does not signal a new vision or a change of scene at that point any more than it does when it is repeated in 7:9. Rather, the vision of the sixth seal continues.

What then does 6:12-17 contribute to chapter 7? In what sense can it be considered necessary background to the vision of the redeemed in that chapter? The simplest answer is that 6:12-17 describes in vivid detail the terrible judgment from which deliverance is promised in chapter 7. We might even argue that 6:12-17 is simply introductory to the vision proper, which comes in chapter 7. If the fifth seal dealt with the suffering people of God, looking toward the day when "the number of their fellow servants and brothers" would be completed (6:11), it is natural that the sixth seal should continue to focus on that group and mark the completion of that number (see 7:4).

The Great Day of Wrath (6:12-17) After a great earthquake the sun turns black and the moon red like blood, the stars fall from the sky, the sky itself crumples like a piece of paper, the mountains slide into the valleys and islands sink into the ocean. Survivors hide in caves and under rocks from more terrible disasters to come. What is wrong with this picture? Most Americans today would probably say, "Everything. It sounds like bad science fiction." However, if we rephrased the question—"What is *missing* from this picture?"—and if we directed it to John and his first-century readers, we would get a very different answer. The picture is not so strange to anyone who has read the Gospels. Jesus told his disciples that "in those days, following that distress, 'the sun will be

---

of our reward?' And Jeremiel the archangel answered them and said, 'When the number of those like yourselves is completed'" (*4 Ezra* 4.35-36; Charlesworth 1983:531).

6:17 Instead of *the great day of their wrath* (referring jointly to God and the Lamb), one of the earliest manuscripts of Revelation, Codex Alexandrinus (A) (as well as the majority of late manuscripts) reads "the great day of his wrath," referring exclusively to the Lamb. This reading, adopted by the KJV, could well be original, for later scribes may have found it easier to attribute "wrath" to God and the Lamb together than to the Lamb in particular.

darkened, and the moon will not give its light; the stars will fall from the sky, and the heavenly bodies will be shaken'" (Mk 13:24-25; compare Mt 24:29; Lk 21:25-26). He immediately added that people "will see the Son of Man coming in clouds with great power and glory. And he will send his angels and gather his elect from the four winds, from the ends of the earth to the ends of the heavens" (Mk 13:26-27; compare Mt 24:30-31; Lk 21:27).

These parallels show what is missing from the picture in Revelation. There is no coming of the Son of Man in the clouds, no gathering of his chosen ones from all over the world. John sees all the terrible events heralding and accompanying the Second Coming of Jesus, but not the coming itself. The prophecy given in 1:7 ("Look, he is coming with the clouds") is almost, but not quite, fulfilled.

The scene echoes Zephaniah 1:14-15: "The great day of the LORD is near. . . . That day will be a day of wrath, a day of distress and anguish, a day of trouble and ruin, a day of darkness and gloom." It is the scene grimly celebrated in the medieval hymn, "Dies Irae, Dies Illa" (in Sir Walter Scott's paraphrase), "That day of wrath, that dreadful day! When heaven and earth shall pass away, what power shall be the sinner's stay? How shall he meet that dreadful day?"

What is striking in the book of Revelation—and strange, perhaps, to the modern reader—is that the wrath is *the wrath of the Lamb* (v. 16). The slaughtered Lamb of sacrifice in the center of the throne is no passive victim, but "the Lion of the tribe of Judah." The Lamb's role in judgment should come as no surprise in light of his equality and partnership with *him who sits on the throne* in the worship of the elders, living creatures and all creation (5:13). From that point on, God and the Lamb never act independently, but always in unison. When they act together in judgment, the inevitable question is, *Who can stand?* (v. 17).

The question has its answer in chapter 7, where John sees four angels *standing* at the corners of the earth to preserve a group of *servants of our God* from destruction (7:1, 3) and an innumerable multitude *standing* in the presence of God and the Lamb (7:9). There are indeed those who will "stand" in the great day of wrath, but they must be prepared and protected.

The 144,000 and the Unnumbered Multitude (7:1-17) The first question confronting the reader in chapter 7 is, Why was it so crucial *to prevent any wind from blowing* (7:1). Why should wind bring *harm* to the natural order (v. 3)? There is wind in the destructive scene just described in 6:12-17, but it is only a simile: "the stars in the sky fell to earth, as late figs drop from a fig tree when shaken by a strong wind" (6:13). There the wind did not figure into John's vision, but he used it metaphorically to compare something he had never seen in real life (stars falling to earth) with something familiar to him (ripe figs falling from a tree). Even Jesus used the fig tree as a metaphor for the approaching end of the world (Mk 13:28-29). But in Revelation wind is factored into the imagery, so that the fig tree is not sprouting leaves but losing its fruit—perhaps its leaves as well.

John's beautiful poetic image comes to life as grim reality in chapter 7. The wind becomes part of the vision—and a very real threat—when John sees *four angels standing at the four corners of the earth, holding back the four winds of the earth to prevent any wind from blowing on the land or on the sea or on any tree* (7:1). All the disasters of 6:12-17 are now wrapped up in the single disaster of "wind." Those who live along the seacoast or in an area subject to tornadoes can understand this text better than those who yearn for refreshing breezes in the desert. The terror of wind lives on into the twentieth century in the movie *Twister* and in e.e. cummings' apocalyptic little poem, "what if a much of a which of a wind," where wind serves as a metaphor for catastrophic change. In the face of such disaster, "the single secret will still be man" for cummings. But the situation is viewed quite differently in the book of Revelation, as we will see.

Here, as in the case of the first four seals, John's language echoes the prophecies of Ezekiel, where scattering to the winds was the culmination of a divine judgment that included plague, famine and the sword: "A third of your people will die of the plague or perish by *famine* inside you; a third will fall by the *sword* outside your walls; and a third I will *scatter to the winds* and pursue with drawn sword (Ezek 5:12, italics mine).

These four angels, like the four riders in chapter 6, have been *given* something (Greek *edothē*; compare 6:2, 4, 8), in this case, *power to harm the land and the sea* (v. 2) by releasing the terrible four winds. Instead they hold the winds back, at least for the time being (v. 1). *Another angel,* ceremoniously introduced (v. 2), commands their restraint and supplies the reason for it: *until we put a seal on the foreheads of the servants of our God* (v. 3). Once again the imagery is drawn from the world of Ezekiel's visions, where a "man clothed in linen" was told to "go throughout the city of Jerusalem and put a mark on the foreheads of those who grieve and lament over all the detestable things that are done in it"; those so marked are spared the destruction threatening the city (Ezek 9:4, 6; in later Jewish literature see *Psalms of Solomon* 15.6, "For God's mark is on the righteous for [their] salvation. Famine and sword and death shall be far from the righteous"; Charlesworth 1985:664). John does not claim that he saw this ritual of sealing in his vision, only that he *heard the number of those who were sealed: 144,000 from all the tribes of Israel* (v. 4).

Sectarian groups in every age have seen themselves in John's 144,000 (compare also 14:1). The number has become synonymous with those who are saved, elect or chosen. Springfield, Missouri (population about 140,000), is widely known as "the buckle of the Bible belt." A colleague of mine once joked that when its population reached 144,000 the Second Coming would take place! When sectarian groups grow beyond that magic number, they often begin to interpret Revelation symbolically rather than literally, and in fact there are clues within the text that a symbolic interpretation *is* required. The number 144,000 is something John says he *heard* (v. 4), not something he saw or was permitted to count. There were twelve thousand, he was told, from each of Israel's twelve tribes, in the following order (vv. 5-8): Judah, Reuben, Gad,

---

7:2 The figure designated as *another angel* is described as *coming up from the east* (literally, 'coming up from the rising of the sun'). The description vaguely recalls that of the angel in John's first vision, whose "face was like the sun in all its brilliance" (1:16) and who turns out to be Jesus (1:18). There is no way to confirm such an identification, but clearly this angel is one with special authority over the four who preceded him.

7:5-8 A century after Revelation was written, Irenaeus (*Against Heresies* 5.30.2) noticed the omission of Dan from the list of the twelve tribes and attributed this to a tradition that the antichrist was to come from the tribe of Dan. Such arguments from silence are risky. There is no evidence in Revelation itself that either the antichrist or any other evil force is linked to Judaism or the Jews, much less a particular tribe. Therefore the omission of Dan remains a mystery. Dan is replaced in John's list by Manasseh, one of Joseph's sons (v. 6).

7:9 The mention of palm branches evokes a number of rich associations. In a general sense, palm branches were regarded as a symbol of victory (compare 2 Macc 10:7). More

Asher, Naphtali, Manasseh, Simeon, Levi, Issachar, Zebulon, Joseph and Benjamin (the list being framed by reminders in vv. 5 and 8 that the group was *sealed* against the terrors to come; the NIV fails to repeat the word *sealed* in v. 8).

John's list does not match exactly any of the traditional lists of the tribes of Israel (for example, Gen 35:23-26; 49:1-28; Deut 33:6-25), either in the names or in the order of the names. Most conspicuously, it is a messianic or distinctly Christian list in that it begins with Judah, the ancestor of David and of Jesus, the "Root of David" (5:5). Just as the elder's voice had announced earlier "the Lion of the tribe of Judah" (5:5), so now John *heard* a list of tribes announced beginning with the tribe of Judah. In each case, however, what John immediately *saw* was something quite different from what was announced. Instead of "the Lion of the tribe of Judah" he had seen "a Lamb, looking as if it had been slain" (5:6), and now instead of *144,000 from all the tribes of Israel* he sees *a great multitude that no one could count, from every nation, tribe, people and language, standing before the throne and in front of the Lamb* (v. 9).

In each case John's vision accomplishes a transformation (compare Gundry 1987:260). A Lion is transformed into a Lamb, and 144,000 Jews are transformed into an innumerable multitude from every nation on earth! The great multitude, *wearing white robes and . . . holding palm branches in their hands* (v. 9), break out in worship of God and the Lamb in a manner recalling chapters 4-5 (v. 10) and are answered by the *amen* of *all the angels . . . standing around the throne and around the elders and the four living creatures* (vv. 11-12; compare 5:11-14). At

---

specifically, they recall the Feast of Tabernacles (Lev 23:40), possibly with the promise already in view that "he who sits on the throne will spread his tent over them" (v. 15) and that the "dwelling of God" will be with God's people (21:3). The scene is also reminiscent of Jesus' triumphal entry into Jerusalem just before the Feast of Passover, especially in the Gospel of John (12:12-13, "the great crowd . . . took palm branches and went out to meet him"). Revelation in turn seems to have inspired the vision recorded in *4 Ezra* 2:42-48 (part of an early Christian apocalypse sometimes known as *5 Ezra*). Here "Ezra" sees a vision on Mount Zion of a multitude he cannot count, and he asks an angel, "Who are these, my lord?" He is told, "These are they who have put off mortal clothing and put on the immortal, and they have confessed the name of God; now they are being crowned, and receive palms." Then he asks, "Who is that young man who places crowns on them and puts palms in their hands?" The angel says, "He is the Son of God, whom they confessed in the world" (Charlesworth 1983:528).

this point, *one of the elders* (also familiar from chaps. 4-5) asks John, *"These in white robes—who are they, and where did they come from?"* (v. 13). When John disclaims any knowledge of who they are (v. 14), the elder answers his own question: *"These are they who have come out of the great tribulation; they have washed their robes and made them white in the blood of the Lamb"* (v. 14).

There has been a curious shifting of roles here. We would have expected John to ask the question and the elder to give the answer, just as Jesus' revelation to his disciples in Mark 13 was prompted by questions from four of his disciples (Mk 13:3-4). But a striking feature of Revelation is that John never asks a question in the entire book. In chapter 5 it was not John but a "mighty angel" who asked, "Who is worthy to break the seals and open the scroll?" (5:2). John then wept "because no one was found who was worthy" (5:4), and an elder announced the answer to the angel's question. Here the elder both asks and answers the crucial question, while John is a passive (and ignorant) observer. These visions follow the principle laid down explicitly in another book of early Christian prophecy, the second-century *Shepherd of Hermas,* to the effect that every spirit from God "is not asked questions, but has the power of the godhead and speaks all things of itself because it is from above, from the power of the Divine spirit. But the spirit which is questioned and speaks according to the lusts of man is earthly and light, and has no power, and it does not speak at all unless it be questioned" (Hermas *Mandates* 11.5-6; see Aune 1983:226-27).

The same principle was at work in John's Gospel when Jesus told his disciples, "In that day you will no longer ask me anything" (Jn 16:23), and the disciples said, "Now we can see that you know all things and that you do not even need to have anyone ask you questions. This makes us believe that you come from God" (Jn 16:30).

The effect of the elder's initiative is to assure John's readers that the elder's explanation of the innumerable multitude comes from God and can be trusted. The explanation includes both the "prehistory" of the group John sees (v. 14) and a glimpse of what is in store for them (vv. 15-17). The prehistory is familiar to John from 6:9-11, where "the souls of those who had been slain because of the word of God and the testimony they had maintained" (6:9) were told to "wait a little longer" until their full number was complete (6:11). These "souls" have *come out of the great tribulation* by martyrdom, and now the implication is that their number is complete. They can be recognized as the same group by the *white robes* they have been given (7:9; compare 6:11)—like the white garments of the twenty-four elders in heaven. The identification of the souls under the altar with the innumerable multitude before the throne of God testifies to the continuity John sees between the fifth and the sixth seals.

In the real world, blood leaves unsightly stains on white clothing, but in the world of the Revelation blood washes away all other stains and makes the clothing pure and all the whiter. It is important to notice that these martyrs are not cleansed by the shedding of their own blood, but, like all Christian believers, by *the blood of the Lamb* (v. 14; compare 1:5, where John's doxology reminds all his readers that Christ has "freed us from our sins" by the shedding of his blood). Martyrdom has no merit in itself, yet John wants to make very clear to the congregations in Asia that martyrdom is likely to be the price of any serious commitment to Jesus Christ.

If this is so, it is important to assure the churches of the vindication of those who are (or will be) martyred. So the elder's explanation continues. The martyrs' vindication, he points out, consists partly of what John has just seen—that *they are before the throne of God and serve him day and night in his temple* (v. 15)—and partly of what he has not yet seen (vv. 15-17). The conclusion to the sixth seal provides a glimpse of the final blessedness of God's people. God *will spread his tent over them* (v. 15). They will never be hungry or thirsty again, and they will be protected from the scorching heat of the sun (v. 16; compare Is 49:10). The Lamb will become their shepherd, leading them to *springs of living water* (compare 21:6), and *God will wipe away every tear from their eyes* (v. 17; compare 21:4).

The vision of the sixth seal ends in much the same way that the book of Revelation as a whole comes to an end. It is important to remember that John does not actually "see" any of this final blessedness, either here or in chapter 21. Rather, he hears it from a heavenly being, in this case one of the elders, and in chapter 21 "a loud voice from the throne" (21:3) or the very voice of the one "seated on the throne" (21:5). The principle of vindication is established by what John has seen in verses 9-12, but the particulars are described with a certain reserve, as a promise to be taken on faith. Although John is far more eager than Paul to tell about his visions (contrast 2 Cor 12:1-6), he still adheres to the common early Christian principle that "we live by faith, not by sight" (2 Cor 5:7), "Now I know in part; then I shall know fully, even as I am fully known" (1 Cor 13:12), and "Dear friends, now we are children of God, and what we will be has not yet been made known" (1 Jn 3:2). It is no accident that the breaking of the seventh and final seal will introduce a half hour of silence before the visions resume.

The Opening of the Seventh Seal (8:1-5) As soon as each of the first six seals was opened, John either "saw" something or "heard" something, or both. When the seventh seal was opened, however, he saw nothing and heard nothing *for about half an hour* (v. 1). Half an hour is not a long time, but half an hour of silence can seem like an eternity, whether it is "dead air" on radio or television or a silent dinner for two after a quarrel between a husband and a wife. To get some idea of the effect, imagine that a church youth group is doing a dramatic reading of the book of Revelation. When it comes to Revelation 8:1, it takes the verse literally so that all speech and all action stops—for thirty minutes—while the congregation fidgets and squirms and probably exits.

The silence is total. It is said to be *in heaven* (v. 1) only because

7:17 The statement that *the Lamb . . . will be their shepherd* is not necessarily the mixed metaphor it appears to be. For every flock of sheep, there was normally a ram that acted as "bellwether," or leader of the flock, either in the absence of a human shepherd or as the one that the shepherd would try to control, knowing that the rest would follow. This is the lamb or young ram depicted, for example, in Jewish and Jewish Christian apocalyptic writings such as *Enoch* (90.9-19; Charlesworth 1983:70) and *Testaments of the Twelve Patriarchs* (see *Testament of Joseph* 19.8; Charlesworth 1983:824). Alternatively, if there is a mixing of metaphors, it is based on the fact that the Lamb is Jesus, who is often pictured as a shepherd (Jn 10:11, 14; 1 Pet 2:25). Elsewhere in Revelation, however, Jesus' shepherding activity is directed toward the nations in the sense that he will "rule" (literally "shepherd") them "with a rod of iron" (12:5; compare 2:27). The more gentle shepherding of his own people is the work of Jesus as the Lamb, in the apocalyptic sense of the bellwether of God's flock.

8:1 Long as it may have seemed, *half an hour* is shorter than one hour and is probably intended as a period preliminary to the decisive "hour of trial" mentioned in 3:10, of which we shall hear more in later chapters; see, for example, 9:15; 14:7, 15; also the repeated

heaven has been the scene of all that John has just heard and seen in 7:9-17. If there are sounds on the earth, they play no part in John's vision. What is the purpose of the long silent pause? Is it so that *the prayers of all the saints* can be heard (Beasley-Murray 1974:150)? The *prayers of all the saints* are not mentioned until the half hour is over (v. 3), and when they are mentioned they are not "heard" but offered up as incense. If, as some have suggested, "the seventh seal is the End" (Caird 1966:104), is the silence merely an indication of nondisclosure—as if John were saying, "Next comes the end of all things, but I am not going to reveal that to you just yet"? Or is the silence a dramatic preparation for the resumption of sound and action? Are we waiting for something more? The fact that the silence is broken by a great deal of noise, *peals of thunder, rumblings . . . an earthquake* (v. 5) and the blasts of seven trumpets, argues for the second of these alternatives.

At the end of the half hour comes the expected reference to something John *saw* (v. 2), suggesting that far from being over, the seventh seal is only beginning. What John *saw* is reminiscent of what he saw in the preceding chapter in connection with the sixth seal: first a group of angels (four in one instance, seven in the other) and then *another angel* (v. 3; compare 7:2) who in some way determines their course of action, probably because he is greater than they. This parallel confirms the notion that the half hour of silence did not bring the series of seals to an end, but that the seventh seal is still playing itself out.

The one called *another angel* functions here as a kind of high priest,

---

phrase "in one hour" in the pronouncements of doom on Babylon in 18:10, 17, 19. Rissi (1966:6) makes a similar point, but clouds the issue with a contrast between "the first, dark half of God's great eschatological hour, which the other half, the bright creation, will then follow. Only then is the whole hour of God brought to its fulfillment." The real contrast is not between judgment and blessing, but between partial and total judgment.

8:2 The definite article *(the seven angels)* suggests a group known to John and his readers, yet no "seven angels" have been mentioned before. Possibly John equates them with "the angels of the seven churches" (1:20) or with "the seven spirits" before God's throne (1:4) or with a definite group of angels familiar to his readers (Tob 12:15; see note on Rev 17:1).

8:3 *Another angel* here, like the one so designated in 7:2, is a figure of special authority, functioning as a priest or high priest. The same possibility raised in the previous instance, that this figure in some way represents Jesus Christ, exists here as well. There is no need to settle such issues of identification. These figures are at least functionally equivalent to Jesus in that what they do is what Jesus does (compare the image of Jesus as high priest in the letter to the Hebrews).

ministering on behalf of the larger priesthood comprising the people of God (compare 1:5; 5:10; 7:15). Standing at the altar in heaven, he offers up incense that has something to do with *the prayers of all the saints* (v. 3; compare 5:8). This is the first we have heard of *the altar* since John's vision of souls "under the altar" in connection with the fifth seal (6:9). There John was allowed to hear the prayers of at least one group of Christian believers—those who had been martyred for their testimony (6:10). His use of *all* widens the application to the living as well as the dead (Caird 1966:107). Just as the prayers of martyrs triggered the judgments of the sixth seal, so the prayers of *all the saints* ignite (literally) the judgments of the seventh. As soon as prayer (represented by the *smoke of the incense*) ascends to the altar of God in heaven, *fire from the altar* descends to earth as divine judgment (v. 5). The angel's role abruptly changes from that of high priest, or intercessor, to that of judge, or executioner. The anguished plea of 6:9, "How long until you judge the inhabitants of the earth?" is still being answered, no less in the seventh seal than in the sixth. Prayer is the engine driving the plan of God toward completion.

The altar, traditionally the place of God's mercy, ironically becomes here the very source of divine judgment. John's vision thus dramatizes the Jewish view that mercy and judgment are not two contrasting sides of God's character, but are the same thing. Flannery O'Connor captured this in the dramatic end of her novel, *The Violent Bear It Away* (1988:478), when Francis Tarwater receives his long-awaited prophetic call: "GO WARN THE CHILDREN OF GOD OF THE TERRIBLE SPEED OF MERCY." When the angel pours fire on the earth, John says, *there came peals of thunder, rumblings, flashes of lightning and an earthquake* (v. 5). Such details echo the scene in heaven before the Lamb appeared, when "from the throne came flashes of lightning, rumblings and peals of thunder" (4:5). Phenomena that John saw in heaven now make their appearance on the earth, framing the account of the seven-sealed scroll and the opening of its seals, and suggesting that the series is now at an end.

8:3-4 The manuscripts differ in verse 3 as to the precise relationship between the incense and *the prayers of all the saints*. The analogy with 5:8 suggests that the two are identical, and this is reflected in many later manuscripts that read "to offer up *as incense* the prayers of all the saints" (with "prayers" in the accusative case). But the earliest and best manuscripts

Alternatively, it is possible that these phenomena are intended to introduce the new sequence of seven angels blowing their trumpets, a sequence that will end in much the same way in 11:19: "And there came flashes of lightning, rumblings, peals of thunder, an earthquake and a great hailstorm" (compare also the end of the sequence of seven bowls, 16:18). The great "storm" is under control in heaven because it comes from the very throne of God, but when the angel unleashes it on earth, it brings only turmoil and chaos. The terrible toll of the *fire from the altar* and the resulting thunder, lightning and earthquake (v. 5) are set forth sequentially in the next four chapters, as the seven angels introduced in verse 2 begin to blow their trumpets.

□ The Seven Trumpets (8:6—11:19)

On Mount Sinai, just before the giving of the Ten Commandments, Moses "led the people out of the camp to meet with God, and they stood at the foot of the mountain." This scene from the book of Exodus (19:17) fairly bristles with details that early Christians would later associate with the coming of Jesus Christ, the resurrection and the last judgment. The Israelites were to "be ready" (Ex 19:11), and Jesus told his disciples to be ready for his coming (Mt 24:44). Moses told them to prepare themselves by abstaining from sexual relations (19:15), and Paul urged this standard on his converts because the end was so near (1 Cor 7:1, 8, 29-32). The Israelites were waiting to "meet with God," and Paul expected Christians to "meet the Lord in the air" (1 Thess 4:17). The Sinai revelation was to happen on "the third day" (19:11, 16), and Jesus rose from the dead the third day (for example, 1 Cor 15:4; Mt 16:21; Lk 13:32).

Most significant for an understanding of John's visions in Revelation is that the Israelites saw "thunder and lightning, with a thick cloud over the mountain" and heard "a very loud trumpet blast" (Ex 19:16). When the people gathered, "Mount Sinai was covered with smoke, because

read "to offer up incense *for* the prayers of all the saints" (with "prayers" in the dative case). The NIV rendering, *incense . . . with the prayers,* attempts to incorporate both ideas.

the LORD descended on it in fire. The smoke billowed up from it like smoke from a furnace, the whole mountain trembled violently, and the sound of the trumpet grew louder and louder" (19:18-19). The letter to the Hebrews rehearses the whole scene at Sinai, including the "mountain . . . burning with fire," the "darkness, gloom and storm," and the "trumpet blast" (Heb 12:18-19), with a promise that earth and heaven would be shaken again one last time (12:26-29).

For Paul, the trumpet in particular became part of the scenario of Jesus' return, along with the resurrection of believers in 1 Thessalonians 4:16 ("with a loud command, with the voice of the archangel and with the trumpet call of God, and the dead in Christ will rise first") and 1 Corinthians 15:51-52 ("in a flash, in the twinkling of an eye, at the last trumpet. For the trumpet will sound, the dead will be raised imperishable, and we will be changed"). John, in the same tradition, combines the imagery of "fire from the altar" hurled to earth and "peals of thunder, rumblings, flashes of lightning and an earthquake" (8:5) with the familiar trumpet blast, now "serialized" as seven trumpets in keeping with the sevenfold character of many of his visions.

The First Four Trumpets (8:6-13) As was the case with the breaking of the seven seals, the first four trumpets in the sequence are set apart from the last three. At the end of the fourth trumpet, John hears an eagle *flying in midair call out in a loud voice: "Woe! Woe! Woe to the inhabitants of the earth, because of the trumpet blasts about to be sounded by the other three angels!"* (v. 13). The first four judgments are differentiated from the more terrible ones that follow in two ways: first, they affect primarily the natural world rather than *the inhabitants of the earth;* second, each affects only *a third* of the earth, trees and grass (v. 7), the sea, sea creatures and ships (vv. 8-9), rivers and springs of fresh water (vv. 10-11), and the sun, moon and stars (v. 12), respectively. The limitation to one-third leaves room for more terrible destruction to come,

---

8:7 The association of fire and blood is natural in contexts of martyrdom. Specifically, *fire mixed with blood . . . hurled down upon the earth* recalls Jesus' double pronouncement in Luke 12:49, "I have come to bring fire on the earth, and how I wish it were already kindled! But I have a baptism to undergo, and how distressed I am until it is completed!" The interchangeability of blood and fire is demonstrated in each of the first two trumpets: in the first, a mixture of the two (plus hail) results in the burning of earth and its vegetation;

whether in connection with the last three trumpets or the later visions. Still, one-third is more than one-fourth. Eugene Boring (1989:135) notes that "in the first cycle, one-fourth of the earth's inhabitants were struck (6:8); in this cycle the scale goes up to one-third," adding wisely, "to inquire whether this is a third of the original whole, or a third of what remained after one-fourth had been struck would be a wrong question; John works with the imagination, not calculators."

The four areas affected—earth, sea, fresh water and sky—made up the whole of the human environment as the ancients perceived it. These four spheres were what Jews and Christians acknowledged as God's creation (compare 14:7). Despite the discovery of new oceans and continents, even the exploration of space, these four—earth, sea, fresh water and sky—are still the natural components of the human environment as we define it today. Already in the sixth seal, John had begun to view some of these spheres of creation as potential spheres of the creator's judgment. He had seen four angels "holding back the four winds of the earth from blowing on the land or on the sea or on any tree" (7:1). All the terror inherent in the metaphor of wind is now to be unleashed as the trumpets blow. Yet wind plays no explicit role in the trumpet series. Fire takes its place, probably with reference to the Sinai scene. Just as the traditional trumpet of God is multiplied by seven in the book of Revelation, so the Lord's descent in fire on Mount Sinai (Ex 19:18), echoed in John's "fire from the altar" (Rev 8:5), is serialized in the first three trumpet blasts: *hail and fire mixed with blood . . . hurled down upon the earth* (v. 7), *something like a huge mountain, all ablaze . . . thrown into the sea* (v. 8) and *a great star, blazing like a torch, fell from the sky* (v. 10). For John, no less than for the author of Hebrews, "our God is a consuming fire" (see Heb 12:29).

Three of the four judgments echo the plagues of the Exodus, preceding the giving of the law at Mount Sinai: *hail* in connection with the first trumpet (v. 7; compare Ex 9:23-25), the sea's turning to *blood*

---

in the second, a mountain of fire thrown into the sea unaccountably turns the sea to blood.

8:9, 11 Although the first four trumpets have largely spared humans, the statements that *a third of the ships were destroyed* (v. 9) and that *many people died* from bitter waters (v. 11) show that there were at least some exceptions. That *many* died, however, not a third, suggests that humans are not the primary target at this point. When they become the target (9:15, 18), the operative fraction will again be "a third."

in the second (vv. 8-9; compare Ex 7:20-21) and darkness in the fourth (v. 12; compare Ex 10:21-23). Yet Mount Sinai, not the Exodus, dominates the imagery, at least up to this point. *Fire,* not hail or blood, is what damages earth, trees and grass (v. 7; contrast Ex 9:25). When a third of the fresh waters turn *bitter* (v. 11), not bloody, it is more like the waters of Marah after the departure from Egypt (Ex 15:23) than the plagues themselves. Finally, the dimming of the light of sun, moon and stars by one-third (v. 12) is far from equivalent to the "darkness that can be felt" or "total darkness" that covered Egypt (Ex 10:21-22). Yet these reminders of the Exodus alert us to watch for more as the visions continue. The controlling theme is closer to the theme of Sinai—fire from heaven.

When the angel blows the second trumpet, the scene echoes Jesus' promise to his disciples that "if anyone says to this mountain, 'Go, throw yourself into the sea,' and does not doubt in his heart . . . it will be done for him" (Mk 11:23). In Revelation the mountain is no ordinary mountain, but a vehicle for fire sent down from God. It is as if Mount Sinai itself, *all ablaze* (v. 8; compare Heb 12:18) has been taken up and thrown into the sea. "Later Christian piety, prompted by Paul (Gal 4:25) and Hebrews (12:18-21), saw in Mount Sinai the terrors of the old law which condemns the sinner " (Sharrock 1987:388). In *The Pilgrim's Progress,* for example, John Bunyan's Christian

> was afraid to venture further, lest the Hill should fall on his head: wherefore there he stood still, and wotted not what to do. Also his burden, now, seemed heavier to him, than while he was in his way. There came also flashes of fire out of the Hill, that made Christian afraid that he should be burned: here therefore he sweat, and did

8:11 The Hebrew word for *wormwood* (literally "bitter food") was rendered into Greek by the Jewish translator Aquila with a slightly different form of the word used here (*apsinthion,* changed here into a proper name, Apsinthos). Although this variation of the word is feminine in Greek, John makes it into a masculine name because the Greek word for *star* is masculine and probably also because fallen "stars," or angels, were commonly assumed to be male in Jewish apocalyptic literature (for example, *1 Enoch 67,* in Charlesworth 1983:15-16).

8:12 The notion that the light not only of the day but also of the night should be dimmed by a third may seem strange to us until we remember that in the Hebrew Bible night was by no means totally dark. God made "two great lights—the greater light to govern the day and the lesser light to govern the night" (Gen 1:16), and the stars too were created "to give

quake for fear (Sharrock 1987:63).

Although the book of Revelation makes no such link between its Sinai imagery and "the curse of the law" (Gal 3:13; 4:25), it is still true that John views the throwing of the fiery mountain into the sea as an act of God's grace on behalf of God's people. Hard as it may be to accept (because we are not accustomed to thinking of God as the author of destruction), this is the case with each of the first four trumpets. They are God's answer to "the prayers of the saints" (8:3).

Even the star that falls from the sky in connection with the third trumpet is a messenger of God. It is easy for us to think otherwise, since C. S. Lewis gave the name "Wormwood" to an agent of Satan, the nephew of the infamous Screwtape and recipient of *The Screwtape Letters*. But the star called *Wormwood* in John's vision is no satanic messenger. Rather, it is the personification of something God threatens to do to God's people when they allow themselves to be deceived by false prophets (see Jer 23:15, "I will make them eat bitter food [KJV wormwood] and drink poisoned water, because from the prophets of Jerusalem ungodliness has spread throughout the land"; compare Jer 9:15). Given the mischief of the Nicolaitans and "Jezebel," the situation in Asia Minor in John's day was similar to the one lamented by Jeremiah.

When the fourth trumpet sounded (v. 12), nothing fell from the sky. But the dimming light of sun, moon and stars, and consequently of both day and night, sent a signal that the worst was yet to come. This impression is confirmed by the voice of an eagle or vulture directly overhead, announcing three even more terrible "woes" or judgments against the earth's inhabitants.

---

light on the earth" (Gen 1:17). Because the fourth trumpet affects sun, moon and stars alike, it makes the day more like night and the night darker than before.

8:13 *As I watched, I heard* is literally "and I saw, and I heard." The combination of the two sensory verbs is odd (compare 5:11). The reference to seeing is probably just a reminder that John is still recording a vision (he has not used this favorite verb of his since v. 2). The emphasis is not on the appearance of the eagle flying overhead, but on the grim message John "hears" it announcing: *Woe! Woe! Woe.* Natural histories in ancient times (including Aristotle and Pliny) classified the vulture as a type of eagle, and vultures (because they fed on carrion) were customarily a sign of impending death (see Mt 24:28; Lk 17:37; also Rev 19:17, where "all the birds flying in midair" are viewed in a similar way).

The Fifth Trumpet, or First Woe (9:1-12) Back in the 1970s, my wife and I and our two boys lived for a few months at an ecumenical study center outside Jerusalem. One afternoon my son spotted a large scorpion in our apartment. We tried bug spray on it with little effect. It seemed in no hurry to go anywhere, so we called our friend Elias, the Palestinian Christian who worked the front desk. His advice was, "Don't do anything! Wait for me and I will be right down." We assumed Elias had an old Arab formula handed down from his ancestors and approved by the management for dealing with scorpions. When he arrived, Elias stared at our unwanted guest for a second or two. Then in one sudden move he brought his right foot down quick and hard on the tile floor, crushing the tiny monster to a pulp. This has been a standing joke in our family ever since. We all knew that any one of us could just as easily have done what Elias insisted on doing for us. The serious side is the reason we did not act—intimidation and fear of the unknown. The hostility between humans and certain creatures of the earth is very ancient, and in the Bible it becomes a symbol of the great conflict between good and evil. Jesus told his disciples in Luke, "I saw Satan fall like lightning from heaven. I have given you authority to trample on snakes and scorpions and to overcome all the power of the enemy; nothing will harm you" (Lk 10:18-19).

The Opening of the Abyss (9:1-6) In John's vision of the fifth trumpet in Revelation, the power and promise given to Jesus' disciples in the Gospel of Luke is turned upside down. Here it is not Satan who falls from heaven to earth, but *a star* (9:1), recalling the star Wormwood a few verses earlier (8:11). The fact that this star had *fallen* does not imply some kind of defection or rebellion against God. It falls as any star might seem to fall, based on ancient observations of meteorites or comets (compare 6:13). This star, like Wormwood, is a messenger from God, but the judgment it brings is even more terrible. It does not strike the earth or poison the waters, but with *the key to the shaft of the Abyss* (v. 1) opens a pit into the very heart of the earth. From the pit, or Abyss, comes smoke *like the smoke from a gigantic furnace,* darkening the sun and sky (v. 2). "Then from the smoke," John writes, "came locusts on the earth, and they were given authority like the authority of scorpions of the earth" (v. 3 NRSV). The situation is exactly the reverse of Luke

10:19. Instead of humans having "authority to trample on snakes and scorpions" and protection from "harm" or injury, the "authority" or *power* is that of scorpions (v. 3), and the strange demonic locusts that wield this authority use it precisely to *harm* or injure human beings (v. 4).

The words of woe just preceding this section (8:13) now begin to be borne out. The plagues introduced by the trumpets are getting worse and worse. The terrible locust plague now described is differentiated from the preceding four trumpets in that it affects humankind first of all, while the natural targets of natural locusts—grass, plants and trees—are protected (v. 4). These are no ordinary locusts, such as those that attacked Egypt in Moses' time (Ex 10:1-15). About them it was written, "Never before had there been such a plague of locusts, nor will there ever be again" (Ex 10:14). John's locusts are more like the locusts in Joel's vision centuries later, "A nation has invaded my land, powerful and without number; it has the teeth of a lion, the fangs of a lioness. It has laid waste my vines and ruined my fig trees. It has stripped off their bark and thrown it away, leaving their branches white" (Joel 1:6-7; see also 2:1-11).

Joel's locust plague, like John's, heralds nothing less than "the Day of the Lord" (Joel 2:1, 11), yet in Joel the invaders are still part of the natural order. In John's vision they are supernatural demons from the Abyss. Natural locusts do not physically attack humans, but John's locusts do, with the sting of the scorpion (vv. 4-5). Natural locusts, according to a biblical proverb, have no king (Prov 30:27), but these locusts do—*the angel of the Abyss, whose name in Hebrew is Abaddon, and in Greek, Apollyon* (v. 11).

This brings us to another difference between the fifth trumpet and the first four. They were, as we have seen, judgments from God and from above, in keeping with the description in 8:5 of an angel who (in response to "the prayers of all the saints") took "fire from the altar, and hurled it on the earth." The fifth trumpet, by contrast, introduces a judgment from below, from *the Abyss,* or depths of the earth (vv. 1, 2, 11), and consequently from the evil powers that live under the earth, associated with death, destruction and the grave. God, of course, is still sovereign over the whole process, for the *star . . . fallen from the sky* (v. 1) was *given* the key to the Abyss, and the terrible locusts *were given* the sting of scorpions (v. 3) and *were told* not to harm plants or trees, *but only those people who did not have the seal of God on their foreheads* (v. 4). As often in biblical language, the passive voice points to God as the one who does the "giving" and the "telling"—and who also sets limits to the judgment. John adds that the locusts *were not given power to kill them, but only to torture them for five months* (v. 5).

The situation is reminiscent of the book of Job, where the righteous Job suffered terribly at Satan's hand, but only because God permitted Satan to put him to the test (see Job 1:6-12; 2:1-6). The difference is that the ones suffering in connection with the fifth trumpet are not the righteous people of God, but rather "the inhabitants of the earth" (8:13), further described here as those who did not have the seal of God on their foreheads (v. 4). John's language shows that he remembers from his earlier vision the sealing of God's people on their foreheads for protection (7:3-8). Those "144,000" (7:4), transformed before John's eyes into "a great multitude that no one could count, from every nation, tribe, people and language" (7:9), are the only ones spared from the terrible plague of locusts. For them, Jesus' promise of "authority" (Lk 10:19) still applies, with the caution Jesus added: "Do not rejoice that the spirits submit to you, but rejoice that your names are written in heaven" (Lk 10:20). But for the moment we hear nothing of them.

The Locusts and Their King (9:7-12) Visitors to a recent exhibit at the Museum of Science in Boston viewed huge models of a number of common garden insects, enlarged hundreds of times over. Such a visit makes us all grateful that God created the world and its creatures on the scale he did! John, building on the prophet Joel's comparisons of

---

9:5 The time period *five months* sets limits to the plague and is probably derived from the normal life span of the locust (Charles 1920:1.243). The locusts in this vision present a strange mixture of the normal and the abnormal.

9:7-9 These verses are framed by a comparison of the locusts to horses (vv. 7, 9), probably not individually but corporately, as a conquering army. The reference to *crowns of gold* (v. 7) contributes to this image of victory or conquest (compare the heavenly elders of 4:4 and the rider on the white horse in 6:2). E. B. Elliott (1847:1:410) argued seriously that the faces were not simply *human faces* (v. 7), but specifically faces of men (that is, with beard or mustache), and supplied an imaginative drawing to make his point—all in the interest of proving they were the invading Arab Muslims of the seventh century (411-13). Although it is intriguing to imagine these creatures as bisexual, with men's faces and *women's hair* (v. 8), the word used with faces is normally an inclusive term for human

locusts to lions (Joel 1:6) or to horses galloping into battle (Joel 2:4), affords us a terrifying glimpse of what a different scale might look like. Such comparisons also occur in Middle Eastern poetry and folklore, both ancient and modern (see Beasley-Murray 1974:162). John's vivid description (vv. 7-10) serves to underscore and heighten the horror of the preceding account of the demonic invasion. We learn, for example, that the scorpionlike authority (v. 3) of the locusts was no abstraction, but that John perceived them with actual *tails and stings like scorpions* (v. 10), with the power to inflict intense physical pain. Small wonder that in those days people *will seek death, but will not find it; they will long to die, but death will elude them* (v. 6).

The awful description ends by introducing the locusts' king, *the angel of the Abyss, whose name in Hebrew is Abaddon, and in Greek, Apollyon* (v. 11). The Hebrew *Abaddon* is commonly translated "Destruction," and it is closely associated with "death" or "the grave" (see Job 26:6; 28:22; Ps 88:11; Prov 15:11). But instead of the word normally found in ancient Greek translations of these passages (*Apōleia,* "Destruction"), John uses the personalized *Apollyon* ("Destroyer"), in keeping with his point that this destructive power is personal—both a *king* and an *angel.* John Bunyan, in *The Pilgrim's Progress,* transformed *Apollyon* into an almost human adversary. Even though he had "scales like a fish . . . wings like a dragon, feet like a bear, and out of his belly came fire and smoke, and his mouth was as the mouth of a lion," Apollyon reasoned with Christian like any human enemy to turn him from the path to which he was called, and finally engaged him in single combat (Sharrock 1987:102-5). "In all but the name," wrote H. B. Swete (1908:120), this Apollyon was "a creation of Bunyan."

---

beings, not males in particular. The reference to women's hair does not imply that these locusts were seductive—they are hardly that! Rather, it reinforces the impression—borne out by the personified King Apollyon in verse 11—that in the world of the Bible ultimate evil, like ultimate good, wears a human face.

9:11 The naming of the king, or *angel of the Abyss,* first in Hebrew and then in Greek, lends a kind of solemnity and significance to this figure (compare the naming of the places where Jesus was presented to the people in Jn 19:13 and where he was crucified in 19:17; also the inscription over the cross in three languages in Jn 19:20). The Hebrew *Abaddon* would be mysterious and evocative to John and his readers, but the section ends with the Greek name *Apollyon,* which carries the meaning in their own language and admirably sums up the effect of the fifth trumpet as a whole—"the Destroyer."

In the book of Revelation, Apollyon is personal but far from human. Some interpreters (for example, Caird 1966:120) identify this *king,* or *angel of the Abyss,* with the fallen star that first released the terrible locusts from *the shaft of the Abyss* (v. 1). Although stars can sometimes represent angels in John's visions (as in 1:20), this angel is more likely one of the locusts from the Abyss. He is named in connection with John's description of them, and like them belongs to the Abyss itself, just as the angels of the seven congregations belong to their respective congregations (1:20; chaps. 2-3) or "the angel of the waters" (NRSV) in a later vision belongs to the "rivers and springs of water" that are turned to blood (16:4-5).

The point of the naming is to call attention to the destructive effects of the locust invasion (Beckwith 1922:563), in much the same manner that the name "Wormwood" calls attention to the bitter effects of that figure. If the result of the third trumpet (8:11) was "bitterness," the result of the fifth trumpet is "destruction." A still further possibility is that the name "Apollyon" was intended also to suggest the Greek god Apollo, who in John's time was widely associated with prophecy, and therefore in the minds of early Christians with false prophecy (see 6:1; Kerkeslager 1993:119). Just as "Wormwood" recalled biblical denunciation of false prophets (see Jer 23:15), so "Apollyon" calls to mind false prophecy in the Graeco-Roman world.

"Destruction" (whether in Hebrew or Greek) is more terrible than "bitterness," yet a voice now breaks in to remind us that even this is not the end: *The first woe is past; two other woes are yet to come* (v. 12). Whether these are John's words or words that he hears, they recall the threefold "woe" of the eagle flying overhead in 8:13 and are to be understood as a continuation or resumption of that announcement. The same will be true in 11:14. John does not reintroduce the vulture or eagle here, but its presence is implied.

The Sixth Trumpet, or Second Woe (9:13—11:14) The sixth trumpet, like the sixth seal (6:12—7:17), is much longer than the other members of the series. The difference in length is again commonly explained by assuming an interruption, or interlude, in the series (this time consisting of 10:1—11:13). There are two reasons for this: (1) John participates in the action in chapter 10, rather than just observing it; (2) if the trumpets represent an actual sequence of events that will take place before the end of the world, it is hard to imagine chapter 10 as part of that sequence. Will John return to earth someday, take and eat a scroll from the hand of a gigantic angel, as he does in that chapter? Probably not. It is easier to suppose that the time sequence has been interrupted, that we are now suddenly back in John's own time, and that John is experiencing a renewal of the prophetic call he received in chapter 1, in preparation for greater terrors to come.

These would be perfectly valid points if the trumpet series were a literal recital of events to happen on earth, in just that order. But it is not. Rather, it is a literal recital of what John saw. The series points to the terrible reality of God's judgment on the world. But that judgment (whenever and however it may come) will not simply be a rerun of John's visions. When chapters 9-10 are viewed as accounts of John's visionary experiences on the island of Patmos in the late first century, there is no need to suppose any kind of break or interruption between them. Even within the so-called interlude, John is explicitly reminded that the trumpet sequence is still going on (10:6-7). Just as chapter 7 belongs to the sixth seal, so 10:1—11:13 should be read as part of the sixth trumpet, not as a time-out or an intermission standing outside the series. The sixth trumpet, therefore, includes not only the judgment proper (9:13-19) but also considerable material bearing on the human response to this judgment and the preceding ones (9:20—11:13).

The Opening from the East (9:13-16) The judgment proper falls into the same two parts as the judgment just described under the fifth trumpet: (1) an opening or a "release" of demonic invaders against the earth and its inhabitants (vv. 13-16); (2) a detailed—and frightening—description of these invaders (vv. 17-19). The locusts of the previous vision were loosed from "the Abyss" by a fallen star (vv. 1-3), while in the present vision four angels are loosed from their place of restraint *at the great river Euphrates* (v. 14), far to the east of Patmos and Asia Minor. If the first invasion seemed to come from the pit of hell, the second is from "outside," from beyond the eastern borders of the Roman Empire. People in many cultures (including our own) have at times feared and hated the unknown or little-known peoples in distant lands. The Romans feared the Parthians beyond the Euphrates as a barbarian horde ready to sack the empire at the slightest sign of weakness. Some Americans from time to time have feared what they called the "yellow peril," whether from the Japanese in World War II, or from communist China and Korea in the Cold War, or Japan with its economic competition today. Those of a more imaginative bent fear aliens from outer space. The imagery of the sixth trumpet evokes just such cultural anxieties—and more.

The structure of the scene, in which one angel (the one blowing the trumpet) releases four terrible angels *to kill a third of mankind* (v. 15), evokes the earlier vision in which one angel cautioned four others *not* to send destructive winds over the earth "until we put a seal on the foreheads of the servants of our God" (7:1-3). In both instances the prospect is of judgment from the east (compare 7:2), and in both instances John hears a momentous number announced: 144,000 in chapter 7, promising hope and protection, and *two hundred million* here (v. 16), threatening death and destruction. The angels in this vision, *kept ready for this very hour and day and month and year* (v. 15) are suddenly transformed into a mounted army of staggering proportions, literally "two myriads of myriads" or twice ten thousand times ten thousand. The abrupt shift presupposes that *the four angels* are in charge of these demonic cavalry in much the same way that the four angels of 7:1-3 were in charge of the four winds. But instead of holding them back, they now release them to wreak havoc on the earth.

Description of the Horses (9:17-19) John's account of the origin of the invaders is followed by a vivid description of them (just as for the locusts). The description only heightens our sense of terror as we move from the fifth trumpet to the sixth. The horses John sees are not simply a means of transportation for human soldiers. Horses and riders are described together as one complex and terrible creature, like the centaur of Greek mythology. They are not human but demonic, and their job is to carry out the commission of *the four angels* from the Euphrates *to kill*

9:13 The voice *from the horns of the golden altar that is before God* recalls 8:3-5, and it may be intended to make a similar point, that the awful judgments about to come are in response to "the prayers of all the saints" (8:3-4). The *horns,* or projections at the four corners of the

a third of mankind (v. 15; compare v. 18).

While the locusts in the preceding vision had "tails and stings like scorpions" (v. 10), these horses had tails *like snakes* (v. 19) with similar power to injure (again, see Jesus' promise of authority over both "snakes and scorpions" in Lk 10:19). Even worse, *out of their mouths came fire, smoke and sulfur,* viewed as three distinct *plagues* bringing death to one-third of the human race (vv. 17-18). If the first four trumpets brought "fire" on the earth (8:7, 8, 10), and the fifth, "smoke from the Abyss" (9:2), the sixth adds *sulfur* to the conflagration. These *three plagues of fire, smoke and sulfur* (v. 18) will become basic elements in John's subsequent visions of eternal punishment (compare 14:10-11; 18:9, 18; 19:3, 20; 20:10; 21:8). "Sulfur" in the King James Version becomes "brimstone," creating the expression "fire and brimstone" for preaching based on the fear of hell.

The Response to the Invasion (9:20-21) For the first time, John gives full attention to the human response to these divine judgments. He has mentioned the human response twice before, but only in passing, as a way of dramatizing the severity of the judgments themselves, first in 6:15-17, where people hid in caves and cried out to the mountains to fall on them, and second in 9:6, where they desired death but did not find it. This time the human response is *in spite* of the severity of the judgment, not because of it. The point is made twice (vv. 20, 21) that these terrible judgments did *not* bring about repentance or a change of heart among those who were not killed.

It is natural to ask whether *these plagues* (v. 20) are the *three plagues of fire, smoke and sulfur* under the sixth trumpet (v. 18) or the whole trumpet series up to this point. But the question is moot because the *three plagues* of verse 18 are the only ones in the entire series specifically designed to be lethal to human beings (see v. 15). More illuminating is John's characterization of *the rest of mankind* that *did not repent* (vv. 20-21). His own moral values come to expression in his list of their vices: *worshiping demons, and idols of gold, silver, bronze, stone and wood—idols that cannot see or hear or walk (v. 20);* also *murders, their magic*

---

altar in heaven, correspond to those on the altar Moses was directed to make in the desert (Ex 27:2; 30:1-3).

arts, their sexual immorality or their thefts (v. 21).

The vices John lists are characteristic of the Gentile world. John is at one with Judaism in his sharp denunciation of Graeco-Roman society. His list is based in part on the Ten Commandments (Ex 20:1-17), which explicitly forbid idolatry, murder, adultery and theft. He stands squarely in the tradition of the prophet Jeremiah, who ridiculed idolatry in Babylon (Jer 10:1-16; compare the apocryphal *Letter of Jeremiah*), and of the apostle Paul, who condemned Gentile idolatry and immorality (Rom 1:18-32) and equated idol worship with the worship of demons (1 Cor 10:19-20). John probably still has in mind those false prophets in Christian congregations who advocated "sexual immorality" and eating "food sacrificed to idols" (Rev 2:14-15, 20). John's disturbing vision is that none of the judgments described up to now have succeeded in bringing about repentance or any change of heart in an evil world. The surviving inhabitants of the earth are like Pharaoh in the face of the plagues on Egypt in Moses' time: their hearts are hardened and they will not repent. Exodus preserves the sovereignty of God by insisting that God hardened Pharaoh's heart (Ex 7:14, 22; 8:15, 19, 32; 9:7, 12, 34-35; 10:1, 20, 27; 11:10; 14:4, 8). No such statement occurs here. On the contrary, it appears that if God's purpose is to bring the world to repentance (compare 2 Pet 3:8-9), it has failed—at least for the time being.

The Angel with the Open Scroll (10:1-10) The failure of God's purpose is not the last word. In order to transcend failure and bring about repentance, human participation is required—and human suffering. Therefore John himself becomes an actor in the unfolding drama. He sees *another* angel (10:1) in addition to the four who had released the terrible invading cavalry from the east (9:14-15). This angel is distinguished from those four, and from most angels in John's visions, by being called *mighty*, or strong. The only "mighty angel" we have met before is the one John had seen in heaven "proclaiming with a loud voice, 'Who is worthy to break the seals and open the scroll?'" (5:2). The mighty angel in the present scene also has "a loud voice" (NASB) *like*

9:21 *Magic arts,* or "sorceries" (NRSV; Greek *pharmakoi*), will be mentioned again in John's lists of those to be thrown into "the fiery lake of burning sulfur" (21:8) and of those to be excluded from the new Jerusalem (22:15). The conflict between Christianity and the practice of magic in Asia Minor (specifically Ephesus) is evident already in the book of Acts (19:13-16, 18-19).

the roar of a lion (v. 3). Moreover, the *rainbow above his head* (v. 1) recalls the rainbow encircling the throne of God in John's first glimpse of heaven (4:3), while the comparison of his face to *the sun* recalls the angel in John's introductory vision (1:16) who identified himself as the risen one (1:17-18).

In short, this *mighty angel* has an aura of divinity about him that prompted some older commentators to see him as none other than Jesus Christ himself. This is highly unlikely, yet the angel does represent God, or the power of God, in a way that most other angelic figures do not. He stands astride land and sea as one who is sovereign over both (v. 2; compare God's judgment on the land and the sea in connection with the first two trumpets). Although he is not Christ in person, he can be viewed as a divine agent acting on behalf of God and the Lamb. That Jesus uses certain angels to represent him in John's visions will become explicit in 22:16: "I, Jesus, have sent my angel to give you this testimony for the churches."

The *mighty angel* here, like the one in 5:2, is introduced in connection with a scroll (v. 2). The scroll in chapter 5 was last seen in the possession of the Lamb, and if this angel holds the same scroll, now open, it is clear that he is acting as the Lamb's agent or representative. Most commentators hesitate to identify the two scrolls because the first was called simply "a scroll" (Greek *biblion,* 5:1), while this one is *a little scroll* (using a diminutive form, *biblaridion,* vv. 1, 9, 10). Moreover, John mentions it as if seeing it for the first time (v. 2). Yet later (v. 8) he is told to take *the scroll* (Greek *to biblion*) from the angel's hand, indicating that the terms "scroll" and "little scroll" are used interchangeably. Perhaps the scroll is "little" only in relation to the gigantic angel who holds it. Its most conspicuous characteristic is that it lies *open* in the angel's hand (vv. 2, 8). By contrast, the scroll in chapter 5 was sealed. The overriding question in that chapter was when and by whom it would be opened (compare 5:2, 3, 5, 9). The simplest conclusion is that the scroll John will take from the angel's hand in this chapter is none other than the

10:1 *Another mighty angel* is literally "another angel, a mighty one." John is not looking all the way back to 5:2 and claiming that this is a different "mighty angel" from the one mentioned there. Nor is he necessarily implying that the two are the same. He is merely describing the two in a similar way (see also 18:21).

scroll taken by the Lamb in chapter 5 (see Mazzaferri 1989:271-74; Bauckham 1993:80-81). John has witnessed the breaking of its seals (6:1—8:5), so there is no reason why the scroll should not be *open*. Just as in chapter 5 the Lamb took the scroll in the presence of a "mighty angel" in order to open it, John must now take the open scroll from a mighty angel's hand in order for the plan of God to run its course (vv. 8-11).

First, however, the mighty angel and *a voice from heaven* (v. 4), acting together, supply a kind of fanfare to raise our level of excitement and expectancy. When the angel shouted, *the voices of the seven thunders spoke* (v. 3). John is about to write down their messages when the heavenly voice stops him: *Seal up what the seven thunders have said and do not write it down* (v. 4). Richard Bauckham rightly observes that "the process of increasingly severe warning judgments is not to be extended any further" because "such judgments do not produce repentance" (Bauckham 1993:82). He implies, however, that *the seven thunders* were somehow canceled simply because John did not write them down. On the contrary, John's point is that he has heard and therefore knows far more than he is telling. If anything, the seven thunders are more mysterious and more frightening for *not* being described in detail. Like the best modern writers of horror and fantasy (M. R. James, for example), John knows that sometimes "less is more," and that understatement can be an effective vehicle for wonder and suspense.

Nevertheless, the suppression of the seven thunders does hasten matters toward their conclusion. The mighty angel backs up the command not to write them down by swearing a solemn oath (vv. 5-7). His gesture of raising his right hand toward heaven (v. 5) recalls the "man clothed in linen" in one of Daniel's visions. He announced an

10:6 The angel's announcement, *there will be no more delay,* was translated in the KJV "that there should be time no longer," influencing the words of the well-known gospel song: "When the trumpet of the Lord shall sound, and time shall be no more." But this is a mistranslation. There is no "timeless eternity" in the book of Revelation. When the seventh trumpet sounds, and "our Lord and his Christ . . . . reign for ever and ever" (11:15), John anticipates not the end of time, but an expanse of time that has no end. More appropriate to his purpose is the last verse of the hymn "Amazing Grace."

10:7 The tense of the verb *will be accomplished* is not future, but in Greek the aorist, or

interval of "a time, times, and half a time" before the prophecies would be fulfilled (Dan 12:7). The mighty angel, by contrast, swears that *there will be no more delay* (v. 6). Like the figure in Daniel, he swears *by him who lives for ever and ever.* But adds to this oath an elaborate reference to God's sovereignty as creator over the sky and earth and sea and everything in them (v. 6). This comes as a further reminder of the first four trumpets, with their demonstrations of God's power over each of these spheres of the created order (see 8:7-12).

The solemn assurance that *there will be no more delay* should not be taken literally. We have, after all, twelve more chapters to go. All it means is that seven thunders will not intervene before things move to their conclusion.

That the fulfillment is still future to John is shown by the expression *in the days when the seventh angel is about to sound his trumpet* (v. 7). This does not happen until 11:15, after a period spread out over at least forty-two months (11:2) or 1,260 days (11:3)—the prophetic equivalent of Daniel's "time, times and half a time" (see note on 11:2). The accent falls less on *no more delay* (v. 6) than on the fact that what is to come is God's *mystery* (v. 7). Because the future is in God's hands, it is bright, despite all the terrible things John has seen. *Mystery* does not imply a deep, dark secret. On the contrary, it is an open secret, or divine plan, that God *announced to his servants the prophets* (v. 7). The word "announce" is literally "to preach the gospel, or good news" (Greek *euangelizō*). The purpose of the mighty angel's oath is to assure John that the "bad news" of the first six trumpets is not God's last word. But in order to transform "bad news" into "good news," John himself must be drawn into the action, and with him all the people of God.

John's part in the realization of *the mystery of God* is made known to him by an experience similar to one that the prophet Ezekiel had (Ezek

---

past tense (*etelesthē*), corresponding to the prophetic perfect tense in Hebrew. It is as if the mystery "is accomplished" already in God's sight and from John's perspective as a prophet. Although the phrase *his servants the prophets* echoes the Hebrew Bible (Amos 3:7; Dan 9:6; 10; Zech 1:6), it is likely that the angel is referring not to Old Testament prophets but to Christian prophets in John's own time (see, for example, 11:18; 22:9). This is confirmed by every other use of the word "prophet" in the book of Revelation (see also Eph 3:4-5, where the "mystery of Christ" is not made known to "other generations as it has now been revealed by the Spirit to God's holy apostles and prophets").

10:10 The command "take it and eat it" differs slightly from Ezekiel's language and recalls

2:9—3:3). Again the "voice from heaven" (vv. 4, 8) and the "mighty angel" act together (vv. 8-11). The voice tells John to take the scroll from the angel's hand. When he does so, the angel gives him further instructions: *Take it and eat it. It will turn your stomach sour, but in your mouth it will be as sweet as honey* (v. 9). The thought of eating the scroll instead of reading it is arresting. It is a thought that would probably not have occurred to any of us had we been writing the story. It appears that the common metaphor of "devouring" an interesting book has been taken literally!

We must know Ezekiel's story in order to understand what is going on. Ezekiel too was told to eat a scroll and "then go and speak to the house of Israel" (Ezek 3:1). Unlike John, Ezekiel had seen the scroll actually being unrolled. "On both sides of it were written words of lament and mourning and woe" (Ezek 2:9). When he ate it, "it tasted as sweet as honey" (Ezek 3:3), suggesting that Ezekiel's message would be sweet to him, though bitter to his hearers. John's experience is more complex. Nothing is said of what is written on the scroll, but the message is *sweet as honey* in John's mouth and *sour* in his stomach (v. 10). Even though John (and his fellow prophets) have the sweet privilege of hearing and delivering God's "good news" (v. 7), their prophecies will inevitably bring them sorrow and suffering. John knows this, for he is already a "brother and companion in the suffering and kingdom and patient endurance that are ours in Jesus." He is on Patmos "because of the word of God and the testimony of Jesus" (1:9).

The Prophecy of the Two Witnesses (10:11—11:14) John's experience with the mighty angel and the scroll is at once interpreted by an anonymous pronouncement summarizing what is to be the subject matter of his prophecy: You must prophesy again about many peoples, nations, languages and kings (v. 11). This raises a question: where in the book of Revelation does John prophesy again about such persons

---

at least one early Christian formula for celebrating the Lord's Supper (see Mt 26:26). The exchange between the angel and John is set in a chiastic (*a-b-b-a*) pattern: first, the angel tells John the scroll will be (*a*) sour in the stomach, but (*b*) sweet in the mouth; then, when John eats the scroll, he finds it (*b*) sweet in the mouth, but (*a*) sour in the stomach. The effect of the arrangement is to highlight the bitterness of prophecy, not so much for the hearers as for the prophets themselves.

11:1-2 The distinction between *the temple* (Greek *naos*) and *the outer court* (Greek *aulē*) serves as a reminder that "temple" in the book of Revelation consistently refers to the

and groups? Or for that matter, where in the book has he prophesied before? He has narrated a series of visions, but is this what is meant by prophesying? Are his prophecies to be spoken or written? Such questions make this one of the more difficult passages in a difficult book.

It is best to read on, ignoring the chapter division. In 10:11 John *was told* something (literally "they told me"), while in 11:1 he *was given* something. The voice from heaven (10:4, 8) and the mighty angel (10:5-7, 9-10) are now out of the picture, yet John is still receiving his instructions, as a true prophet must always receive them, from above. First he is told that he *must prophesy* (10:11); then he is given a prophetic action to perform (11:1-2). Clearly the latter is part and parcel of the former.

The prophetic action consists of measuring *the temple of God and the altar* and *the worshipers there* (v. 1). To *measure* here means to secure or establish, just as it does later in relation to the new Jerusalem (21:15; compare Ezek 40:3; Zech 2:2), and to "measure" those who worship is perhaps (as the NIV has it) to *count the worshipers*. Everywhere else in the book of Revelation, the "temple" and the "altar" are in heaven, not on earth in the city of Jerusalem. Even in the new Jerusalem of the future, John will "not see a temple in the city, because the Lord God Almighty and the Lamb are its temple" (21:22). It is likely, therefore, that John is being told here to measure the heavenly temple or sanctuary, not the earthly one. If so, *the outer court,* said to be "excluded" and not measured (v. 2) is a place on earth—or perhaps the earth itself.

In any event, it is a place now *given to the Gentiles,* who will *trample on the holy city for 42 months* (v. 2). Whether the scene of the prophecy to follow is the whole earth or specifically the *holy city* of Jerusalem (made desolate by the Romans in A.D. 70) is an open question at this point. That the old Jerusalem plays a role in this prophecy is made likely by the parallel between John's language and that of an earlier prophecy of Jesus found in Luke: "Jerusalem will be trampled on by the Gentiles

---

temple proper, or sanctuary, not to the entire temple area encompassing the courtyard and surrounding buildings (the latter in Greek is *hieron,* which never occurs in Revelation). From John's perspective, God's temple is now in heaven (compare Heb 9:11-14, 23-24), while the earth (with Jerusalem as its center) is the temple's unprotected outer court, the scene of the coming great conflict between good and evil. Accordingly, the *worshipers* in the temple of God (v. 1) are not human beings, whether Jews or Christians, but heavenly beings, including the twenty-four elders and four living creatures mentioned in chapters 4-5.

until the times of the Gentiles are fulfilled" (Lk 21:24). This period of Gentile domination is seen in the book of Revelation as either *42 months* (v. 2) or *1,260 days* (v. 3), that is, three and a half years (precisely one-half of seven).

In verse 3, the anonymous voice speaking to John takes on a kind of personality: *And I will give power to my two witnesses*. This can only be the voice of God, for God is clearly the source of the witnesses' authority, yet the voice goes on to speak in the third person of *the Lord of the earth* (v. 4), *a breath of life from God* (v. 11) and *the God of heaven* (v. 13). This is characteristic of many biblical oracles in which God speaks through a prophet, partly from God's own perspective in heaven and partly from that of the prophet who delivers the message on earth. The oracle does not end after verse 4 (where the NIV and the NRSV end it with their quotation marks), but continues to the end of the sixth trumpet and the announcement of the third woe (v. 14). This is God's voice speaking through John, as John fulfills his commission to *prophesy again about many peoples, nations, languages and kings* (10:11; compare *every people, tribe, language and nation,* 11:9).

Who are John's "two witnesses"? Identifications have been varied and sometimes eccentric, ranging from the apostles Peter and Paul martyred in Rome (Munck 1950) to two seventeenth-century London tailors named John Reeve and Lodowick Muggleton! The latter interpretation created a sect known as the Muggletonians, which lasted for three hundred years. In America, the Shakers identified the witnesses as the male and female aspects of God, linked both to Christ's first coming (as Jesus of Nazareth) and second coming (as Mother Ann Lee, founder of the Shakers).

The context suggests that in some way the testimony of the two witnesses corresponds to John's own. In 10:11 he is told to prophesy, and in 11:3, 6 he describes the witnesses doing just that. By referring to them as *the two olive trees and the two lampstands* (v. 4), he recalls a

11:2-3 The time period designated as *42 months* (v. 2) or *1,260 days* (v. 3) is equivalent to Daniel's "a time, times and half a time" (Dan 12:7; compare Rev 12:14). This is based on understanding "a time" as a year and "times" as two years, yielding a total of three and a half years, or half of seven. In prophetic calculation a year was commonly rounded off to 360 days (12 months of 30 days each). By dividing the classic symbolic number seven in half, John seems to make the point that tribulation will end and victory will come sooner than expected (as in Mk 13:20, "If the Lord had not cut short those days, no one would

vision of Zechariah (Zech 4:2-3), with the accompanying message, "'Not by might nor by power, but by my Spirit,' says the LORD Almighty" (Zech 4:6). Olive trees (with their oil) and lampstands (with their light) are appropriate images for the Spirit of God, and John has already used lampstands as a metaphor for the seven congregations to which he writes. The witnesses, therefore, should be understood as vehicles of the Holy Spirit, representing Christian prophecy or the church in its prophetic ministry to the world, whether in John's time or ours.

The confrontation John describes is a virtual war (vv. 5-13). The mission of the two witnesses is to *their enemies* (vv. 5, 12), otherwise identified as those *from every people, tribe, language and nation* (v. 9), or *the inhabitants of the earth* (v. 10). "The inhabitants of the earth" are precisely those on whom the flying eagle in John's vision had earlier pronounced three woes, corresponding to the last three trumpets (8:13; compare also 3:10; 6:10). There are striking similarities between the mission of the two witnesses and the trumpet series as a whole. At the sounding of the first three trumpets, fire fell to earth (8:7-11), and in the case of the witnesses *fire comes from their mouths and devours their enemies* (v. 5). The second trumpet turned a third of the sea to blood (8:8-9), and the two witnesses *have the power to turn the waters into blood,* and in fact *strike the earth with every kind of plague as often as they want* (v. 6). The implication is that all the plagues described in connection with the first four trumpets are now under the control of the two witnesses! In addition, they *have power to shut up the sky so that it will not rain during the time they are prophesying* (v. 6), a power associated in biblical tradition with the prophet Elijah (1 Kings 17:1; Lk 4:25; Jas 5:17). It is not hard to see why many commentators have linked the two witnesses in some way to the biblical figures of Moses, who turned Egypt's waters to blood, and Elijah, who not only sent drought and famine over Israel but called down fire from heaven

survive. But for the sake of the elect, whom he has chosen, he has shortened them").

11:6 It is no coincidence that it is not to rain for the 1,260 days of the witnesses' testimony (*during the time they are prophesying;* compare v. 3) and that the drought in the time of Elijah was said to have lasted an equivalent "three and a half years" (Lk 4:25; Jas 5:17). The detail is not found in 1 Kings 17-18 and probably rests on early Christian interpretations of the story as an example of divine judgment in the last days.

at Mount Carmel (1 Kings 18:36-38).

The echoes of the first four trumpets suggest that John's prophecy of the witnesses be read as a conscious transformation of the entire trumpet series. We have had other such transformations: a lion into a lamb (5:5-6) and 144,000 Jews into a crowd without number from every nation on earth (7:4-9). Here the transformation is that the people of God themselves become the executors of divine judgments. In the trumpet series their role was largely passive: God sent judgment on the earth in response to their prayers (8:3-5), and they were protected from harm by virtue of having "the seal of God on their foreheads" (9:4; compare 7:3-4), but otherwise they were out of the picture. Now they are very much in the picture, in the persons of their representatives, the two witnesses. They have been given *power to strike the earth with every kind of plague* (v. 6) and have *tormented those who live on the earth* (v. 10).

The transformation of the fifth trumpet and the first part of the sixth comes in verses 7-13. The two witnesses are invincible *during the time they are prophesying* (v. 6), but when the 1,260 days are over, they become vulnerable to attack by *the beast that comes up from the Abyss* (v. 7). John speaks of *the beast* as if it has been mentioned before, but this is not the case. We will hear more of him in chapters 13 and 17, but the reference here is very abrupt, *unless* we recall the king of the locusts under the fifth trumpet, "the angel of the Abyss, whose name in Hebrew is Abaddon, and in Greek, Apollyon" (9:11). Whether or not John has consciously transformed Apollyon into the beast from the Abyss, the terminology of the fifth and sixth trumpets is echoed in John's references to the beast's making "war" (v. 7, NRSV; compare 9:7, 9) against the two witnesses and "killing" them (v. 7; compare 9:15, 18, 20). The deadly war of invading locusts and cavalry against the earth's inhabitants is here transformed into a war of *the beast that comes up from the Abyss* against

11:8 By naming the city *figuratively* (Greek *pneumatikos,* "spiritually") as *Sodom and Egypt,* John characterizes it as both desolate and evil. The name "Sodom," applied to Jerusalem already in Is 1:9-10, is used here not so much to call attention to the sins of the biblical Sodom (Gen 18-19) as to evoke an image of ruin or desolation (compare Jude 7). *Egypt* (not even a city!) was in Jewish memory the place of slavery and oppression from which God had set Israel free. The prophetic name calling implicit in such language for Jerusalem finds its closest New Testament parallel in Paul's reference to "Hagar" (Gen 16), who "corresponds to the present city of Jerusalem, because she is in slavery with her children" (Gal 4:25).

God's people and their prophets.

In this way, John reintroduces the idea of martyrdom, which surfaced briefly in connection with the fifth and sixth seals (6:9-11; 7:14), but has played no role up to now in the trumpet series. At verse 7 the accent shifts from "testimony" to martyrdom. The English word *martyr* is derived from *martyria,* the Greek word for "witness" or "testimony," yet ironically it is only when their *martyria* is finished (v. 7) that the "witnesses" are martyred. Ironically too, their goals are realized not by their power to bring all kinds of terrible plagues on the earth (vv. 5-6), but by their own violent deaths at the hands of the beast (vv. 7-10). The familiar Christian "gospel," the story of suffering and death followed by vindication—whether of Jesus or his faithful disciples—is what transforms the ending of the trumpet series from nonrepentance (9:20-21) to repentance (11:13).

The abject defeat and shame of the two witnesses is sketched in some detail in verses 8-10. Their bodies lie in public view, unburied, the most tragic of destinies for the devout Jew (Jer 8:1-2; 14:16; Tob 1:16-18). The period of their shame, *three and a half days* (v. 9), ironically recalls their three-and-a-half-year period of invincibility (v. 3). The witnesses lie in the main street or public square of *the great city, which is figuratively called Sodom and Egypt, where also their Lord was crucified* (v. 8). This designation sends mixed signals. "The great city" in John's subsequent visions (16:19; 17:18; 18:10, 16, 18, 19, 21) is "Babylon the great" (14:8; 16:19; 17:5), used apparently as a symbolic name for Rome (17:18). Yet the words *where also their Lord was crucified* seem to identify the city as Jerusalem, *the holy city* of verse 2. If he had meant Rome, John could easily have said that the city was "figuratively called Babylon." But he referred instead to *Sodom and Egypt* (v. 8), leaving the identification open.

It is perhaps wisest to think of the city more generally as one embodying the values of human culture in rebellion against God—like

---

The expression *where also their Lord was crucified* could suggest that Jesus too died on the main street or in the center of Jerusalem rather than "outside the city gate," as is commonly assumed (see Heb 13:12). In the second century Melito of Sardis, writing from the very region to which the book of Revelation was sent, placed Jesus' crucifixion "in the center of Jerusalem," or "in the middle of the main street, even in the center of the city, while all were looking on" (Melito of Sardis, *On the Passover* 94; Hawthorne 1975:171). But John probably intends to say only that *the great city* was the city where Jesus died, not that the witnesses' deaths were in any way reenactments of his own.

Augustine's "earthly city" over against the "City of God," or John Bunyan's "City of Destruction" or "Vanity Fair" in contrast to the "Celestial City" in *The Pilgrim's Progress.* It is indeed Jerusalem, but Jerusalem understood as the center of the world (compare Ezek 5:5; 38:12) or, as one ancient Jewish book put it, "in the midst of the navel of the earth" (Jubilees 8.19; Charlesworth 1985:73). It is no longer recognizable as a holy city because it has been *given to the Gentiles* (v. 2). There is nothing distinctly Jewish about it, since its inhabitants are those *from every people, tribe, language and nation* (v. 9), or simply *the inhabitants of the earth* (v. 10).

The rescue of the two witnesses comes as *a breath of life from God entered them, and they stood on their feet* (v. 11). Their resurrection is not from the grave, like Jesus' resurrection, because their bodies lie unburied. Their vindication is as public as their shame, for *terror struck those who saw them* (v. 11) and they are taken up to heaven *while their enemies looked on* (v. 12). Accompanying this visible resurrection is *a severe earthquake* destroying a tenth of the city and killing seven thousand people, with the result that *the survivors were terrified and gave glory to the God of heaven* (v. 13). The expression *gave glory to the God of heaven* implies that the end of the story is repentance (compare 14:7, "Fear God and give him glory. . . . Worship him who made the heavens"; also the reference in 16:9 to those who "did not repent and give him glory" NRSV).

The transformation of the trumpet series is now complete. What could not be accomplished by six terrible plagues (see 9:20-21) is accomplished through the martyrdom and vindication of the people of God. The grimly increasing ratio of destruction on the earth, from one-fourth (6:8) to one-third (8:6-12), is now reversed. Only one-tenth of the people

---

11:12 Some ancient manuscripts read "I heard" instead of *they heard* in connection with the voice from the sky saying *come up here.* This reading is almost certainly influenced by the account in 4:1, where John himself heard a voice saying virtually the same words to him. The first person does not fit the present context, which is not a narrative of anything John himself saw or heard. From verse 3 on, it is a prophetic story told by God or by a divine messenger. The best and most widespread textual evidence favors the third person, *they heard.*

11:13 Because the city is Jerusalem, it is tempting to think of its repentance as that of the Jews or of Israel (see Beckwith 1922:584-85, 604), in the tradition of Paul and Romans 9—11. As Paul describes the Jews' situation in his day (as in Elijah's), there were seven thousand who had not "bowed the knee to Baal" (Rom 11:4), while "the rest were hardened"

in the city are destroyed, while nine-tenths are spared. The extended sixth trumpet has achieved at last the purpose of the series as a whole—repentance on earth and worship of God among some at least of the earth's inhabitants. At this point (v. 14), the eagle's voice breaks in again to introduce the last of three "woes" (compare 8:13; 9:12). But even the meaning of *woe* is transformed as the trumpet series moves into its seventh and final phase, since what immediately follows is not "woe" in the usual sense, but victory and vindication for the people of God (vv. 15-18).

The Seventh Trumpet, or Third Woe (11:15-19) We all know the feeling summed up by the expression "the future is now." It may be graduation, marriage, the birth of a first child or a long-awaited trip to some faraway place. Someday it will be retirement, and one day it will be the hour of death. It is something we knew was coming, something anticipated and imagined for years, with excitement and joy or with dread. Sooner or later a time comes when it is upon us, and we experience either realization or disappointment or relief, depending on what our expectations were and how closely their fulfillment matched them.

John's expectations about the seventh trumpet must have been a strange mixture of excitement and dread, not unlike those of any Christian facing simultaneously the mystery of death and the hope of heaven. On the one hand John had been warned of three terrible "woes" to come on the earth, but had only witnessed two of them (8:13; 9:12). One remained, possibly the worst of all, and it was to come "soon" (11:14). Yet he had also been told that "when the seventh angel is about

(Rom 11:7 NRSV). In Revelation the figures are reversed: seven thousand die in the earthquake, while "the rest," that is, the *survivors,* give glory to God! Still, there is no real hint of a Jewish presence in 11:1-13. The enemies of the two witnesses are consistently "the inhabitants of the earth" in a general sense (v. 10), those "from every people, tribe, language and nation" (v. 9). Even the term *the God of heaven* is used in Scripture of God mostly in relation to non-Jewish people or nations (Rev 16:11; also Ezra 1:2; Dan 2:17-19, 36-44; Jon 1:9). If the repentance is that of the Jews or of Israel, it is the repentance of a secularized Israel so completely "given to the Gentiles" (v. 2) that it has lost its Jewish identity. Ironically, the city regains its Jewish identity precisely by acquiring a Christian identity, as it responds belatedly to the mission of the two witnesses.

to sound his trumpet, the mystery of God will be accomplished, just as he announced to his servants the prophets" (10:7). Now that he hears the trumpet, it sounds more like the fulfillment of a promise than an oracle of woe. *Loud voices in heaven* announce that *the kingdom of the world has become the kingdom of our Lord and of his Christ, and he will reign for ever and ever* (v. 15).

Clearly the announcement introduces a major division in the book. At once the twenty-four elders in heaven, who have not been heard from as a group since the opening throne-room scene in chapters 4-5, fall on their faces in worship, just as they did twice in that opening scene (4:10; 5:8), offering thanks to God for what he has done and what he is about to do (vv. 16-18). It appears that these verses form a kind of *inclusio* with chapters 4-5, framing the seven seals and seven trumpets and preparing the way for still more visions to follow.

At the same time, the singular expression, *the kingdom of the world,* echoes the prophecy just completed about "the great city" of this world, "which is figuratively Sodom and Egypt" (v. 8). The world has many cities and "many peoples, nations, languages and kings" (10:11), but John knows, just as Augustine knew in his City of God, and Bunyan knew in *The Pilgrim's Progress,* that these are all *one* city, all *one* kingdom, whether we call it the City of Man or the City of Destruction or Vanity Fair. Only when that city's citizens "were terrified and gave glory to the God of heaven" (v. 13) was it possible to say, *The kingdom of the world has become the kingdom of our Lord and of his Christ.* The seventh trumpet is significant, therefore, both in relation to chapters 4-11 generally and to the end of the sixth trumpet in particular.

The dual phrase, *of our Lord and of his Christ,* recalls previous references to "the one sitting on the throne" together with "the Lamb" (5:13; 6:16; 7:10), but echoes more closely the language of Psalm 2: "Why do the nations conspire and the peoples plot in vain? The kings

---

11:15 The word *kingdom* only occurs once in the Greek text (literally, "the kingdom of the world has become [that] of our Lord and of his Christ"). The KJV reading "kingdoms of this world" is based on very weak manuscript evidence. Probably a scribe misread the Greek singular as a plural on the assumption that the world contains many kingdoms, not just one. The KJV translators then supplied "kingdoms" in the second instance, leading to the odd notion that God will take over each of the kingdoms of this world, or (alternatively) that there is one kingdom of "our God" and another of "his Christ."

of the earth take their stand and the rulers gather together against the LORD and against his Anointed One" (or "his Christ," Ps 2:1-2). Although G. B. Caird may have exaggerated in stating that John here "begins an exposition of Psalm ii" extending through several chapters (Caird 1966:141), much of the latter half of the book of Revelation will be given over to answering the psalmist's question. With the end of the Cold War, and in the face of many "small" crises all over the world (at this writing Russia, Bosnia, Haiti, Rwanda and Zaire), the ancient question reasserts itself with as much urgency as ever. Why indeed is there so much turmoil among the nations?

The song of the twenty-four elders recalls God's self-revelation just before John's first vision (1:8), but with one significant difference. God is described not as the one "who is, and who was, and who is to come, the Almighty," but now as *Lord God Almighty, the One who is and who was* (v. 17). God is no longer "to come" because God *has* come in power. The elders' song is a thanksgiving *because you have taken your power and have begun to reign* (v. 17). The occasion for God's great assertion of power is stated very briefly, in the spirit of Psalm 2: *The nations were angry* (v. 18). God's anger is in direct response to the anger of the nations. As one recent translation aptly puts it, "The nations rose in wrath, but your day of wrath has come" (REB; compare 6:17). In a similar vein, the song concludes that the time has now come *for destroying those who destroy the earth* (v. 18).

The first four trumpets might easily have left the impression that God was destroying the creation with fire from heaven, but by now the trumpet series has been transformed. Responsibility for the damage rests not with God, but with those who provoked God's anger. We have met them briefly, as the beast from the Abyss (11:7) or as "the great city . . . called Sodom and Egypt" (11:8). We will meet them again in varied forms in later chapters. The concluding reference to *destroying those who destroy the earth* (v. 18) is strangely similar to Paul's solemn warning to

11:19 The *ark of his covenant* was a box made at God's direction (Ex 25:10-22; 37:1-9) that was placed first in the tabernacle in the desert and later in Solomon's temple. It contained "the gold jar of manna, Aaron's staff that budded, and the stone tablets of the covenant" (Heb 9:4). When Solomon's temple was destroyed, according to Jewish tradition, the ark was hidden in the earth until the last day (see note at 2:17). Now it appears, appropriately enough, in heaven because in the book of Revelation the temple itself is in heaven.

the Corinthians: "Don't you know that you yourselves are God's temple and that God's Spirit lives in you? If anyone destroys God's temple, God will destroy him; for God's temple is sacred, and you are that temple" (1 Cor 3:16-17). Here in Revelation, it is as if the whole earth is God's temple, the "outer court" of his sanctuary in heaven (compare 11:2), given over to the Gentiles—or nations—for a limited time, but now holy once again and ready to be reclaimed.

Between the stern words of retribution that frame verse 18 are corresponding words of justice and reward. It is likely that the rewarding of *your servants the prophets and your saints and those who reverence your name, both small and great,* as well as the destruction of the earth's destroyers, takes place at the final resurrection in connection with *judging the dead*. This final judgment will eventually turn out to be a complex process in two stages (compare 20:5, 11-15), but in keeping with traditional Jewish expectations, the elders' song announces it as a single event involving reward for the righteous and punishment for the wicked (compare Mt 25:46; Jn 5:28; Acts 24:15). The righteous are here divided into three groups: Christian prophets (compare 10:7), ordinary believers, or "saints," whose prayers triggered the series of seven trumpets (5:8; 8:3-4), and unbelievers who learned to fear and worship God at the end of the trumpet series (11:11, 13). As subsequent chapters will show, the judgment of *those who destroy the earth* is not limited to the final resurrection (20:11-15), but begins already with the fall of the city called "Babylon" (14:8 11; chaps. 16-18) and the defeat of the armies of "the kings of the earth" (19:17-21).

The divine response to the elders' song is the sudden opening of *God's temple in heaven* (v. 19), protected by John's prophetic act of measuring at the beginning of the chapter (11:1). Within God's temple *the ark of His covenant appeared* (v. 19 NASB), followed shortly by two more "appearances" (all with the same Greek word for "appeared," *ōphthē*: first, "a great and wondrous sign appeared in heaven" (12:1) and then "another sign appeared in heaven" (12:3). The appearance of the ark of the covenant is God's acknowledgment of the thanksgiving just offered by the twenty-four elders. John's glimpse of the ark is the nearest he comes in all his visions to a glimpse of God. The repetition of the words "appear" and "in heaven" accent the continuity between God's self-disclosure in the temple and the disclosure of conflict and victory in the next four or five chapters (compare also 15:5). In this sense the seventh trumpet is open-ended, encompassing all the rest of the book of Revelation and announcing in advance the end of the story.

At the same time the trumpet series, like that of the seven seals, is terminated by a "storm" in heaven reminiscent of Mount Sinai: *flashes of lightning, rumblings, peals of thunder, an earthquake and a great hailstorm* (v. 19; compare 8:5).There will be more visions and more judgments, but no more trumpets. The double series that began with the seven-sealed scroll in chapters 4-5 is now at an end. Although there is definite continuity between chapters 11-12, there is at least a momentary pause in the action. Many readers have found this as good a place as any to divide the book of Revelation into two approximately equal parts: chapters 1-11 and chapters 12-22.

□ Two Great Signs and Their Interpretation (12:1-17)

The mystery of Christmas is unfolded in various ways in the New Testament. In one account it is the story of poor visitors in Bethlehem who give birth to a child "destined to cause the fall and rising of many in Israel, and to be a sign that will be spoken against, so that the thoughts of many hearts will be revealed," with a warning to the mother that "a sword will pierce your own soul too" (Lk 2:34-35). In another account the infant Jesus is threatened by Herod the Great and taken to Egypt by his parents when Herod "gave orders to kill all the boys in Bethlehem and its vicinity who were two years old and under" (Mt 2:16).

The third story, less well known, is a kind of transformation of the second. A pregnant woman is threatened by a great dragon that intends to "devour her child the moment it was born." But when she gives birth, the male child is "snatched up to God and to his throne," while the woman flees to the desert to "a place prepared for her by God" (Rev 12:4-6). Wherever we look, the mystery of Christmas is linked to danger and to the ancient conflict between good and evil. This particular expression of the conflict has the look of certain myths that were current in several cultures in John's time and before (see Yarbro Collins 1976). For our purposes, however, the point at issue is not the origin of the imagery, but the uses to which the imagery is put in John's vision and in the testimony he bears to the seven churches in Asia Minor.

The Two Signs (12:1-6) As the trumpet series ended, John was looking into the very temple of God in heaven (11:19). Now his vision continues with a panorama of events starting in heaven but running their full course on earth. He describes two great "signs" in heaven: first, the pregnant woman (vv. 1-2) and second, *an enormous red dragon with seven heads and ten horns* (vv. 3-4). The two meet in a brief confrontation (vv. 4-6), but its outcome is inconclusive and its meaning unclear until an interpretation is given (vv. 7-18).

The geography of the conflict is uncertain. *Heaven* refers to the place where God dwells in a holy temple (11:19) and also to the sky, as John perceived it from Patmos (vv. 1, 3). The woman in the first sign dominates the sky. It is both day and night, somehow, for the sun, moon and stars are all visible at once. The woman is *clothed with the sun, with the moon under her feet and a crown of twelve stars on her head* (v. 1). The dragon too is in the sky at the beginning, for *his tail swept a third of the stars out of the sky and flung them to the earth* (v. 4). But does the birth of the child take place in the sky or on the earth? The statement that the child was *snatched up to God and to his throne* (v. 5) while *the woman fled into the desert to a place prepared for her by God* (v. 6) allows us to infer that both the child's birth and the woman's confrontation with the dragon took place on earth. Even though John's vision is a panorama spread across the sky, it deals with events both in heaven and on earth.

The child in the vision is Jesus, for John identifies it as *a son, a male*

12:1 The *woman clothed with the sun* is the one character in the vision whose identity is not immediately clear. If the child she bears (v. 5) is Jesus, is she the Virgin Mary? It would be difficult to make sense of verses 6, 13-16 as Mary's personal history. If she is threatened by "the ancient serpent" of Genesis 3:15, is she Eve? Although the mother of the human race could perhaps have been transformed by John's vision into an ideal of womanhood or motherhood, the same problem exists. What are we to make of her protection in the desert for *1,260 days* or "a time, times and half a time"? More plausibly, like two other women in the book of Revelation (17:18; 21:9-10), she represents a city or a community. In the Old Testament and early Judaism a woman with child could represent the people of Israel (Is 26:17) or specifically "Zion," the city of Jerusalem (Is 66:7-8). The latter identification continued in early Christianity (Gal 4:26; 4 Ezra 2:15-32, 40-41). In our text the mixture of trouble and hope during the 1,260 days recalls 11:1-13, suggesting that the subject matter of the two passages is similar—the checkered fortunes of the old Jerusalem after the destruction of the city and temple in A.D. 70.

child, who is to rule all the nations with a rod of iron (v. 5 NRSV). Earlier the risen Jesus had promised the church at Thyatira "authority over the nations—'He will rule them with an iron scepter . . . just as I have received authority from my Father" (2:26-27). But when he is *snatched up to God and to his throne* (v. 5), Jesus disappears from the vision, and interest shifts to the woman and her fate. At the end of verse 6 the outcome of her encounter with the dragon remains uncertain.

The Interpretation of the Signs (12:7-17) The gaps and abrupt changes in verses 1-6 are explained in part by the rest of the chapter. Verses 7-18 look like a doublet of these opening verses, as if John were drawing on two different accounts of the same vision. Whether he is or not, he seems to be using the second account to interpret and clarify the first. It is as if John had asked God (or an angel) the meaning of what he had just seen in verses 1-6 and received verses 7-18 as an answer. Yet as we noticed earlier (see 7:13-14), John never in all his visions asks God questions. In some instances an angel answers without being asked, but now there is no angel to do the explaining, and John himself assumes the interpreter's role. In verses 7-9 he elaborates and clarifies his description of the dragon, which is reinforced in verses 10-12 by a voice he hears in heaven. In verses 13-16 he expands similarly on the dragon's conflict with the woman. Verses 17-18 mark a transition to a further stage in the vision.

The Dragon's Past and Present (12:7-9) John identifies the dragon repeatedly (v. 9) as *the ancient serpent, the devil* (compare 2:10) and

12:5 G. B. Caird (1966:149) has argued that "by the birth of the Messiah John means not the Nativity but the Cross." He claims that John is "continuing his exposition of the second psalm, begun in the vision of the seventh trumpet" and that in Psalm 2 "it is not at his birth but at his enthronement on Mount Zion that the anointed king is addressed by God, 'You are my son; today I have begotten you.'" But the theory does not work. First, Caird assumes that Christ's death is equivalent to his enthronement, but neither Psalm 2 nor our text makes any mention of Christ's death. Second, the dragon does not try to prevent the child's being born, but attempts to destroy him *after* he is born, a plan that makes no sense if the apparent 'birth' is actually Christ's enthronement as king. The common view that the story moves directly from Jesus' birth to his ascension is therefore preferable. Jesus' death is not mentioned because (1) John consistently uses other images to present the death, above all the slaughtered Lamb, and (2) his accent here is on Jesus' identity as the offspring or child prophesied in Gen 3:15.

Satan (compare 2:9, 13, 24; 3:9). He is further described by the evil he does: "leading the whole world astray" (v. 9) and "accusing" the people of God (v. 10). The dragon's remote past is defined by the term *ancient serpent,* which links him to the story of Adam and Eve in the Garden of Eden (Gen 3:1, 14-15). The assumption that the serpent in the garden is the devil in disguise is common today in popular Christianity, but was by no means self-evident in John's time. Like the serpent in Genesis, the dragon in Revelation is seen as the enemy of the woman. The story told in this chapter and the next reads like an interpretation of God's curse on the serpent in Genesis 3:15: "And I will put enmity between you and the woman, and between your offspring and hers; he will crush your head, and you will strike his heel."

This enmity was present already in verse 4, where the dragon confronted the woman to *devour her child the moment it was born.* Although the child *was snatched* from danger (v. 5), John left the impression in verse 6 that the conflict was far from over, and in fact he will return to it soon in more detail. First, however, comes a graphic description of the dragon's more recent past (vv. 7-9): *And there was war in heaven. Michael and his angels fought against the dragon, and the dragon and his angels fought back. But he was not strong enough, and they lost their place in heaven. The great dragon was hurled down. . . . He was hurled to the earth, and his angels with him.*

Such language raises the question of whether or not John has in mind a specific event of the recent past, perhaps the same event to which Jesus referred when he told his disciples, "I saw Satan fall like lightning from heaven" (Lk 10:18). It is possible, but not likely. Rather, the account of *war in heaven* rests on a conclusion drawn from John's own experience and from the vision just recorded. From experience John knew that Satan was very much in evidence on earth (compare 2:9-10, 13, 24; see also 1 Pet 5:8), and he attributes this to his recent expulsion from heaven. In the vision, the dragon's tail *swept a third*

12:7 *Michael* is mentioned in the Hebrew Bible only in Daniel, where he is "one of the chief princes" (Dan 10:13), "your prince" (addressing Daniel, 10:21) and "the great prince who protects your people" (12:1). Only in the New Testament is he called "the archangel" (Jude 9) and portrayed with an army of angels, as here.

12:10 For Satan as *accuser* of the people of God, see Job 1:6-8; Zech 3:1. In early Jewish

of the stars out of the sky and flung them to the earth (v. 4). That *stars* can mean angels was established already in the interpretation of an earlier vision (1:20). From this John could infer the downfall of the dragon and his angels.

The Voice in Heaven (12:10-12) Before resuming the story of the dragon and the woman (v. 13), John hears a *loud voice in heaven* reflecting on the significance of the dragon's fall (vv. 10-12). The event invites comparison with stars that fell to earth in two earlier scenes: the star called "Wormwood" in connection with the third trumpet (8:10-11) and the star with the key to the Abyss in connection with the fifth (9:1). The first star poisoned rivers and springs of water, and the second brought severe injury and pain on the earth's inhabitants. Similarly, the dragon's expulsion from heaven means *woe to the earth and the sea, because the devil has gone down to you! He is filled with fury, because he knows that his time is short* (v. 12).

Yet the differences outweigh the similarities. The announcement by the heavenly voice has the form of a song or hymn, and it is a hymn of joy more than of woe. The dragon's fall means that *now have come the salvation and the power and the kingdom of our God, and the authority of his Christ* (v. 10). The echo of the seventh trumpet (see 11:15) assures the reader that the outcome of the conflict on earth is not in doubt, even before it begins. This conflict will end as the war in heaven ended—with the defeat of the dragon and his cohorts. More specifically, Satan's fall from heaven means that his traditional role as *accuser* of the people of God is at an end, for he has no more access to God in heaven (v. 10). The perspective is much the same as Paul's in his letter to the Romans (Rom 8:33-34, 38):

> Who will bring any charge against those whom God has chosen? It is God who justifies. Who is he that condemns? Christ Jesus, who died—more than that, who was raised to life—is at the right hand of God and is also interceding for us. . . . No, in all these things we are more than conquerors through him who loved us.

---

literature, Michael and Satan are sometimes set over against one another as defender and accuser, respectively (as, for example, in the midrash on Exodus, *Exodus Rabbah* 18.5). In the New Testament, Jesus Christ commonly takes over Michael's role as defender or intercessor (for example, 1 Jn 2:1-2; Heb 7:25), but in the present passage (as in Jude 9) the traditional Jewish imagery is still at work.

No longer the accuser of God's people, Satan assumes the role of deceiver of the world and of the nations (v. 9). But the voice in heaven makes clear from the start that God's people will not fall victim to his deceit. The voice shifts momentarily out of the time frame of John's vision to reveal in advance the outcome of the impending conflict: *They overcame him by the blood of the Lamb and by the word of their testimony; they did not love their lives so much as to shrink from death* (v. 11; compare Paul's "more than conquerors" in Rom 8:37).

In this pronouncement the "overcomers" of chapters 2-3 are identified as Christian martyrs. Their victory over the dragon comes not by physical prowess, nor even by purity or good works, but solely by their willingness to face martyrdom for Jesus Christ. They will be victorious in exactly the same way in which Jesus the Lamb was victorious—through their deaths.

The optimistic tone of verses 10-11 is maintained even in verse 12, with its mixture of joy and woe. The joy is the joy of angels in heaven over their defeat of the dragon (see vv. 7-9) and over the saints' victory on earth. The *woe* of verse 12 echoes the "third woe" announced just before the seventh trumpet (11:14), but is tempered by the assurance that the dragon's *time is short* to torment the earth and its inhabitants. The "short time" corresponds to the "1,260 days," or three and a half years, of the woman's flight to the desert (v. 6; see note on 11:2, 3). Whenever this time period is mentioned in the book of Revelation, the accent is on the shortness of the time (not seven, but half of seven), in the spirit of Jesus' promise about shortening the days of trouble "for the sake of the elect, whom he has chosen" (Mk 13:20; compare Mt 24:22).

The Dragon and the Woman (12:13-16) Frustrated in his attempt to devour the woman's child (v. 5), the dragon pursues the woman herself. This explains her flight to the desert described in verse 6. Like Israel in ancient times (Ex 19:4), the woman is carried by *the two wings of a great eagle* to her place of protection for *a time, times and half a time* (compare Dan 7:25; 12:7). Hers is the promise of Isaiah, that "those

12:14 Most English translations conceal the fact that the phrase *a great eagle* actually has the definite article in Greek ("the great eagle"). This could imply that it is not just any eagle, but one mentioned before in John's visions, presumably the eagle that announced the three woes on the earth's inhabitants (Rev 8:13).

who hope in the LORD will renew their strength. They will soar on wings like eagles; they will run and not grow weary, they will walk and not be faint" (Is 40:31).

The dragon in his pursuit of the woman abruptly becomes *the serpent* (vv. 14-15), recalling once more his identity as "the ancient serpent" (v. 9) and the curse on the serpent in the Garden of Eden (Gen 3:15). The "enmity" between serpent and woman now becomes open conflict. In an extraordinary scene the earth, regarded from earliest times as a woman, often as Mother Earth, comes to the rescue of one who is herself both woman and mother. The earth is personified over against the dragon, or serpent. He *spewed water like a river, to overtake the woman and sweep her away with the torrent* (v. 15), but the earth in turn *helped the woman by opening its mouth and swallowing the river that the dragon had spewed out of his mouth* (v. 16). The dragon, who had tried to *devour* or "eat up" the woman's child (Greek *katesthiō,* v. 4), meets his equal here in a creature of God *swallowing* or "drinking up"(Greek *katapinō*) his deadly stream of water. Yet the woman's real protector is God, who had prepared the desert as her place of refuge on earth (vv. 6, 14). The earth is simply the instrument by which God keeps the woman safe.

The Dragon's Departure to the Sea (12:17) The dragon has now been defeated and frustrated at every turn. First he was driven out of his place in heaven (vv. 4, 7-9). Next he failed in his attempt to devour the woman's child (vv. 4-5), and when he tried to destroy the woman herself in her own "place" of refuge prepared by God (vv. 6, 13-16), he failed again. Three strikes and out—almost! The dragon's last recourse is to *make war against the rest of her offspring—those who obey God's commandments and hold to the testimony of Jesus.* To this end he leaves the desert and is seen standing *on the shore of the sea* (v. 17).

If the woman's child was Jesus (v. 5), who are *the rest of her offspring,* who *obey God's commandments and hold to the testimony of Jesus?* They can only be the Christian communities to which John was writing. The patient reader who has been asking, What has all this to do with me?

12:17 The word *offspring* (Greek *sperma,* literally "seed") is normally used either of the male sperm or of children in relation to a father (for example, "Abraham's seed," Gal 3:29), but not a mother. The unusual construction suggests that Genesis 3:15, an exception in which the word *is* used of the woman, is still in mind.

finally has an answer. Here if anywhere we find ourselves in these confusing middle chapters of the book, for the *war* between the dragon and us will play itself out in the scenes shortly to follow. It now becomes evident that John's visions bring to realization a two-part interpretation of the ancient prophecy addressed to the serpent in Genesis 3:15: "I will put enmity [1] between you and the woman [fulfilled in Rev 12], and [2] between your offspring and hers" [fulfilled in Rev 13].

The woman's "offspring" in the first instance is Christ (12:5), but the focus of attention is not on the conflict between the dragon and Christ (which is in the past), but on the conflict between the dragon's "offspring" (not yet identified) and the followers of Christ, those who *obey God's commandments and hold to the testimony of Jesus*. That will be the subject of the next chapter.

□ The Two Beasts and Their Deception (13:1-18)

The NIV locates the sentence *The dragon stood on the shore of the sea* at the beginning of chapter 13. This is not the case, however, either in modern Greek editions of the text or in the NRSV, both of which include this sentence with chapter 12 (as 12:18, a verse that does not exist in the NIV). I for my part have followed the versification of the RSV, which also places the pronouncement in chapter 12, but as part of verse 17. The tendency to place it in chapter 13 seems to have begun with certain later Greek manuscripts that read *estathēn*, "I stood" *on the shore of the sea*. The effect of this reading was to place *John* on the shores of Patmos, with the verb "I stood" preliminary to the *I saw* of 13:1. But the earlier, better manuscripts, as well as all modern translations (including the NIV), read *estathē*, "he stood," locating *the dragon* by the sea and linking him unmistakably with the beast's emergence *out of the sea* in 13:1 (see Michaels

13:1 The NIV consistently refers to both beasts in the chapter as "he," while the NRSV uses the pronoun "it." A good case can be made for either alternative. On the one hand, "it" is appropriate because the word for "beast" in Greek is neuter and because within John's vision the two beasts are obviously animals, not humans. On the other hand, they act like persons, and the beast from the sea is widely understood to represent an individual antichrist figure. The beast's number, after all, is "man's number" (13:18). Because I am trying to read the text from within John's vision, I have generally used "it" on the theory that what John saw was an "it," not a "he." Moreover, there is an ambiguity as to whether these beasts represent individuals or institutions.

1992:81-82). Because the latter reading is presupposed here, I have included the statement with chapter 12. The new character in the story is *the beast coming out of the sea,* and it is appropriate that chapter 13 should begin with him.

The Beast from the Sea (13:1-10) John's use of *I saw* (vv. 1, 2) marks a return to the first-person narrative style that dominated chapters 4-10. In chapters 11-12 John could say something "appeared" in the sky or in heaven (11:19; 12:1, 3) without specifying that it appeared to him personally. In the account of the dragon and the woman, the expression "I heard" in 12:10 was the only reminder that John himself was still in the picture. But now he abruptly becomes an eyewitness to the events he describes:

> *And I saw a beast coming out of the sea. He had ten horns and seven heads, with ten crowns on his horns, and on each head a blasphemous name. The beast I saw resembled a leopard, but had feet like those of a bear and a mouth like that of a lion. The dragon gave the beast his power and his throne and great authority. One of the heads of the beast seemed to have had a fatal wound, but the fatal wound had been healed.* (13:1-3)

Several points in the scene are worth noticing. First, a family resemblance between the dragon and the beast is evident. The dragon in chapter 12 had "seven heads and ten horns and seven crowns on his heads" (12:3), while the beast from the sea in chapter 13 has *ten horns and seven heads, with ten crowns on his horns.* Only the number and placement of the crowns vary. Second, although it is not stated in so many words that the beast is the dragon's "offspring," this is suggested by a setting in which the dragon seems to call the beast out of the sea and gives it *his power and his throne and great authority* (v. 2). Finally, the beast's fatally

13:3 Although I refer frequently to Genesis 3:15, certain inconsistencies in John's imagery suggest that he is not attempting a full-blown exposition of this classic text. He is simply drawing on some of its details to illumine the new story he has to tell. For example, in the Lamb's case there was no explicit reference to Genesis 3:15, for the Lamb was not injured in the heel or the foot. The Lamb's followers, in fact, who are also "slain" or "slaughtered" (6:9), are later said to have been "beheaded" (20:4) for their testimony. As for the serpent, or dragon, he is not himself bruised or wounded, as Genesis 3:15 might suggest, but simply defeated.

wounded head (v. 3; compare vv. 12, 14) recalls a significant detail in the ancient prophecy from Genesis about the serpent and the woman: "And I will put enmity between you and the woman, and between your offspring and hers; *he will crush your head,* and you will strike his heel" (Gen 3:15, italics mine).

Clearly the beast from the sea bears the battle scars of the combat prophesied in that ancient text. The statement that one of the beast's heads *seemed to have had a fatal wound* could be literally translated "was as if slaughtered to death," reminding us that when the Lamb first appeared in John's visions he too was "standing as if . . . slaughtered" (5:6 NRSV; the same Greek word). Something more is presupposed here than the "war in heaven" and the conflict between the dragon and the woman described in chapter 12. The beast's wounded head suggests a *previous* encounter between the Lamb and the beast, probably centered in Christ's death on the cross. Both the Lamb and the beast were "slaughtered" or "slain" in that encounter, yet both are "alive" (1:18; 13:14), and each in his own way is a "victor" or "conqueror" or "overcomer" (for the Lamb, see 3:20; 5:5; 17:14; for the beast, 6:2; 11:7; 13:7).

No other figure in the book of Revelation has captured readers' imaginations quite like the beast of chapter 13. Above all, the challenge at the chapter's end to "calculate the number of the beast, for it is man's number . . . 666" (v. 18) has drawn a chorus of responses from John's time down to the present, many forged in the heat of later but now long-forgotten controversies, and none very convincing. The general public (and often the church too) tends to view John's description of the beast either as the stuff of which science fiction is made or as a club to wield against personal or national enemies. Academic biblical scholars, by contrast, are more than willing to leave both the imagery and

13:5 The abruptness of the statement that the beast has authority "to do" (or *to exercise his authority*) for 42 months is softened in later manuscripts by substituting "to do what he wants" or "to make war." But the shorter, more difficult reading is correct.

13:6 It is not surprising that the idea of blaspheming God is extended to include blaspheming God's name, for God's name is the same as God's person. What is unusual is that the blasphemy extends to God's *dwelling place* [Greek *skēnē*] *and those who live* [Greek *tous skēnountas*] *in heaven*. Near the end of this book, a voice will announce that "the dwelling *[skēnē]* of God" is with human beings and that "he will live *[skēnōsei]* with them" (21:3). Until then it can be assumed that God's *dwelling place* is not on earth with

what it represents back in the distant past, on the grounds that John was making a veiled political statement about the Roman Empire in his own time. On this view, the beast is the empire, its many heads are a series of emperors, the wounded head is Nero, the first persecutor of Christians, who had died and, according to some versions of a popular legend, was expected to return to power with an army of the hated Parthians (for a summary, see Keener 1993:796, who concludes that "Rome would have taken serious offense at the implications of this exiled prophet John had the authorities read and grasped the symbolism of his book").

Widely held as this interpretation is among scholars, it is not without difficulties. For example, did John himself actually believe the so-called *Nero redivivus,* or reborn Nero, myth? If he did, are Christians today obliged to believe it? If he did not, was he guilty of deceiving his readers by playing on their superstitions and fears? If Nero is the mortally wounded head, how could he have been wounded by Christ, the woman's offspring, in keeping with Genesis 3:15? What could the death of Christ possibly have to do with Nero's death? To a large degree the interpretation of the beast as Nero is derived not from chapter 13 itself, but from chapter 17. As the vision of chapter 13 unfolds, neither John himself nor someone reading his prophecy for the first time has the benefit of the detailed explanation that is supplied four chapters later (17:7-18). The latter interprets in explicitly political terms the things John sees in 17:1-6, but it is by no means evident that the explanation there is also meant as a key to the visions of chapter 13.

The principle of reading John's visions (1) in the order in which he claimed to have seen them and (2) as if reading them for the first time should be respected and maintained. Then the reader is not in such a

---

humans but in heaven with the angels—presumably the same "dwellers" [*hoi . . . skēnountes*] in heaven who were told to "rejoice" at the dragon's fall to earth (12:12) and who themselves had a hand in his defeat (12:7-8). The close kinship between the Christian community and the angels was seen in connection with the angels of the seven congregations, and it will be reinforced later when an angel twice claims to be John's fellow servant (19:10; 22:9). Blasphemy against angels was no less a problem in early Christianity than the worship of angels (see Jude 8-9; 2 Pet 2:10-11), and John condemns it here by linking it to both blasphemy of God and the persecution of Christians.

hurry to move from vision to historical reality, and a door is opened to a rather more universal, less political reading of the text. On such a reading, the question to be asked is not, Where will we see this beast again later in the book? but, Where have we seen this beast before? The answer is clear: in 11:7, where John was told that "when [the two witnesses] have finished their testimony, the beast that comes up from the Abyss will attack them, and overpower and kill them." The description matches that of the beast in chapter 13. He too "comes up," in this case *out of the sea* (v. 1); he too "attacks" (that is, "makes war") against the people of God: he too "overpowers" or "conquers" them (v. 7) and "kills" many of them (vv. 10, 15). The vocabulary is similar, and there is good reason to conclude that "the beast from the Abyss" (11:7) and "the beast from the sea" (13:1) are one and the same. After the passing mention in chapter 11 (and possibly even earlier under the name "Apollyon" in 9:11) John now provides the beast with a more formal introduction.

The most conspicuous biblical reference point for John's beast from the sea is Daniel's dream of four great beasts from the sea, the first like a lion with eagle's wings, the second like a bear, the third like a leopard, and the fourth, different and more terrible than the others, with ten horns (Dan 7:1-7). In John's vision the order of the first three is reversed (leopard-bear-lion), and Daniel's four beasts have been rolled into one. Or, to put it another way, Daniel's terrible, unidentified fourth beast seems to have "swallowed" its three predecessors and to have taken on the distinguishing characteristics of each. This should further caution us against identifying John's beast too quickly or too exclusively with one specific empire or political system, whether past or future. We should first appreciate John's vision as a vision and should try to put ourselves inside the fascinating (though frightening) world it creates for us.

13:7 The entire sentence, *he was given power to make war against the saints and to conquer them,* is omitted in some important manuscripts, including p^{47} and A. The fourfold repetition of the phrase *was given* in verses 5 and 7 could easily have led to the accidental omission of a line as a scribe's eye skipped over one of the four occurrences of the phrase. But it is also possible that this sentence was introduced into the text later to coincide with 11:7. If it is omitted, the chapter gives no details of the beast's persecution of Christians.

13:8 The original text does not say that Christ died before the world was created, despite widespread use of the phrase *the Lamb that was slain from the creation of the world.* This

The beast's agenda corresponds to that of the dragon: the dragon was the deceiver of "the whole world" (12:9), and the beast throughout chapter 13 carries out that deception. John implies that the healing of the beast's mortal wound is itself a deception, producing amazement over *the whole world* (v. 3) and leading people on earth to worship both the dragon and the beast (v. 4). The beast's authority prevails on earth *for forty-two months* (v. 5; compare 11:2), and by the end of that time *all the inhabitants of the earth* will worship it (v. 8).

The dragon's further goal of persecuting Christians (12:17) is also evident, though rather less conspicuous in the beast's career. The beast is given *a mouth to utter proud words and blasphemies* (v. 5), and he opens it *to blaspheme God, and to slander his name and his dwelling place and those who dwell in heaven* (v. 6). The last phrase probably refers to angels, viewed as heavenly counterparts to Christian believers on earth. The actual persecution of Christians is mentioned explicitly only in verse 7, yet persecution is clearly implied by the prophetic appeal to John's readers in verse 10: *If anyone is to go into captivity, into captivity he will go. If anyone is to be killed with the sword, with the sword he will be killed. This calls for patient endurance and faithfulness on the part of the saints.* The appeal is based on Jeremiah 15:2: "Those destined for death, to death; those for the sword, to the sword; those for starvation, to starvation; those for captivity, to captivity" (compare the four horsemen of Rev 6:1-8).

The significance of the brief prophetic oracle in verse 10 can scarcely be overestimated. Time and again, from the ill-fated Muenster kingdom of the sixteenth-century Anabaptists to David Koresh at Waco in the 1990s, the book of Revelation has been linked in the public mind to violence, war and armed rebellion. The book has been blamed for everything from social revolutions in Latin America to the nuclear arms race during the Cold War. John's oracle here gives the lie to all such

would be untrue. He died in real history, in the first century in Jerusalem, even though his death was foreknown and destined "before the creation of the world" (1 Pet 1:20). Our text speaks rather of the beast "whose name has not been written from the creation of the world in the book of life of the slain Lamb" (see Michaels 1992:92-94 and compare 17:8, where Jesus' death is not even mentioned). The NRSV avoids the error of the NIV, but falls into another by connecting the phrase "whose name has not been written . . . in the book of life" with "everyone" (as in 17:8) instead of the beast.

interpretations, whether offered by those who would justify violence or those who would consign Revelation to the scrap heap because of the violent world it evokes. The book is most emphatically *not* a call to arms, but a call *for patient endurance and faithfulness on the part of the saints* (v. 10).

The burning question in the minds of John's readers must have been, If all these terrible things are going to happen in the world, what should be our response? The answer of this text—and of the whole book of Revelation—is that the response of Christians must be one of nonresistance and nonretaliation: first, because armed resistance will be futile in any case and second (and more importantly), because God and the Lamb have already guaranteed them victory. Those who "overcome" do so not with the sword, but with "the blood of the Lamb" and "the word of their testimony" (see 12:11). For the present, John is saying, until the beast's forty-two months are up (v. 5), those destined for imprisonment will go to prison and those destined for death will be killed. The sole responsibility of Christians is to be faithful and to wait out the storm. God and the Lamb will intervene in due time. John's point is not unlike that of Paul in Romans 12:19-21:

> Do not take revenge, my friends, but leave room for God's wrath, for it is written, "It is mine to avenge; I will repay," says the Lord. On the contrary:
>
> "If your enemy is hungry, feed him;
> if he is thirsty, give him something to drink.
> In doing this, you will heap burning coals on his head."
>
> Do not be overcome by evil, but overcome evil with good. [Compare Prov 25:21-22 LXX]

Where John differs from Paul is that Paul still had confidence that the state "does not bear the sword for nothing," but is "God's servant, an agent of wrath to bring punishment on the wrongdoer" (Rom 13:4). Because of developments in the Roman Empire since Paul's time,

---

13:10 Almost all ancient manuscripts record the last part of John's prophetic appeal differently, with an active rather than a passive verb and with the helping verb "must": "If anyone kills with the sword, with the sword he must be killed." Only Codex Alexandrinus (A), our single most reliable manuscript, has the passive *if anyone is to be killed*. But the other reading is suspect because of the possible influence of Matthew 26:52, "all who draw

John has lost confidence in the state. Instead of the state's executing God's wrath on wrongdoers, it will now be a case of God's executing wrath on the state. This will come in the next six chapters, which have given the book of Revelation its reputation as the most violent book in the New Testament. Without question, the reputation is deserved. Yet it does not follow that the book fosters violence among its readers. The very opposite is true. The call to *patient endurance and faithfulness on the part of the saints* (v. 10) is a call to peace, a call to leave the judgment of our enemies in the hands of God and the Lamb. In our day it is mostly those who have abandoned the belief that God will destroy evildoers with fire from heaven who take it upon themselves to do exactly that.

The Beast from the Earth (13:11-18) The expression *then I saw* (v. 11) introduces a new phase of John's vision (compare "I saw" in vv. 1, 2). Now he sees *another beast,* this one *coming out of the earth* instead of the sea. Earth and sea are interchangeable in the sense that either can be regarded as the realm of death or the dead. Either can become, under certain circumstances, an "abyss," or bottomless pit (9:1-2, 12; 11:7). The two beasts, however, are not quite interchangeable. The beast from the earth, called in later visions "the false prophet" (16:13; 19:20; 20:10), is in no way a rival or a competitor of the beast from the sea, but on the contrary is strictly subordinate to the first beast. Its mission is not to exalt itself or to demand worship for itself, but solely to make sure that the earth's inhabitants worship the first beast (vv. 14-15). Possibly John's readers noticed here a kind of twisted parallel to the Christian triad of Father, Son and Holy Spirit. In early Christian thought (especially in John's Gospel) Jesus does nothing on his own authority, but glorifies the Father who sent him, speaking and acting only on the Father's authority (Jn 5:19, 30). Similarly the Spirit of truth acts on Jesus' authority and glorifies Jesus alone (Jn 16:13-14). This is why some commentators have referred

the sword will die by the sword," and perhaps also Revelation 11:5. More likely the passive is correct, and the sole source of John's text was Jeremiah 15:2 (Metzger 1971:750). Whichever reading is adopted, the text is warning Christians against armed resistance of any kind.

to the dragon and the two beasts in Revelation as a kind of "evil trinity" (Beasley-Murray 1974:244).

Most people voting for a candidate or looking for a leader say they want a "doer," someone who "gets things done," not just a talker. The so-called little horn in one of Daniel's famous visions was said to have had "a mouth that spoke boastfully" (Dan 7:8), and in our chapter of Revelation the first beast was "given a mouth to utter proud words and blasphemies" (v. 5). If the second beast is indeed a false prophet, it too deals largely in words, speaking *like a dragon* (that is, like *the* dragon, v. 11).

Yet it cannot be said that these figures are all talk and no action. On the contrary, the verb "to do" or "to make" (Greek *poieō*) is very conspicuous in John's account of his vision, more so than is apparent in translation. The first beast is given authority to "do" (that is, to exercise his authority) for forty-two months (v. 5) and (in most manuscripts) to "make" war against Christian believers (v. 7). The second beast "does" (that is, exercises) *all the authority of the first beast on his behalf,* and "makes" *the earth and its inhabitants worship the first beast* (v. 12). It also "does" (that is, performs) *great and miraculous signs,* so as to "make" fire come down from the sky in full public view (v. 13). The second beast is given power to "do" this and other signs in order to deceive the earth's inhabitants, telling them to "make" (or *set up*) an image in honor of the first beast (v. 14). The second beast then gives this image life and speech, and "makes" (that is, causes) those *who refused to worship the image to be killed* (v. 15). Finally, the second beast "makes" (that is, forces) *everyone, small and great, rich and poor, free and slave, to receive a mark on his right hand or on his forehead, so that no one could buy or sell unless he had the mark, which is the name of the beast or the number of its name* (vv. 16-17).

All the verbs noted are forms of *poieō* "to do," in Greek. The two beasts are indeed the "doers" in the troubled world of John's vision. But

---

13:11 The statement that the second beast had *two horns like a lamb* (in contrast to the first beast's ten horns, v. 1) suggests that this beast (known elsewhere in the book as "the false prophet") is a kind of counterfeit Christ, for the Lamb in the book of Revelation is quite consistently Jesus Christ. One obvious objection to this could be that Jesus the Lamb has seven horns (5:6), not two, but John's point in our chapter is more subtle: the second

where is this troubled world? When will all these terrible things take place? We can read and understand what John is saying, but what is he saying it about? Will the drama of Revelation 13 be acted out literally in our world, and if so, where? In the United States, in some Third World dictatorship, or everywhere at once? No passage in the entire book has captured the human imagination to quite the extent this one has. Many Americans who have little or no interest in believing or practicing anything found in the Bible suddenly become literal-minded fundamentalists when it comes to the *mark* of the beast (v. 17) and the mysterious *666* (v. 18). Some of their interpretations place the passage in the world of the occult or science fiction, while others propose conspiracy theories about the European Common Market, rampant computer technology, the increasing prevalence of credit and debit cards, personal identification numbers and the like. As a result, many serious Christians avoid the chapter altogether and with it, too often, the entire book of Revelation.

It is important to remember that virtually all the main verbs in verses 12-18 are present tense. This is obscured to some extent in the NIV, which seems to take them as "historical" present tenses, governed by the past tense, "I saw," in verse 11. They come through in the NIV, therefore, as past tenses: *he exercised* (v. 12), *he performed* (v. 13), *he deceived* (v. 14), *he forced* (v. 16). This is legitimate, but it should not cloud the fact that what John sees is something going on even as he watches. Literally, the second beast "is exercising" the first beast's authority and "is making" the earth's inhabitants worship the beast (v. 12). It "is performing" great signs (v. 13), "is deceiving" the earth's inhabitants (v. 14) and "is forcing" everyone to bear the first beast's mark on the hand or the forehead (v. 16). All this *could* simply be the style of prophetic narrative. It is, however, more likely that John is suggesting that what he saw was in some sense going on in the Roman Empire even as he wrote. John's purpose is not to construct a scenario for a specific series of events in the distant future,

beast has two horns like *a* lamb, not seven horns like *the* Lamb. Instead of making a direct comparison between this beast and Christ, he simply draws on the same pool of imagery. Compare Matthew 7:15, "Watch out for false prophets. They come to you in sheep's clothing, but inwardly they are ferocious wolves."

but to interpret (not literally, but very imaginatively) certain developments in his own day. Once we stop looking for a blueprint of the future, we can gain insight from the picture he paints into the conflict between good and evil in every generation—including our own.

Three aspects of John's description of the second beast's activities are particularly instructive. First, there is a strong accent on idolatry, with a characteristically Jewish insistence that the worship of idols is based on deception (see 2:14, 20; 9:20). The second beast *deceived the inhabitants of the earth* when he *ordered them to set up an image in honor of the beast,* and *was given power to give breath to the image of the first beast, so that it could speak* (vv. 14-15). Second, the relationship between the two beasts is like that between the state and a state church. The beast from the sea is a secular political power, while the beast from the earth is a religious institution fostering worship of the first beast. The idolatry in question is thus defined as idolatry of the state. In John's day the state was the Roman Empire, but the vision is fulfilled in every generation whenever the state, with the help of religious institutions, tries to make itself the object of worship or to claim for itself allegiance that belongs to God alone.

John's vision is not so much protesting against some isolated aberration in the first century A.D. as staking out the limits of good citizenship. As long as the state is simply the state, an institution created by God (as it was for Paul in Rom 13:1-7) or at least tolerated by God (as it was for Peter in 1 Pet 2:13-17), it is possible for a Christian to be a good and loyal citizen. But when the state oversteps its bounds so as to become God, good citizenship is no longer an option. The battle lines are drawn, even though the Christian's role in the battle is a passive one governed by the counsel of verse 10: "if anyone is to go into captivity, into captivity he will go," and "if anyone is to be killed with the sword, with the sword he will be killed."

The third characteristic of the narrative in verses 11-18 is that "the saints" are not explicitly in the picture at all. These verses deal solely with the effect of the beasts' activities on *the earth and its inhabitants* (v. 12). The accent is not on "war against the saints" (as in v. 7), but on the deception and subjection of the general public, *small and great, rich and poor, free and slave* (v. 16). Implicit, however, is the assumption that these repressive public measures demand an appropriate response from Christian believers, a response indicated in verse 18 by *this calls for wisdom,* corresponding to "this calls for patient endurance and faithfulness" in verse 10. The invitation to anyone who *has insight to calculate the number of the beast* (v. 18) is clearly directed to John's Christian readers.

The number *666* is commonly regarded as an example of gematria, an ancient numbers game in which each letter of the alphabet was assigned a numerical value. Any name could be encoded in a number representing the total of the letters in the name. John makes it clear that *666* is *man's number,* or "the number of a person" (NRSV). The problem is that with a bit of ingenuity many prominent names in every generation can be made to add up to 666. One commentator wrote that such identifications "lead to nothing just because they lead to everything" (Hendriksen 1939:273). The numbers work quite well, for example, with the name Adolf Hitler.

But in order to convey any meaning at all to John's original readers, *666* must have pointed to a name they recognized in their own time. The most common suggestion is Nero Caesar. But as Robert Mounce has pointed out (1977:264), "this solution asks us to calculate a Hebrew transliteration of the Greek form of a Latin name, and that with a defective spelling." When the Latin form of the name is transliterated directly into Hebrew, the result is 616, and sure enough, in the western Roman Empire where Latin was dominant, there were manuscripts in which the number was recorded as 616 (Irenaeus noticed this already in the late second century in his *Against Heresies* 5.30). Clearly, the scribes who copied the book of Revelation were familiar with gematria, and it may well have played a part in John's riddle. Yet because of its indeterminacy no solution based on that phenomenon alone is likely ever to be proven or to find general acceptance.

A more cautious approach starts from the simple recognition that *666* is linked to the characteristic interest in the number seven throughout the book of Revelation as a number of completeness or perfection. The number *666* falls short of the magic seven three times over—at the level of hundreds, tens and single units. William Hendriksen (1939:182) defined its message as "failure upon failure upon failure." The point is subtly different from the dividing of seven in half to yield three and a half years, the equivalent of the "42 months" or "1,260 days." These numbers, as we have seen, represented a divine limitation on the authority of the dragon or the beast, while the number *666* attempts to characterize the beast himself. At the very least, the ancient philosophical notion of evil as a lack or a deficiency of the good seems to be at work in John's mysterious *number of the beast.*

Beyond this, the interpreter—any interpreter—is on thin ice. For what it is worth, some (for example, Rissi 1966:76) have pointed out that *666* is what is called a triangular number, that is, the sum of every whole number from one to 36. Thus if we were to lay out on a sheet one dot, then two, then three, then four and so on up to thirty-six, we would form a triangle made up of 666 dots. The number 36 is of interest not only because it is the square of six but because it too is a triangular number, the sum of every whole number from one to eight. In geometrical terms the two-dimensional triangle becomes a kind of pyramid. In a later vision (17:11), the beast will be called "an eighth" after a series of seven, and the argument is that *666* in chapter 13 is in some way equivalent to "an eighth" in the later chapter. This suggestion, although speculative, is of interest because Revelation 17:11 is introduced similarly: "This calls for a mind with wisdom" (17:9). It can only be evaluated, however, in the context of the later reference.

The most important thing for the modern reader to remember in connection with the celebrated *666* of verse 18 is that its purpose is to characterize, not identify, the beast. If the name Nero Caesar is somehow concealed here, the point is not that the beast from the sea *is* Nero, but that the beast is *like* Nero in its character and evil acts. Clearly the emperor Nero in the sixties was the major oppressor and persecutor of Christians within the historical memory of John's readers. If *666* is simply an expression of evil as anything that falls short of the good, then its

13:18 If *666* is intended as a number that falls three times short of the completeness or perfection suggested by the number seven, it is worth noting that the Christian *Sibylline Oracles* in the fourth century A.D. used the number 888 (three times *exceeding* perfection) to represent the name of Jesus (Greek *Iēsous*): "Then indeed the son of the great God will

purpose is to dramatize the point that the beast is evil and therefore to be resisted at all costs, and possibly also that it is doomed to "failure upon failure upon failure," as the next few chapters will show.

In any event, the modern reader should give priority to verse 10, "this calls for patient endurance and faithfulness," over verse 18, ***this calls for wisdom***. The believer's responsibility is not to know everything in advance, but to be faithful no matter whether the threat to faith comes from the final antichrist figure itself or from one of its many predecessors—for example, false prophecy as represented by the rider on the white horse in chapter 6. In our preoccupation with the beast in Revelation, we should not forget the words of 1 John 2:18: "Dear children, this is the last hour; and as you have heard that the antichrist is coming, even now many antichrists have come. This is how we know it is the last hour." It is every bit as vital for Christians to resist the "many" as "the one."

□ The Firstfruits and the Harvest (14:1-20)

The two parts of this chapter (vv. 1-5 and 6-20) are unified by the fact that *firstfruits* (14:4) imply a *harvest* (14:15-16). In the Hebrew Bible every firstborn, human or animal, belonged to the Lord (Ex 13:2), so the "firstfruits," or initial yield of every crop, were set aside as a sacrificial offering (for example, Lev 2:9-14; Neh 10:35-37). God's portion of the harvest was given to God up front, as it were. In the New Testament, "firstfruits" is used as a metaphor for something given in advance, anticipating a greater benefit or "harvest" to come. This can be the resurrection of Jesus anticipating the resurrection of believers (1 Cor 15:23), the Spirit as a gift from God pointing to future resurrection (Rom 8:23), the first converts in a particular region holding out the promise of more converts to come (Rom 16:5; 1 Cor 16:15) or reborn Christians offering hope for the rebirth of God's creation (Jas 1:18).

Our passage is unique within the New Testament in that the 144,000 as sacrificial "firstfruits" anticipate a "harvest" seen not as blessing or

come, incarnate, likened to mortal men on earth, bearing four vowels, and the consonants in him are two. I will state explicitly the entire number for you. For eight units, and equal number of tens in addition to these, and eight hundreds will reveal the name" (*Sibylline Oracles* 1.324-29; Charlesworth 1983:342).

salvation, but as judgment, a harvest rather like John the Baptist's, in which the Harvester was to "clear his threshing floor" and "gather the wheat into his barn," but "burn up the chaff with unquenchable fire" (Lk 3:17). John's glimpse of the 144,000 on Mount Zion is but a brief respite between the wrath of the beasts against them in the preceding chapter and the wrath of God on their behalf in the harvest that follows.

The Redeemed of the Earth (14:1-5) "Sweet is the melody, so hard to come by," according to songwriter Iris DeMent. Few of us can write music, and some (myself included) have trouble even carrying a tune. In any choir or congregation, it is easy to tell when someone is singing offkey. In the realm of the spirit it is more difficult. When a preacher has the words right, it is natural to assume that the "music" is there too, in the sense that the messenger's life and character authentically embody the truth of the message. Words, after all, are what the Christian gospel is all about, or so we are told. But every once in a while we hear someone about whom we have to say, "The words are theologically correct, but where is the melody?" Calvin Miller in his imaginative sketches *The Singer* and *The Song* has reminded us of the "music" of the Christian message, and nowhere is this music more evident than in John's vision of the redeemed on Mount Zion. What distinguishes these 144,000 from the rest of the human race is something very simple. They are able to learn a song (v. 3).

The Reward of the 144,000 (14:1-3) The turmoil of conflict is over, and the people of God, *144,000* strong, now stand triumphantly with the Lamb on Mount Zion. They have *his name and his Father's name written on their foreheads* (v. 1), most emphatically *not* "the mark of the beast" (13:17). The two beasts of the preceding chapter are nowhere to be seen. We are not told just how the conflict was resolved, but John gives us a momentary glimpse of its outcome. *Mount Zion* (occurring only here in the book of Revelation) is a place on earth, not in heaven, for the voice heard next is a voice *from heaven* (v. 2). *Zion* was the name of the mountain on which David built the earthly Jerusalem

14:1 Possibly *Mount Zion* is equivalent to the unnamed "mountain great and high" from which John later views the new Jerusalem (21:10). The earthly Jerusalem was in fact surrounded by several high hills or mountains, including Mount Zion. In contrast to the

centuries before, and whenever John refers to "the holy city" or "the new Jerusalem" in the Revelation (3:12; 21:2, 10), it is always "coming down out of heaven from God," and therefore located on earth. Up to this point in the visions, "mountains" have been pictured as either threatened (6:14-16) or threatening (8:8), but *Mount Zion* is a place of victory and rest for the *144,000.*

This group of the redeemed includes both the 144,000 Israelites from 7:1-8 and the "great multitude that no one could count" from 7:9-17. Just as "the Lion of the tribe of Judah" (5:5) remained in some sense a lion even after he had been transformed into the Lamb (5:6), so the 144,000 continue to be the 144,000 even after their transformation into an unnumbered crowd. They have lost their explicit identification with the twelve Jewish tribes listed in 7:5-8, but they have gained other distinguishing features.

They are identified first as those *redeemed from the earth,* and their reward is the privilege of learning *a new song* (v. 3). Because they are redeemed, there is reason to believe that redemption will be the theme of their song. The only "new song" mentioned before in Revelation was that of the living creatures and elders in heaven (5:9), and it was a song of redemption: "because you were slain, and with your blood you purchased men for God from every tribe and language and people and nation." It was accompanied by the music of harps (5:8), and the word for "purchased" in its lyrics was the same word used here of the 144,000 in the phrase *redeemed from the earth* (v. 4). This time the song comes not from the living creatures and elders themselves, but from an anonymous voice *from heaven* in their presence, *like the roar of rushing waters and like a loud peal of thunder,* and *like that of harpists playing their harps* (v. 2). Both the words and the music are left to our imaginations.

Their Identity and Qualifications (14:4-5) In keeping with his practice of identifying certain figures he has seen by explaining who or what they "are" (1:19-20; 4:5; 5:6, 8; 7:14; 11:4), John now becomes more specific about the 144,000: *These are those who did not defile themselves*

book of Revelation, the only other reference to "Mount Zion" in the New Testament defines it as "the heavenly Jerusalem" (Heb 12:22), probably in the sense that it is still in heaven (compare "the Jerusalem that is above," Gal 4:26).

with women, for they kept themselves pure. They follow the Lamb wherever he goes (v. 4). He defines the phrase *redeemed from the earth* more carefully by adding, "They have been redeemed from humankind as first fruits for God and the Lamb, and in their mouth no lie was found; they are blameless" (v. 4 NRSV; the NIV has *purchased from among men*). Such are their qualifications for learning the new song.

The phrase *follow the Lamb wherever he goes* confirms the impression of chapter 7 that the 144,000 are Christian martyrs, and that the "number" of the martyrs is now "complete" (6:11). The Lamb was first seen as if "slain" or "slaughtered" (5:6), and to *follow the Lamb wherever he goes* is to be "slain" as he was and for his sake (6:9). The martyrs' death, moreover, is viewed as sacrificial, like the death of the Lamb. For this reason, they are described as *blameless* (Greek *amōmos*), a term referring to moral purity that also means "unblemished" when applied to an animal chosen for sacrifice (as in 1 Pet 1:19, where Christ is compared to "a lamb without blemish or defect"). Two specific aspects of their moral purity are singled out: the first is that they *did not defile themselves with women, for they kept themselves pure* (v. 4; literally "for they are virgins"); the second is that *no lie was found in their mouths* (v. 5).

The most problematic feature of the vision for most readers today is that these 144,000 who are redeemed from the earth are male and celibate (Yarbro Collins 1984:129-31). According to one kind of feminist reading, "Women in the Apocalypse are victims—victims of war and patriarchy. The Apocalypse is not a safe space for women" (Pippin 1992:80). But this passage includes something to offend almost everyone, not just feminists and not just those who are "sexually active" (to use the modern euphemism), but women in general, men in general (they, after all, are the martyrs), married men in particular, married clergy of both sexes and all who have not taken vows of lifelong celibacy!

We can avoid such sweeping literalism by keeping two key factors in mind. First, a likely reason why the 144,000 are male is that they were male when first introduced in 7:4 as "sons of Israel" (RSV). The enumeration of twelve thousand from each tribe (7:4-8) sounds very

14:4 The Greek word used here and elsewhere in the New Testament for *firstfruits* is *aparchē*. Two very early manuscripts divide it as *ap' archēs*, "from the beginning," yielding the translation, "These were redeemed . . . from the beginning" (compare "from the creation

much like the mustering of a male army, and military imagery is common enough in connection with the prospect of martyrdom (see, for example, 1 Pet 5:6-9). Ritual sexual purity was considered a necessary qualification for going into battle (see Deut 23:9-10; 1 Sam 21:5; 2 Sam 11:11). Second, the ideal of sexual purity is thoroughly in keeping with the value system of the book of Revelation as a whole. Negatively, the congregations to which the book is written are warned against sexual immorality as well as idolatry (2:14, 20). The reference here to avoiding defilement *with women* can be read as an implicit warning (in advance) against "Babylon the Great, the Mother of Prostitutes" (17:5), who "made all the nations drink the maddening wine of her adulteries" (14:8; compare 17:1-6). Certainly this "defilement with women" has nothing to do with marriage, and the text should not be read as commanding literal, lifelong celibacy. Marriage, in fact, is a positive image for salvation in the book of Revelation, for the redeemed become in John's final visions the "bride" or "wife" of the Lamb (19:7-8; 21:2, 9; 22:17). The ideal of virginity or celibacy in a spiritual sense is essential to such imagery. As Paul put it, "I am jealous for you with a godly jealousy. I promised you to one husband, to Christ, so that I might present you as a pure virgin to him" (2 Cor 11:2).

Individually, then, the redeemed are seen here as male because they are martyrs, and in that sense soldiers. To call these men "virgins" is the same as saying that they *follow the Lamb wherever he goes,* a phrase combining the ideals of martyrdom and military allegiance. The other side of the coin, however, is that *corporately* they are female precisely because they will be wedded as "bride" or "wife" to Christ the Lamb. They will be seen as "the new Jerusalem . . . prepared as a bride beautifully dressed for her husband" (21:2). *All* corporate communities, in fact, are personified as women in this book, whether as mother (chap. 12), prostitute (chap. 17) or bride (chap. 21). To personify the redeemed individually as male and corporately as female, while confusing to us, says nothing about their actual gender. In its own strange way, and without conscious intent, the book of Revelation echoes the principle

of the world" in 13:8). But "firstfruits" is far more likely because of the sacrificial implications of verse 5 and in relation to the harvest to follow (vv. 6-20).

that there is neither "male nor female, for you are all one in Christ Jesus" (Gal 3:28).

As for the claim that *no lie was found in their mouths* (v. 5), this too reflects the values of the book as a whole. There is nothing more abhorrent to John than those who pretend to be something they are not, whether Jews (2:9; 3:9), apostles (2:2) or prophets (2:20; also 16:13; 19:20; 20:10). Near the end of the book the list of those consigned to the lake of fire ends with "all liars" (21:8), while the list of those excluded from the new Jerusalem ends with "everyone who loves and practices falsehood" (22:15). Possibly John's words are influenced by the early Christian image of Jesus as unblemished Lamb or suffering Servant, who "committed no sin, and no deceit was found in his mouth" (1 Pet 2:22 NRSV; compare Is 53:7-9), implying that Christians are those who follow his example. But the primary characteristic of the 144,000 is their sacrifice, as made explicit in the phrase *offered as firstfruits to God and the Lamb* (v. 4).

The Harvest (14:6-20) The mention of "firstfruits," with the stipulation that the sacrificial victims are "blameless" (14:4-5), leads us to expect that the "harvest" will soon begin, and we are not disappointed. John sees the harvest carried out in another of his sequences of seven. Like the judgments introduced by the trumpets, it is the work of seven angels, but this time only the first three are numbered. The judgment is ceremoniously announced by three angels (vv. 6-12), punctuated with a voice from heaven (v. 13), and then carried out by four more angels (vv. 14-20). The earth itself is harvested first (vv. 14-16), and finally the earth's inhabitants (vv. 17-20). Only as the judgment is actually carried out is it explicitly defined as a harvest (vv. 15-16, 18-19).

The Three Angels (14:6-12) John sees next *another angel* (v. 6; compare 7:2; 8:3; 10:1) proclaiming *the eternal gospel* (v. 6). Because he has seen no angels individually since the seven that blew the seven trumpets (8:2—11:19), it is natural to infer that this angel, commencing a new sequence, is *another* in addition to those seven. The angel is

---

14:6 Those who *live on the earth* (literally "sit on the earth") are presumably the same as the "inhabitants" of the earth" (6:10; 8:13; 13:8, 12, 14; 17:2, 8; compare 3:10; 11:10), yet possibly without the strong negative connotations of the more common phrase. The

flying in midair, that is, directly overhead, like the eagle or vulture that announced the three woes terminating the trumpet series (8:13).

This *eternal gospel* to all the earth's inhabitants is a strange gospel in two respects. First, it is not "good news" (as the term *gospel* suggests), but quite the opposite—much like the "woe, woe, woe" of the eagle in the earlier vision (8:13). Second, and more surprising, there is nothing distinctly Christian about the message. The angel's *eternal gospel* does not mention Jesus Christ and contains no promise of salvation. Yet it is the only instance of the noun *gospel* in the entire book of Revelation. *The eternal gospel* is perhaps best understood on the analogy of Jesus' own proclamation of the kingdom of God ("The kingdom of God is near. Repent and believe the good news" or "gospel," Mk 1:15; compare Mt 4:17). That proclamation had two parts: an announcement ("the kingdom of God is near") and a command ("repent!"). John's *eternal gospel* has the same two parts, but in reverse order: first a command, *Fear God and give him glory,* and then an announcement, *for the hour of his judgment has come.* The announcement of God's judgment is equivalent to one aspect of the announcement of God's kingdom, for the coming of the kingdom involves judgment as well as salvation. In the case of the command, *fear God and give him glory* is a fairly exact equivalent to "repent" (see 16:9), except that John's vision spells out further implications of this repentance: *Worship him who made the heavens, the earth, the sea and the springs of water* (v. 7).

The analogy with Jesus' "gospel of the kingdom" helps us to understand how the angel's proclamation here can also be described as "gospel." The very word "eternal," in fact, is probably linked to the absence of anything explicitly Christian about the angel's message. There is something almost contradictory about the terms "eternal" and "gospel." The Christian "gospel" by definition is new—"good news"—implying that God has done a new thing in the world by sending Jesus as Messiah or Savior. "Eternal," on the other hand, refers to that which has always been true.

Fear God and give him glory is the God of Israel's message to the

association here with *every nation, tribe, language and people* suggests that this is also the group from which the redeemed are drawn (5:9; 7:9; compare also the phrase "redeemed from the earth" in v. 3).

Gentile world always and everywhere—whether the Messiah has come or not. It closely resembles the "good news" Paul and Barnabas brought to the citizens of Lystra, "telling you to turn from these worthless things to the living God, who made heaven and earth and sea and everything in them" (Acts 14:15). Such a "gospel" is pre-Christian, Christian and post-Christian, and in that sense "eternal," for it is a call to the earth's inhabitants to repent, leave their idols, and turn to the one true God (compare Acts 17:24-31; 1 Thess 1:9). It puts into words the implied message of the seven trumpets, a message that went unheeded when humans "did not repent of the work of their hands; they did not stop worshiping demons, and idols," and did not "repent of their murders, their magic arts, their sexual immorality or their thefts" (9:20-21).

The call to *fear God and give him glory* also makes explicit the message that *was* heeded when "a tenth of the city collapsed . . . and the survivors were terrified and gave glory to the God of heaven" (11:13). The worship demanded is worship of God the Creator, and the spheres of creation (*the heavens, the earth, the sea and the springs of water*) correspond to the spheres of God's judgment according to the first four trumpets (compare 8:7-12).

A *second angel* follows with a message apparently directed to the same audience (v. 8). This time the message focuses specifically on *Babylon the Great,* an ancient city about which we have heard nothing so far in the book of Revelation. Like other cities, Babylon is personified as a woman, in this case an immoral woman. The angel's proclamation echoes Isaiah 21:9 ("Babylon has fallen, has fallen! All the images of its gods lie shattered on the ground!") and Jeremiah 51:7 ("Babylon was a gold cup in the LORD's hand; she made the whole earth drunk. The nations drank her wine; therefore they have now gone mad"). The new element in the text of Revelation is the definition of Babylon's wine as *the maddening wine of her adulteries*. We will hear more of "Babylon" and her "wine" in 16:19 and throughout chapters 17 and 18. For now it remains simply an allusion to the prophets, and to Israel's memory of oppression at the hands of a foreign empire long ago. Yet we sense that

14:8, 10 *The maddening wine of her adulteries* is literally "the wine of the passion [Greek *thymos*] of her fornication." The corresponding phrase in verse 10, *the wine of God's fury* is literally "the wine of the passion [Greek *thymos*] of God." There is a play on words here

Babylon the Great is also linked somehow to the two beasts and the more contemporary oppression described in the preceding chapter.

The voice of *the third angel* makes it explicit: *If anyone worships the beast and his image, and receives his mark on the forehead or on the hand, he, too, will drink of the wine of God's fury, which has been poured full strength into the cup of his wrath* (v. 9; compare 13:15-16). The warning confirms our suspected link between the beast of the preceding chapter and Babylon, with *the wine of God's fury* as Babylon's appropriate punishment for *the maddening wine of her adulteries* (v. 8). Yet for the time being *Babylon the Great* remains unidentified. John's original readers may have known her identity, but we do not—at least not without looking ahead to chapter 17.

The *third angel* adds that those who worship the beast and receive its image *will be tormented with burning sulfur in the presence of the holy angels and of the Lamb* (v. 10). The *smoke of their torment* will ascend forever, and they will have *no rest day or night* (v. 11). Although the language of these verses has contributed mightily to traditional Christian images of hell, it is difficult to say whether or not "hell," as commonly understood, is in view here. Why, for example, is the torment going on *in the presence of the holy angels and of the Lamb,* thus (apparently) in heaven itself? The announcement seems related to a celebration of Babylon's doom five chapters later: "Hallelujah! The smoke from her goes up for ever and ever" (19:3). That celebration too goes on in heaven (19:1). Probably both scenes are momentary previews of "hell" and hell's finality in "the lake of fire" (19:20; 20:10, 14; 21:8), not the reality itself.

There is no way to be certain whether the word to Christian believers that immediately follows (v. 12) is a continuation of the third angel's speech or simply John's prophetic appeal to his readers, in the manner of 13:10 ("this calls for patient endurance and faithfulness on the part of the saints"). The words here are virtually the same: *This calls for patient endurance on the part of the saints who obey God's commandments and remain faithful to Jesus* (compare 12:17). The effect of placing

because the Greek word *thymos* can mean either anger or sexual passion (see Caird 1966:185). In this sense the punishment fits the crime: the immoral passion of Babylon is punished by the passionate anger of a righteous God.

the appeal here is to make the alternatives (either worshiping the beast and receiving its mark or remaining faithful to Jesus Christ) as clear and as stark as possible.

The Voice from Heaven (14:13) The series of angels flying overhead is abruptly interrupted by a voice from the same direction. This voice, like the prophetic appeal preceding it, is directed to Christian readers. It is addressed to John first and commands him, *Write!* with the intention that what he writes will go out to the seven congregations. In both pronouncements (vv. 12, 13), the time frame is no longer the future that John has been scanning in his vision, but the present in which both John and his seven congregations actually live. The reason for saying this is the phrase *from now on*. In the vision that began at 14:1, the number of the martyrs was complete (at 144,000), but here the number is not yet complete. More will *die in the Lord,* and they are pronounced *blessed*. The Spirit in reply defines their blessedness: *Yes . . . they will rest from their labor, for their deeds will follow them*.

The situation recalls the fifth seal (6:11), where the souls of the martyrs were told to "wait" (literally "rest") until their number was complete. In both passages those who die as martyrs are said to be at rest, in contrast to the worshipers of the beast, for whom "there is no rest day or night" forever (14:11). The martyrs' rest is from *their labor* in the sense of toil and hardship, but the Spirit adds that *their deeds will follow them*. As H. B. Swete renders it, "They shall rest from their labors—I say not from their works, for their works go with them" (Swete 1908:188). The martyrs' wearisome efforts will be over, but their accomplishments follow them into heaven (contrast Heb 4:10, where Christians do rest from their "work," or "works," just as God did after creation). In the messages to the seven congregations, the risen Jesus

14:12 The phrase *obey God's commandments and remain faithful to Jesus* is literally "keep the commandments of God and the faith of Jesus" (compare NRSV). As in Romans 3:26, "the faith of Jesus" is ambiguous, for it can mean either Jesus' faithfulness to God or our faithfulness to Jesus. The ambiguity is intentional, for the presupposition of our faithfulness to Jesus is his identity first of all as God's "faithful witness" (1:5; compare 3:14).
14:13 The phrase *"Yes," says the Spirit* looks like a standard expression used by early Christian prophets (Aune 1983:282). Each of the seven prophetic messages in chapters 2-3 includes a command to "hear what the Spirit says to the churches" (2:7, 11, 17, 29; 3:6, 13, 22), while in the book of Acts the prophet Agabus at Caesarea introduces a prophetic

knew both the hardships and the lasting accomplishments of his people (2:1). He was able to tell whether or not their good deeds were genuine (2:9, 19; 3:1, 8, 15). In the case of the martyrs there is no question about their deeds, for they die *in the Lord,* having maintained their faith and obedience to the end.

The time-honored custom of reading this text at funerals suggests that the prophetic announcement could apply not just to martyrs in the strict sense of the word but to all Christian believers. Nothing much is said in the book of Revelation about natural death from sickness, accident or old age. Because there was so much violence in the society in which the book was written, the emphasis is almost entirely on persecution and martyrdom. Yet if any text in the book is applicable to natural death, this one is. The outlook is much the same as that of a roughly contemporary Jewish text that has nothing to do with martyrdom: "Moreover at the time of a man's departure, neither silver nor gold nor precious stones nor pearls go with him, but only the Law and good works" (Pirke Aboth 6.9; Danby 1933:461). Probably John's intent is that the martyrs first, but beyond them all who die *in the Lord* (that is, as faithful Christians), have the right to claim the promises of this verse.

The Next Two Angels (14:14-16) The series of angels in the sky continues unnumbered. Two pairs appear. An angel seated on a cloud holds a sickle, and then another angel comes and commands the first angel to reap a harvest. This happens twice, so that the harvest takes place in two stages. The first of the four is not called "another angel" (as in vv. 6, 8 and 9) but *one like a son of man.* In contrast to the angel with the "eternal gospel" (v. 7), who looked like an eagle or a vulture, this figure looks human. But in contrast to the one "like a son of man" in John's opening vision (1:13), this figure never identifies itself as Jesus.

---

warning to Paul with the words, "The Holy Spirit says," or, "Thus says the Holy Spirit" (Acts 21:11). *Yes* always introduces a response (compare 1:7; 16:7; 22:20), in this case John's response as a prophet to the voice from heaven telling him to "write."

14:14 As in 1:13 (see note), the quotation marks in the phrase *one "like a son of man"* should be dropped. Quotation marks suggest a biblical citation (the NIV footnote proposes Dan 7:13), but it is unlikely that any such citation is intended. The NRSV's "one like the Son of Man" is also incorrect because it gives the impression that the angel on the cloud either was Jesus or looked like Jesus. The point is not that the angel looked like Jesus of Nazareth or like a figure in Daniel's vision, but simply that it looked like a human being.

Still, it is tempting to think of this figure as Jesus because it is seated on a cloud, recalling imagery in which Jesus the Son of Man is to come "in clouds" (Mk 13:26), or "on the clouds" (Mt 24:30), and "send his angels and gather his elect from the four winds" (Mk 13:27). Probably the vision is intended to evoke just such images, but without implying that the figure on the cloud actually is Jesus in any literal sense. This figure does not "send" the other angels, but on the contrary takes his orders from the angel *out of the temple* that follows him (v. 15).

A better interpretation is that both these angels (the last four, in fact) are *functionally* equivalent to Jesus in that what they accomplish is what he accomplishes: the judgment of the world. This is signaled by the description of the first figure *seated* on a white cloud (v. 14), as John will later see Christ "seated" on a white horse (19:11) and God "seated" on a white throne (20:11)—settings in which they will execute judgment. The cry of the next angel, *Take your sickle and reap, because the time to reap has come, for the harvest of the earth is ripe* (v. 15), echoes the announcement that "the hour" (that is, the *time*) for God's judgment had come (v. 7). The only difference is that now it is addressed not to humans facing the judgment (it is too late for them), but to the messenger about to carry it out. The messenger quickly does what he is told. Still sitting on the cloud, he *swung his sickle over the earth and the earth was harvested* (v. 16).

The Last Two Angels (14:17-20) The statement that "the earth was harvested" has a ring of finality to it, but the harvest is not over. Two more angels appear, the first *out of the temple in heaven* (v. 17), like the angel who issued the command to harvest the earth, and the second *from the altar* (v. 18). As before, the first angel is carrying a sharp sickle, and the second gives the order to use it.

The harvest that now ensues is far more graphic and terrible than the earth harvest so briefly described in verses 15-16. It is a destructive

---

14:20 *The city* in the phrase *outside the city* has the definite article, suggesting a specific city mentioned before. One possibility is "Babylon the Great" (v. 8), but *outside the city* suggests a city that is spared, not "fallen" like Babylon. A better option is another "great city," the earthly Jerusalem, where Jesus was crucified (see 11:8), a tenth of which was destroyed by an earthquake while "the survivors were terrified and gave glory to the God of heaven" (11:13). In chapter 14 Jerusalem is represented by "Mount Zion," the home of the 144,000 (v. 1), and it is plausible that this city would be protected from the bloody harvest carried out in fire and blood. The angel commanding it is the angel *who had charge of the fire* (v. 18)—perhaps the same angel who earlier "took the censer, filled it with fire from the altar, and hurled it on the earth" (8:5). Here as in the earlier vision, destructive judgment comes, ironically, from the altar in heaven, the place of mercy and the focus of Christian worship. If the first stage of the harvest was a generic "harvest of the earth," presumably of wheat or some other grain, this is to be a grape harvest—the "vintage of the earth" (v. 19 NRSV; literally "the vine of the earth"). The dark red juice of grapes suggests the image of blood and violent death. The grape clusters are cut off with the sickle and thrown *into the great winepress of God's wrath* and *trampled in the winepress outside the city, and blood flowed out of the press, rising as high as the horses' bridles for a distance of 1,600 stadia* (vv. 19-20).

What scene anywhere in the book of Revelation is as gruesome as this one? Moreover, why does the harvest take place in two such contrasting stages? One possibility is that the "harvest of the earth" corresponds to the first four trumpets (8:6-13), which affected only the natural creation, while the "vintage of the earth," or grape harvest, matches the last three trumpets (9:1—11:19), which brought injury and death to humans as well. A more likely interpretation is that this harvest, like the one John the Baptist predicted in Matthew and Luke, involves both salvation and destruction, but with emphasis on the latter. The Baptizer spoke of "one more powerful than I," who would "clear his threshing floor" and "gather the wheat into his barn, but . . . burn up the chaff with unquenchable fire" (Lk 3:17). Instead of wheat and chaff, the vision in Revelation contrasts the bloodless harvest of grain with the bloody *winepress of God's wrath* (v. 19).

Because he has displayed so clearly the victory of the redeemed in 14:1-5 (and will do so again in 15:2-4), the accent of John's vision of harvest is on the destruction of the wicked, not the salvation of the

---

harvest. Some commentators have conjectured that the length of the great river of blood (*1,600 stadia*, or 200 miles, a stadium, or furlong, being about 600 feet) approximates the length of Palestine from north to south, but the approximation is not very close. The dimension, therefore, neither confirms nor denies the identification of the city as earthly Jerusalem. All that can be said is that 1,600, like 144,000, is a square multiplied by a power of ten (4 x 4 x 100; compare 12 x 12 x 1000) and thus an appropriate symbol of completion or consummation, in this case of divine judgment.

righteous. Writing against the background of America's own Civil War bloodbath, Julia Ward Howe captured something of the spirit of this graphic vision in her famous lines,

Mine eyes have seen the glory of the coming of the Lord;
He is trampling out the vintage where the grapes of wrath are stored;
He has loosed the fateful lightning of His terrible swift sword;
His truth is marching on.

If the trampling of the vintage is the work of angels in this vision, it is unmistakably Christ's own work in a later passage, where the one who treads the winepress of the fury of the wrath of God Almighty is immediately identified as king of kings and lord of lords (19:15-16). Once more the four angels of the harvest are functionally equivalent to Jesus, the Son of Man and the Judge. Their bloody work of retribution is his as well. Not everyone agrees. Caird, for example (1966:191-94), understands the bloodbath not as God's punishment of the wicked but as the deaths of Christian martyrs at the hands of their oppressors. John's purpose, he says, is "to make a profound disclosure about the great martyrdom, to show that the bloodbath of persecution, which might appear to be the total defeat of the church, was to the eyes of faith the ingathering of the elect and the means whereby the Son of Man would turn the slaughter of his saints into the downfall of his enemies" (1966:243).

The difficulty with this view is that the number of the martyrs is already complete (14:1-5). The grape harvest is more easily understood as God's wrath against those responsible for their deaths. In John's view, martyrdom is *not* its own reward. The martyrs are victorious only because their deaths are followed by actual resurrection and actual judgment against their enemies. Caird's interpretation seems motivated more by a desire to downplay the wrath and vengeance of God than by the actual language of the text. Christian piety has followed a sounder instinct in pointing out an ironic parallel between Christ (through his angels) treading the bloody winepress of God's wrath here, and Christ enduring God's wrath against sin on the cross by shedding his own blood. The further irony that both this judgment and the judgment of

15:1 The *great and marvelous sign* here corresponds to the "great and marvelous" deeds

sin at Jesus' crucifixion took place *outside the city* (see Heb 13:12 and perhaps Mt 21:39) may well be intentional.

☐ The Seven Last Plagues (15:1—16:21)

Critics of television have pointed out that too many hours spent in front of the tube are ruining the attention span of us all, young and old alike. Politicians running for office speak less and less to complex issues, resorting instead to sound bites of a minute or less. John's visionary experience in the book of Revelation must have been more like watching television than reading a book, and yet his attention span is better than mine as I try to follow the plot of his work. So much happens so quickly in Revelation that I find it all too easy to forget what has gone before. John himself does not forget, but picks up the thread of earlier visions accurately and often unexpectedly. Nowhere is this more evident than in the fifteenth chapter, where he picks up details from chapters 4, 8, 12 and 14.

The Third Great Sign in Heaven (15:1-8) When John claims that *I saw in heaven another great and marvelous sign,* he recalls for us the "great and wondrous sign" in heaven in 12:1 ("a woman clothed with the sun") and "another sign . . . in heaven" in 12:3 ("an enormous red dragon"). The third sign, so long in coming, consists of *seven angels with the seven last plagues—last, because with them God's wrath is completed* (v. 1). The terrible harvest of chapter 14 is not quite the end; there is one more series to come.

The seven angels are introduced ceremoniously, as were the angels who began blowing the seven trumpets in chapter 8. In that chapter John saw first the seven angels with their trumpets (8:2). Then "another angel" came and presented "the prayers of all the saints" like incense at the altar in heaven, filled the censer with fire from the altar and poured the fire on the earth in judgment (8:3-5). Finally the seven angels went into action, blowing their trumpets one by one (8:6—11:19). The pattern here is similar. John sees first the seven angels (15:1). Then instead of the saints' prayers entering heaven, the saints themselves appear (vv.

celebrated in verse 3, that is, the judgments that the *seven angels with the seven last plagues* will carry out in the next chapter.

2-4). Finally the seven angels go into action (vv. 5-8) with *seven golden bowls filled with the wrath of God* (v. 7), which are then poured out on the earth one at a time (16:1-21).

Why is the judgment triggered by "the prayers of the saints" in the first instance and by the presence of the saints themselves in the second? The common theme is sacrifice. Prayers are regarded as sacrifice represented by incense (8:3-5). The deaths of the martyrs have also been pictured as sacrificial in nature (14:1-5). Here too the redeemed have come through the blood and the fire of martyrdom. They stand at the sea of glass in heaven (compare 4:6), its shining surface reflecting the fire and torches surrounding it (compare 4:5), as well as the fire of persecution out of which the martyrs have come. They are specifically identified as those victorious over the beast and his image and over the number of his name (v. 2). Evidently they are the same group as the 144,000 in the preceding chapter, except they are no longer on "Mount Zion" but in heaven, with harps given them by God (v. 2), corresponding to the harps from heaven that played the "new song" that only the 144,000 were able to learn (14:2-3). Having learned the song, they are now ready to sing it. This image of the redeemed playing harps is probably the source of many modern depictions, in cartoons and in the public imagination, of humans becoming angels and playing harps all day long as their principal occupation in heaven.

The image in its context has a very serious purpose. John identifies

---

15:2 Some commentators interpret the *sea of glass mixed with fire* as an image for the Red Sea (red being the color of fire), with the implication that the saints, like Israel in the time of Moses, have crossed the Red Sea. This is unlikely. Nothing is said about the redness of the fire, and the sea is not a stormy Red Sea with "a wall of water" on either side (Ex 14:22), but something like a sheet of clear glass (see 4:6). The Red Sea comes into the discussion only because of the mention of the "song of Moses" (v. 3). There are few if any parallels between this song and the song attributed to Moses after the crossing of the Red Sea in Exodus 15.

The mention of *those who had been victorious over the beast and his image and over the number of his name* does not imply that the beast is finally defeated (as in 17:14, for example, and 19:20). The text says literally that they were victorious *from* [Greek *ek*] the beast and his image and the number of his name. The point is that the death of the martyrs at the hands of the beast meant victory for them in that they escaped the beast's power through their deaths.

15:3 Instead of *King of the ages,* the best ancient Greek manuscripts (including Codex Sinaiticus and the first hand of Codex Alexandrinus) read "King of the nations" (see NRSV), the new song as the song of Moses the servant of God and the song of the Lamb (v. 3). Quite clearly, it is not a song about Moses or about the Lamb, but the song of both jointly about the Lord God Almighty, celebrating the power and justice of the God of Israel and "King of the nations" (v. 3 NRSV) and introducing the last series of God's righteous judgments. Like the "eternal gospel" proclaimed from heaven (14:6), the song is not distinctively Christian. It encompasses the worship of Jew and Christian, Hebrew and Greek, Moses and the Lamb alike. Indeed it sounds like a postscript to the "eternal gospel," asking, Who will not fear you, O Lord, and bring glory to your name? For you alone are holy (v. 4). The song is Jewish to the core, yet comes to a focus in the expectation of Jew and Christian alike that all nations will come and worship before you, for your righteous acts have been revealed (v. 4).

The song (vv. 3-4) serves to place the judgments to follow in the setting of God's holiness and justice. When it is finished (v. 5), John sees *the temple,* or sanctuary in heaven, opened for the second time in his visions (compare 11:19). It is not like the magnificent Jerusalem temple destroyed by the Romans in A.D. 70, or even the temple first built by Solomon. John defines it rather as *the tabernacle of the Testimony,* corresponding to the tent where Moses and the people of Israel experienced the glory of the Lord in the desert after the Exodus (Ex 38:21; 40:34; compare Acts 7:44). It was called the tent of "testimony," or "covenant," because it contained the ark of the covenant. Even though

---

anticipating the hope expressed in verse 4 that "all nations will come and worship before you." Probably the NIV translators judged that the reading "King of the nations" had been unduly influenced by verse 4, but more likely *King of the ages* crept into the text as a standard liturgical expression familiar to scribes (see 1 Tim 1:17, "to the King eternal," but literally "to the King of the ages").

15:6 Instead of seven angels *dressed in clean, shining linen* (Greek *linon*), some important ancient manuscripts have them "dressed in clean shining stone" (Greek *lithon*). Because later scribes would more likely have changed "stone" to "linen" in a text describing clothing than the other way around, "stone" (represented in English by the Wycliffite version of 1380 and the Rheims New Testament of 1582) is the more difficult reading and thus probably the original one. If so, the angels' appearance recalls the description of God as like "jasper and carnelian" (literally "jasper and carnelian *stone*," 4:3) or of the new Jerusalem "with the glory of God, and its brilliance was like that of a very precious jewel, like a jasper, clear as crystal" (literally "like a very precious *stone,* like a jasper, clear as crystal," 21:11; see Michaels 1992:82-83).

the ark is not mentioned here, what John sees recalls his earlier vision of the ark in the sanctuary (11:19). Thus the seven bowls begin precisely where the seven trumpets ended.

As the seven angels *receive seven golden bowls filled with the wrath of God* from one of the four living creatures (v. 7), John sees the sanctuary *filled with smoke from the glory of God and from his power,* so that *no one could enter the temple until the seven plagues of the seven angels were completed* (v. 8). This description evokes the scene in the desert after the Exodus, when "Moses could not enter the Tent of Meeting because the cloud had settled upon it, and the glory of the LORD filled the tabernacle" (Ex 40:35). The seven plagues to follow (16:1-21) will reenact several of the Exodus plagues on Egypt, but because these are the *last* plagues (v. 1), the order of the Exodus events is reversed. John sees the glory of God in *the tabernacle of the Testimony* first, and after that the plagues, sent not to free God's people from slavery (the redeemed are already free), but as a last effort to bring the earth's inhabitants, like Pharaoh, to repentance.

The First Three Bowls of Wrath (16:1-7) In the trumpet series there was a break between the first four trumpets (8:7-12) and the last three (signaled by a flying eagle announcing three more "woes," 8:13). In the bowl series, as in the seven judgments of chapter 14, the break is between the first three and the last four, signaled by a solemn exchange between *the angel of the waters* (16:5-6) and *the altar* (v. 7).

The first three bowls parallel the first three trumpets (8:7-12) in that they affect (in sequence) the earth, the sea and the fresh waters. Yet the bowls do not merely repeat the earlier series. The differences are as conspicuous as the similarities. First, the intensity is greater. The trumpet series affected one-third of the earth, sea and fresh water respectively (as well as a third of the sun, moon and stars), while the judgments introduced by the bowls have no such limitation. Second, in contrast to

16:5 The address, *you who are and who were, the Holy One,* recalls the designation of God as the one "who is, and who was, and who is to come" (1:4; compare 1:8; 4:8), except that the third term, "who is to come," is missing, just as it was in 11:17. Both here and in 11:17, the assumption is that now God has already come in power to carry out decisive judgement.
16:6 The phrase *the blood of your saints and prophets* is the first of three in the book of

the earlier series, humans are affected from the start. A third, more important difference is that the bowl series presupposes the conflict in the intervening chapters between the Christian community and the beast. The humans who suffer from these plagues are specifically those *who had the mark of the beast and worshiped his image* (v. 2). Still another difference, reflected perhaps in the fact that all seven judgments are repeatedly called "plagues" (15:1, 8; 16:9; compare 9:18), is that they correspond more closely to the Exodus plagues than do the judgments introduced in the trumpet series.

The first bowl brings *ugly and painful sores* on those who bear the beast's mark (v. 2; see Ex 9:8-12); the second turns the sea *into blood like that of a dead man, and every living thing in the sea died* (v. 3), while the third turns the fresh waters to blood (v. 4; see Ex 7:14-25). In the trumpet series there were no ugly sores or boils; a third of the sea was turned to blood, but as only one detail among several (8:8-9); fresh waters were poisoned but not turned to blood (8:10-11). Here, *the angel in charge of the waters* comments on the judgment of the fresh waters introduced by the third bowl (vv. 5-6), and with a response from *the altar* (v. 7) provides a chorus to the first three bowls and a momentary pause in the action. The pattern of a pronouncement followed by a response introduced by *yes* recalls the earlier exchange between a "voice from heaven" and "the Spirit" about "the dead who die in the Lord" (14:13), also following a series of three angels and preceding the appearance of four more.

Taken together, the angel's pronouncement and the altar's response form a kind of hymn that begins and ends with an acknowledgment of the justice of God's wrath displayed on the earth: *You are just in these judgments, you who are and who were, the Holy One, because you have so judged* (v. 5), and *Yes, Lord God Almighty, true and just are your judgments* (v. 7). Like "the song of Moses . . . and the song of the Lamb" (15:3), the angel's hymn addresses the *Lord God Almighty* (v. 7) and echoes such lines from the previous song as "just and true are your

---

Revelation that seem to distinguish between two groups of Christian martyrs (compare 17:6; 18:24; and possibly 20:4). The *saints* are perhaps any believers killed for their Christian faith and their refusal to worship the beast, while the *prophets* are a more limited group of those who, like the "two witnesses" of chapter 11, have borne active testimony to Jesus Christ and paid for it with their lives.

ways" (15:3), "for you alone are holy," and "your righteous acts have been revealed" (15:4).

The heart of the judgment hymn is the ironic pronouncement in verse 6: *for they have shed the blood of your saints and prophets, and you have given them blood to drink as they deserve.* The sentiments are similar to those expressed in the Jewish apocryphal work Wisdom of Solomon, reflecting on how the plagues were appropriate to the Egyptians' sins: "In return for their foolish and wicked thoughts, which led them astray to worship irrational serpents and worthless animals, you sent upon them a multitude of irrational creatures to punish them, so that they might learn that one is punished by the very things by which one sins" (Wis 11:15 NRSV). Wisdom of Solomon makes no mention of the plague that turned the waters of the Nile to blood (Ex 7:14-25), but in Revelation the same principle applies: those who shed the blood of martyrs are themselves punished with a plague of blood.

The Fourth Bowl (16:8-9) Unlike the first three, this plague is *not* a direct parallel to the plagues on Egypt. The sun, instead of being darkened (as in Ex 10:21-29), *was given power to scorch people with fire. They were seared by the intense heat and they cursed the name of God . . . but they refused to repent and glorify him* (vv. 8-9). The accent on fire recalls not so much the Exodus story as the first three trumpets (8:7-11) with their recurrent theme of fire from the sky. The only similarity to the Exodus story is the defiance of those who suffered from the plague. But their reaction here goes well beyond Pharaoh's persistent hardness of heart. They *cursed* [literally "blasphemed"] *the name of God, who had control over these plagues, but they refused to repent and glorify him* (v. 9). The "eternal gospel" call to "fear God and give him glory" (14:7) has had no visible effect on a defiant and rebellious world.

The Fifth Bowl (16:10-11) This time the bowl is poured out specifically

---

16:10 The fifth bowl echoes in some respects the fourth trumpet, where a third of the light of sun, moon and stars was darkened (8:12). It echoes even more the fifth trumpet, where "the shaft of the Abyss" was opened, and "the sun and the sky were darkened by the smoke

on the throne of the beast, and his kingdom was plunged into darkness (v. 10). The plague of darkness marks a return to the theme of the Exodus, when there was darkness over Egypt, "darkness that can be felt" (Ex 10:21). A kind of cumulative effect of the first five bowls sets in as people *gnawed their tongues in agony and cursed the God of heaven because of their pains and their sores* (v. 11; compare the "painful sores" of verse 2). The verdict after five plagues is the same as after four: *they refused to repent of what they had done* (v. 11).

The Sixth Bowl (16:12-16) The common feature between the sixth trumpet and the sixth bowl is *the great river Euphrates* (v. 12; compare 9:14). Here, instead of 200 million cavalry (9:16-17), John sees *the kings from the East* coming across the Euphrates (v. 12), representing *the kings of the whole world* assembled for a great battle (v. 14). These kings and their armies correspond to the cavalry of the earlier vision and, like those demonic forces, bring trouble to the earth in threes: three plagues of fire, smoke and sulfur in the earlier instance (9:18), and here *three evil spirits that looked like frogs; they came out of the mouth of the dragon, out of the mouth of the beast and out of the mouth of the false prophet* (v. 13). The comparison between these spirits and frogs is the only link between this plague and the Exodus (see Ex 8:1-15).

The *evil spirits* of this verse are literally "unclean spirits," the same phrase used in the Gospel of Mark for demons (see, for example, Mk 1:23; 5:2). John, after telling what he *saw* (v. 13), now speaks as a prophet to confirm the identification of the spirits as *spirits of demons performing miraculous signs,* and to interpret *kings from the East* as *the kings of the whole world* (v. 14). John transforms the Roman fear of Parthian invaders (see 9:14) into a universal confrontation. To him, kings and nations and armies are demon possessed, not just individuals. Twice he states that the evil spirits "gathered them" for battle (vv. 14, 16), giving first the time and then the place of the great final conflict. The time is *the great day of God Almighty* (v. 14), and the place is *the place that in Hebrew is called Armageddon* (v. 16). In giving the time, John gives

---

from the Abyss" (9:2), with the result that humans suffer pain "like that of the sting of a scorpion" and "will seek death, but will not find it" (9:5-6).

away the outcome as well. *The great day of God Almighty* means the day on which *God Almighty* is victorious. There is no suspense about how the battle will turn out, and further glimpses of it in subsequent chapters (17:14; 19:17-21) will only confirm the inevitable.

Between the notation of the time (v. 14) and place (v. 16) of the battle, John's prophetic voice suddenly gives way to the voice of Jesus himself (v. 15). It is the first time Jesus has spoken directly since dictating the seven messages of chapters 2 and 3, and his words sound very much like words from those messages: *Behold, I come like a thief! Blessed is he who stays awake and keeps his clothes with him, so that he may not go naked and shamefully exposed* (v. 15; compare 3:2-4, 18). This word of warning to the book's readers comes very abruptly in its context. Probably the reference to *the great day of God Almighty* (v. 14) suggested the image of "the day of the Lord," which in early Christian instruction was said to come "like a thief in the night," a tradition known to both Paul and his readers in 1 Thessalonians 5:2 (compare also Mt 24:43 and Lk 12:39). For John's readers the words represent a hopeful time shift from that near future day, when, too late for repentance, the world moves inexorably to its doom, back to a present in which there is still time to "Wake up! Strengthen what remains and is about to die," so as to walk with Jesus "dressed in white" (3:2, 5). When *Armageddon* comes, the day of grace will be over. Either we are on God's side—the victorious side—or we perish with those who are deceived by the dragon, the beast and the false prophet.

The word *Armageddon* conjures up twentieth-century images that are mostly foreign to the book of Revelation—above all the image of global nuclear war. The term in its immediate context refers not to a battle but to a place, whether fictional or real. *Armageddon,* or

---

16:16 Another possible etymology of *Armageddon* is "the mount of assembly" (Hebrew *har mô'ēḏ*), according to Isaiah 14:13 the dwelling place of "the king of Babylon," whose downfall is described poetically and in some detail in Isaiah 14:3-23 (Rissi 1966:84). This is attractive because of the verb "gather" or "assemble" in John's immediate context (vv. 14, 16) and because of the obvious link in the context between the dragon, beast and false prophet (v. 13) and "Babylon the Great" (v. 19). Yet it is not easy to see how the name could have evolved from *har mô'ēḏ* to Armageddon. The derivation from Megiddo is more plausible linguistically.

16:17 The mention of the seventh bowl's being poured out *into the air* perhaps anticipates

"Harmagedon" (NRSV), was as strange to the book's original readers as it is to us today. It is a Hebrew name in a Greek book and, unlike the Hebrew name "Abaddon" (9:11), is given in Hebrew only, without a Greek translation. The first syllable, *har,* is the Hebrew word for "mountain," so that the name could be read "mountain of Mageddon" or "mountain of Megiddo."

In the Hebrew Bible, Megiddo was the name of a fortified city and a plain in northern Palestine. The plain of Megiddo was strategically located, a kind of natural battlefield and the scene of one notably disastrous battle, the defeat of King Josiah at the hands of Pharaoh Neco of Egypt (2 Kings 23:29-30; 2 Chron 35:20-24). "Megiddo" may have had connotations similar to "Waterloo" in a more modern setting. But there was no Mount Megiddo nor any mountain near Megiddo. "Harmagedon," or "mountain of Megiddo," therefore, is a contradiction. It is as if we said today that a great battle would take place at "Death Valley Mountain." The strange name may have been chosen deliberately to signal that the place was imaginary, not real, and that the great final "battle" would not be an actual battle at all. In any case, no battle is described in connection with the pouring out of the sixth bowl. Troops are assembled, but nothing happens.

The Seventh Bowl (16:17-21) In place of a battle, the plagues come to an end with a word from God: *out of the temple . . . a loud voice from the throne, saying, "It is done"* (v. 17). The voice calls forth the same phenomena we have seen three times before in John's visions: *flashes of lightning, rumblings, peals of thunder and a severe earthquake. No earthquake like it has ever occurred since man has been on earth, so tremendous was the quake* (v. 18). Each time John had seen and heard these things, more was involved: first at the throne of God, lightning,

---

the giant hailstones of the last plague (v. 21), since hail falls from the sky. We might expect that the air, or sky (if anyone could get there), would be the only safe place in an earthquake. But in this instance the whole created order is in chaos. Everything is collapsing, and there is no refuge anywhere.

16:18 Curiously, the earthquake is characterized similarly to the hail in Exodus. The hail was "the worst storm in all the land of Egypt since it had become a nation" (Ex 9:24; compare v. 18), while the earthquake here is such that *no earthquake like it has ever occurred since man has been on earth* (compare Jesus' prophecy of tribulation in Mk 13:19).

rumblings and thunder (4:5); then at the beginning of the trumpet series, all these plus the earthquake (8:5; compare 6:12; 11:13); finally, at the end of that series, all of the above plus "a great hailstorm" (11:19). With the seventh bowl, the earthquake is described in much greater detail. *The great city split into three parts, and the cities of the nations collapsed. . . . Every island fled away and the mountains could not be found* (vv. 19-20). The hail is also detailed: *From the sky huge hailstones of about a hundred pounds each fell upon men. And they cursed God for the plague of hail, because the plague was so terrible* (v. 21).

The earthquake is a grim counterpart to an earlier one in which "a tenth of the city collapsed. Seven thousand people were killed in the earthquake, and the survivors were terrified and gave glory to the God of heaven" (11:13). But that earthquake struck Jerusalem, and that "great city" was known as "Sodom and Egypt" (11:9). This one is focused on *Babylon the Great* (v. 19), and no glory is given to God. Instead, the oracle of 14:8 comes to fulfillment: "Fallen, fallen is Babylon the Great." Babylon is given *the cup filled with the wine of the fury* of God's wrath (v. 19; compare 14:10). But who or what is Babylon? Why does John consistently refer to Babylon as "she" or "her" (v. 19; 14:8)? Ironically, "she" has been destroyed without ever being formally introduced. Her introduction will come belatedly in the next chapter.

Along with Babylon, John also sees *the cities of the nations* fall (v. 19). These cities are probably meant to correspond in some way to "the kings of the whole world" assembled for battle at Armageddon (vv. 14, 16), but must have also evoked for John's readers the specific cities of Asia where they lived: Ephesus, Smyrna, Pergamum, Thyatira, Sardis,

16:19 It is possible, though far from certain, that the *three parts* into which *the great city* splits are meant to correspond to the three unclean spirits of the preceding plague and, consequently, to the evil triumvirate of the dragon, the beast and the false prophet (see v. 13). Dissension within the ranks of the forces of evil will in any case become explicit in the following chapter (17:16).

16:21 The weight of *about a hundred pounds* is literally "about a talent." The "talent" was a Roman measure of weight equivalent to 125 Roman pounds of twelve ounces each (thus a little less than 100 pounds). It also became a measure of coinage that varied, depending on whether the unit of weight was applied to gold, silver or copper (see Mt 25:14-30). Here the enormous size of the hailstones underscores the destructive finality of the plague of hail.

Philadelphia and Laodicea. Whatever was in store for the respective Christian congregations in each of those cities, John's vision revealed that the cities themselves were doomed to share great Babylon's fate.

As for the *plague of hail,* it recalls for one last time the biblical plagues on Egypt (compare Ex 9:22-26). The statement that those on whom the giant hailstones fell *cursed* or "blasphemed" God explicitly confirms the responses at the end of the fourth and the fifth bowls (vv. 9, 11), and it serves as a final verdict on the entire series. Like the plagues of the Exodus and like the trumpets (9:20, 21), the "seven last plagues" do not bring repentance.

□ Babylon and Her Destiny (17:1—19:10)

The three "great signs in heaven"—"a woman clothed with the sun" (12:1), "a great red dragon" (12:3) and "seven angels with seven plagues" (15:1)—are over. A new stage of the prophecy begins. Its start and its finish are clearly marked. To begin, *one of the seven angels who had the seven bowls* introduces a long and elaborate vision. At the end John falls down to worship the angel and is told not to because the angel is only a fellow servant (19:10). This pattern repeats itself in John's last vision (21:9—22:9). Both visions focus on a city personified as a woman, here an evil woman, Babylon "the great prostitute" (17:1; compare 14:8; 16:19), and there a good woman, Jerusalem the virgin bride.

The Vision of the Woman and the Scarlet Beast (17:1-7) The angel promises to show John *the punishment of the great prostitute* (v. 1) with whom *the kings of the earth committed adultery* (v. 2). The angel's

---

17:1 The phrase *one of the seven angels who had the seven bowls* recalls the self-identification of the angel Raphael in the apocryphal book of Tobit: "I am Raphael, one of the seven angels who stand ready and enter before the glory of the Lord" (Tobit 12:15 NRSV). But the angel here (unlike Michael in Rev 12:7) is not named. There is no way to know which of the seven angels enumerated in chapter 16 this is, nor does it matter.

The detail that the prostitute *sits on many waters* echoes part of an oracle directed to "the people of Babylon": "You who live by many waters and are rich in treasures, your end has come, the time for you to be cut off" (Jer 51:13). The location literally described ancient Babylon with its "numerous canals distributing the waters of the Euphrates through the country about Babylon" (Beckwith 1922:692).

language, focusing on the prostitute's punishment, confirms the notion that the vision extends beyond chapter 17 through 19:10. Her punishment is not specified until 17:16, and it then goes on to occupy chapter 18 and the beginning of chapter 19. The angel begins by carrying John in the Spirit to a desert, where he is shown a kind of tableau, or still life, of the woman sitting on a scarlet beast that was covered with blasphemous names and had seven heads and ten horns (v. 3). The beast is recognizable from an earlier vision (13:1), but the center of the tableau is the seated woman, who is dressed in purple and . . . glittering with gold, precious stones and pearls (v. 4). She is a picture of wealth, extravagance, luxury and ease. John's attention is intently focused on this woman, and he identifies her by the name written on her forehead: BABYLON THE GREAT, THE MOTHER OF PROSTITUTES AND OF THE ABOMINATIONS OF THE EARTH (v. 5). This name, he tells us, is a mystery. He has used the name "Babylon" before (14:8; 16:19), but now he explains that it is a figurative or symbolic name, like "Sodom and Egypt" applied earlier to the city where the two witnesses died (11:8).

The corruption of the woman is evident both in the angel's first mention of her (vv. 1-2) and in John's own observation (vv. 4-6). She is *the great prostitute* (v. 1) and *the mother of prostitutes* (v. 5), the latter

---

17:3 The phrase *in the Spirit* was used in John's opening vision (1:10) and in connection with his first glimpse into heaven (4:2). It will be used again in his vision of the new Jerusalem (21:10). It is possible to read the phrase in 1:10 as programmatic for the entire book, while the other three instances (understood as "in the spirit" or "spiritually") simply make clear that John did not *literally* travel to heaven (in 4:2), or to a desert (here), or "to a mountain great and high" (in 21:10). Rather, he moved around in the world of his visions. It is more likely, however, that the four instances of "in the Spirit" punctuate the book of Revelation as a whole (see introduction). "Spirit" should therefore be capitalized in all four places (as in the NIV), referring to the Holy Spirit, not merely John's inner life (the NRSV has "in the spirit" in all four places, with "in the Spirit" as an alternative in the margins).

17:3 John is taken *into a desert* to see the evil woman on the scarlet beast. Ironically, the desert was also the place where the woman who had given birth in chapter 12 found protection from the serpent, or dragon (12:14). This could raise the question (in the reader's mind or in John's), Are the two women the same? Has the good mother of chapter 12 been transformed into a wicked prostitute? Some (for example, Ford 1975:285) have argued seriously that Babylon and Jerusalem are the same. This is highly unlikely, and yet the ambiguity is perhaps greater from inside the vision than from the standpoint of a sophisticated modern reader who knows how the story ends. John's "astonishment" or "admiration" of this woman (vv. 6-7) suggests that the distinction between good and evil was not as immediately clear to him as it is to us.

The observation that the beast was covered with *blasphemous names* (compare 13:1) is John's way of signaling that he saw more than he is telling. Although one such name is

probably in the sense that she deceived or led other cities astray. Her *adulteries* are compared to wine, with which *the inhabitants of the earth were intoxicated* (v. 2; compare 14:8). John sees in her hand *a golden cup . . . filled with abominable things and the filth of her adulteries* (v. 4). He sees too that she herself is drunk, not with wine and adulteries, but *with the blood of the saints, the blood of those who bore testimony to Jesus* (v. 6). She is the evil genius behind those on earth who "shed the blood of your saints and prophets" and have been given blood to drink (16:6). The fierce rhetoric of John's vision is directed not against the woman's wealth, laziness, or luxurious living, nor against her drunkenness or prostitution. These characteristics are noted, but the vision's real target is the woman's deception of the earth (v. 2), and above all her violence against the people of God (v. 6). In this sense her crimes match those of the dragon (12:9, 17) and the beast (13:7-9).

Only rarely in his visions does John express emotion at what he sees. He collapsed at the feet of the figure who appeared to him in 1:17 and was told, "Do not be afraid." He began to weep bitterly (5:4-5) when "no one was found worthy to open the scroll or look into it" and was told, "Do not weep." Here he is *greatly astonished* at what he has just seen (v. 6), and the angel asks him, *"Why are you astonished?"* In each

---

BABYLON THE GREAT (v. 5), he does not enumerate them all because to do so would itself be blasphemy. Correspondingly, some names are too holy to be revealed (see 2:17; 3:12; 19:12).

17:4 The colors *purple and scarlet* may possibly allude to the lucrative trade in various kinds of dye between Rome and the cities to which John was writing, implying that these cities were contributing to the wealth and consequently to the corruption of Rome (see 18:12, 16). The beast too is "a scarlet beast" (v. 3), a detail not mentioned in chapter 13, unless the color of blood is intended to recall the beast's "fatal wound" (13:3, 12, 14). More likely, the beast's color is simply meant to match the scarlet clothing of the woman.

17:5 The word *mystery* is not part of the inscription on the woman's forehead (as in the NIV). The first part of the verse should be translated, "And on her forehead was written a name, a mystery: 'Babylon the Great'" (NRSV). John does not actually see the word "mystery." He informs his readers that the name "Babylon" is a mystery in that it is a symbolic name, not a literal one (compare the use of the word "mystery" in 1:20).

17:6 *The blood of the saints, the blood of those who bore testimony to Jesus* is a misleading translation, at least to the extent that it implies a precise identification of *the saints* with *those who bore testimony to Jesus.* The phrase corresponds closely to "the blood of your saints and prophets" (16:6), where two groups are in view: faithful Christians generally and Christian prophets in particular (see note on 16:6). That "the prophets" and "the witnesses to Jesus" are the same can be seen by comparing 11:3 and 11:10, and 19:10 and 22:9. The NRSV translation, "the blood of the saints and the blood of the witnesses to Jesus," is therefore to be preferred.

instance John's emotion is calmed and corrected by a heavenly being of some kind (compare also 19:10; 22:9).

What exactly is the emotion here? H. B. Swete (1908:218) defined it as sheer surprise: "The Seer had been invited to see the downfall of Babylon; the angel had offered to shew him her sentence executed. He expected to see a city in ruins. But instead of this there had risen before him on the floor of the desert the picture of a woman gilded, jewelled, splendidly attired, mounted on a scarlet monster, drunk with blood. It was a complete surprise. Who was this woman?" Tina Pippin (1992:57) describes it as something more akin to lust. "The narrator of the Apocalypse of John relates a marvelous feeling on encountering the Whore of Babylon. The female has seductive power. The desire of the male who views her erotic power is brought quickly under control by the angel: 'Why are you so amazed?'"

Pippin is correct that John is being seduced here, yet John's language suggests that he sees Babylon first of all not as a seductive woman, but as a city, "the great city" of 16:19. A man can be "astonished" or "amazed" at the splendor of a world metropolis, but in the case of a sexually alluring woman, "astonishment" is not the right word! The Greek text says, literally, "And seeing her I marveled a great marvel." The archaic accents of the King James Version capture the meaning quite well: "and when I saw her I wondered with great admiration." A man may lust after a prostitute, but rarely "admires" her. John is on the brink of yielding to temptation, but the temptation is not sexual. John's astonishment is more dangerous than that, for it is closer to worship. It recalls the earlier account in which "the whole world was astonished and followed the beast" (13:3; see Caird 1966:214). John is taken in by the beast as much as by the woman. It is not "erotic power" that momentarily beguiles him, but the power and wealth and magnificence that ruled the world in which he lived. Seductive? Yes. Erotic? No.

The Angel's Interpretation (17:8-18) The angel's question, "Why are you astonished?" is virtually equivalent to "Snap out of it!" The angel wakes John from his reverie not only with these words, but with the

17:8 What was said of the beast in 13:8 is said here of the *inhabitants of the earth* who are deceived by the splendor of the beast and the woman. Their names, like the name of

promise of a full interpretation of the "mystery" of the woman and the beast (v. 7). Surprisingly, the interpretation centers more on the beast (vv. 8-17) than on the woman, whose identification comes almost as an afterthought (v. 18). And yet the explanation is again and again linked explicitly to what John has just seen: *the beast, which you saw* (v. 8), *the ten horns you saw* (v. 12), *the waters you saw* (v. 15), and *the woman you saw* (v. 18).

The vision has its own rhetoric independent of John's feelings or temptations, and the angel gives voice to that rhetoric. Conspicuous from the start is a note of humor or parody at the beast's expense—and John's! The beast, says the angel, *once was, now is not, and will come up out of the Abyss and go to his destruction* (v. 8). This of course parodies the designation of God as the one "who was, and is, and is to come" (4:8; compare 1:4, 8), in such a way as to make the beast sound ridiculous. The "Lord God Almighty" is from eternity to eternity, while the beast moves from being to nonbeing to being again, and finally to destruction. God is the one who deserves astonishment, admiration and worship. But foolish people *will be astonished when they see the beast* not although, but because *he once was, now is not, and yet will come* (v. 8; compare 13:3). What ought to evoke ridicule evokes admiration and wonder instead, and even John is implicated.

Yet the beast is not altogether laughable. The note of ridicule is tempered with fear. The beast recalls that mythical monster, sometimes named Rahab and sometimes Leviathan, mentioned in the Hebrew Bible, that "had reared up against God in primeval times and been subdued by him," and would do it again with the same result" (Beasley-Murray 1974:255, who cites Is 27:1; 30:7; 51:9; Ezek 29:3-5). Like the dragon or "ancient serpent" of 12:9, the beast is described as a figure out of the remote past that comes back to haunt the future. Yet ultimately it is doomed to destruction. Such archetypal figures may inhabit our subconscious memories or imaginations, as individuals and as communities, and may therefore call up in us some of the same fears they held for John's original readers. We need only recall H. P. Lovecraft's twentieth-

the beast, *have not been written in the book of life from the creation of the world* (see note on 13:8). In other words, God has not chosen them for salvation.

century horror stories about the monstrous "Old Ones" who once inhabited the earth and are waiting to return to torment anyone foolish enough to rouse them from their age-long slumber. Whether we think of the childhood of the race or the childhood of individuals, the remote past is a haunted place, the stuff of which myths and dreams—and nightmares—are made. So when John hears that the beast *once was, now is not, and will come up out of the Abyss* (v. 8), he is grateful for the added words, *and go to his destruction* (v. 8). So are we.

The angel continues the explanation with a challenge: *This calls for a mind with wisdom* (compare 13:18). The beast's seven heads, the angel claims, are *seven hills on which the woman sits* (v. 9), and at the same time *seven kings* (v. 10). In the symbolism of this book, two different symbols can represent the same reality (for example, both the seven lamps before the throne and the seven eyes of the Lamb represented "the seven spirits of God," 4:5; 5:6). Here one symbol represents two distinct realities. The *seven hills* are the first clue that "Babylon" is actually Rome, for the notion that Rome was built on seven hills was already current among Latin poets (Swete 1908:220, citing Virgil, Horace, Ovid, Martial, Cicero and others). More important is the second part of the interpretation: the seven heads are also *seven kings,* of whom *five have fallen, one is, the other has not yet come; but when he does come, he must remain for a little while. The beast who once was, and now is not, is an eighth king. He belongs to the seven and is going to his destruction* (vv. 10-11). This appears to be a restatement, tilted in a rather political direction, of *once was, now is not, and will come up out of the Abyss and go to his destruction* (v. 8).

More than any other passage in the book of Revelation, the interpretation of the seven horns as seven kings has fostered the notion that John saw the beast as a kind of reincarnation of the emperor Nero, whose brief but gruesome persecution of Christians in the year 64 was vivid in Christian memory. The passage has also figured prominently in efforts to date the book. Identifying the sixth king who now *is* (v. 10) would supply an approximate date of composition for the book of Revelation. Unfortunately that identifi-

17:11 On the *Nero Redivivus* expectation see the Roman historians Tacitus (*Histories* 2.8-9)

cation is not possible. No one knows with what emperor the series of seven begins, nor how to count the three emperors (Galba, Otho, Vitellius) who all reigned in 68-69.

It is true that from the late first century on the popular *Nero Redivivus* superstition held that Nero would return after his death to take power again (see above on 13:3). In identifying one of the beast's heads as *an eighth king* who nevertheless *belongs to the seven* (v. 11), the angel probably alludes to that superstition, not to endorse it as true, but to make the point that the only figure from remembered history to whom the beast might be compared in its cruelty to the people of God was the ill-fated Nero. The point is not that the eighth king is actually *Nero Redivivus*, but that he is like Nero in his character and destiny.

The possible allusion to Nero has cast a shadow on many commentators' interpretation of chapter 13, whether in the reference to one of the beast's heads that "seemed to have had a fatal wound, but its fatal wound had been healed" (13:3) or in the much discussed number "666" (13:18). Yet it is important to keep in mind that the angel is explaining 17:1-6, not chapter 13. Despite the fact that the two visions have one major character in common, the beast, they should not be confused. It cannot be assumed that the *Nero Redivivus* legend is the key to the interpretation of the beast's wounded head in chapter 13. Remember, the beast is introduced in chapter 17 as if for the first time. Its previous escapades in chapters 11 and 13 seem to have been forgotten. At most, it is possible that the mysterious 666 at the end of chapter 13 was intended in some way to anticipate the more complex (and more political) application of the figure given here by the angel, but for the most part the vision of the present chapter is new, and it must stand on its own.

Two important conclusions can be drawn from the angel's words. The first is that the antichrist (if we may borrow that term) is in a general sense the seven-headed beast, and yet at the same time the eighth head or eighth king in particular, who somehow *belongs to the seven* (v. 11). In other words, the antichrist in Revelation is both an institution and a

and Suetonius (*Nero* 57), the Jewish *Sibylline Oracles* (4.119-24, 5.33-34) and the Christian *Ascension of Isaiah* (4.2-4).

person, an empire and an emperor. The second conclusion is that the Roman emperor reigning at the time John wrote the book is *not* this antichrist. Although the presupposition of the entire book is that "the time is near" (1:3; 22:10), it is not actually present. According to the scenario of verses 10 and 11, the sixth emperor *is* and the seventh is yet to come. When he comes, he will *remain for a little while.* Only then will the dreaded eighth emperor, perhaps modeled after Nero, appear on the scene. The angel makes it clear that the vision concerns the future, not the present and not even an immediate future. Although John may have remembered the three emperors within a single year (the year 68-69), the likelihood is that the angel was pointing to an interval of as much as a decade or more before the final conflict and the destruction of the beast.

The interval is just as visible in the next phase of the angel's interpretation. The ten horns of the beast are *ten kings who have not yet received a kingdom, but who for one hour will receive authority as kings along with the beast* (v. 12). The word *kingdom* is here defined by the phrase *authority as kings.* At the time John writes, the ten are not yet kings because they have not yet received kingly authority. Like the seventh king and like the eighth, they belong to the future, and they too will hold sway for an unspecified time, represented by the phrase *one hour.* These kings *have one purpose.* Instead of receiving their authority from the beast, as we might expect, they *give their power and authority to the beast* (v. 13). Where does this authority come from? We are not told, for the moment.

Unlike the seven kings of verses 9-11, the ten kings represented by the beast's ten horns are not a temporal series. They seem to be a confederation or alliance, probably the same alliance identified earlier as "the kings from the East" (16:12) or "the kings of the whole world," gathered for battle at Armageddon (16:14-16). Armageddon, in fact, seems to be in view in the angel's pronouncement that these kings *will make war against the Lamb, but the Lamb will overcome them because*

17:14 The phrase *Lord of lords and King of kings* is appropriate in its immediate context because the Lamb here demonstrates his supremacy over an earthly lord (the beast) and ten earthly kings. But the phrase as applied to the God of Israel has ancient roots: "God of gods and Lord of lords" (Deut 10:17); "God of gods and Lord of kings" (Dan 2:47); "God

he is Lord of lords and King of kings—and with him will be his called, chosen and faithful followers (v. 14). This is the first explicit indication that believers will participate with the Lamb in his victory over the powers of evil. Although they were provisionally "victorious" over the beast in their deaths (15:2), here they are participants in the *final* victory, presumably at Armageddon.

But two qualifications must be noted. First, the victory is primarily the Lamb's, not theirs, for the verb (*will overcome*) is singular, and Christian believers are mentioned almost as an afterthought. Second, the words *called, chosen and faithful* are conditions for participating in the victory, each more specific than the one before: first *called* (compare 19:9), then not only called but *chosen* (see Mt 22:14), and finally, not only chosen but *faithful* (as in 2:10, "be faithful, even to the point of death"). The purpose of these adjectives is similar to that of the seven messages of chapters 2—3: to encourage John's readers to be faithful so as to "overcome" (compare 16:15, in the immediate context of the kings gathering at Armageddon).

In chapter 16 we were given the setting of the battle only. Now we know its outcome, and now we begin to understand how it comes about that the seven-headed beast will finally *go to his destruction* (vv. 8, 11). The angel's account of the ten kings and their ill-advised alliance with the beast is interrupted by an abrupt mention of the "many waters" where the woman was seated (see v. 1). These *waters*, the angel tells John, are *peoples, multitudes, nations and languages* (v. 15). This is another step toward interpreting the woman herself—just in case John missed the reference to the *seven hills*. The "many waters" identified her at first as ancient Babylon (see Jer 51:13), but the angel now reveals that they are only a metaphor. The woman is not an ancient city literally built beside "many waters," or canals, but a city of John's own time with many "tributaries," that is, with many nations and races of people accountable to it politically, culturally and economically. The identification becomes explicit in verse 18: *The woman you saw is the great city that rules over*

of gods and Lord of lords and King of kings" (Dan 4:37 LXX). Here as elsewhere John applies traditional divine titles to the Lamb (compare 1 Tim 6:15 where, according to one interpretation, God, and according to another, Jesus, is "the King of kings and Lord of lords").

the kings of the earth. By this time the identification is unnecessary, for every reader has figured out who the woman is. It is made explicit only to give immediacy and force to the repeated announcements of the woman's doom in the next chapter. The clarity of the identification makes it impossible to argue that the book of Revelation is written in a kind of code to hide from Roman officials what the Christians of Asia Minor thought of them. No Roman citizen could read verse 18 and have any doubt that the prophecy was intended as an oracle against imperial Rome, *the great city that rules over the kings of the earth*.

Into the explicit identification of "Babylon" the prostitute as Rome (vv. 15 and 18), the angel weaves a continuation of the account of the ten kings, now in relation both to the beast and the prostitute (vv. 16-17). For the first time, dissension is evident within the ranks of evil: *The beast and the ten horns you saw will hate the prostitute. They will bring her to ruin and leave her naked; they will eat her flesh and burn her with fire* (v. 16). In these few words, and in the brief *one hour* of the kings' alliance with the beast (v. 12), the destruction of "Babylon" is accomplished. The entire next chapter will be given to a bittersweet celebration and mourning of her gruesome fate. The destruction of the beast and its allies will come later.

Before revealing the identity of the prostitute, the angel supplies one crucial piece of information about the ten kings. The expression *they have one purpose* (v. 13) is now explained, so that we now learn the true source of their authority. The angel tells John that it was God who *put it into their hearts to accomplish his purpose by agreeing to give the beast their power to rule, until God's words are fulfilled* (v. 17). Behind the unified *purpose* or intention of the kings is nothing less than the sovereign purpose of God the Almighty! With this, the angel anticipates the end of the vision when he says, "These are the true words of God" (19:9)—the final verdict from above on all that John has seen and heard.

Earlier it had seemed that the forces of evil had summoned the kings to battle at Armageddon. John had seen "three evil spirits that looked like frogs" coming from the mouths of the dragon, the beast and the false prophet. These he had defined as "spirits of demons performing miraculous signs," going out "to the kings of the whole world, to gather them for the battle on the great day of God Almighty" (16:13-14). Now, as he is allowed to look more deeply into the same events, John is reminded of the sovereignty of God superintending even the thoughts and purposes of the enemy. The so-called dualism of the book of Revelation, we now learn, is an illusion, for the vaunted powers of evil are merely pawns of a righteous God whose power is still unchallenged. Armageddon turns out to be a trap, and God has led them straight into it.

Some modern readers find the book of Revelation offensive because it presents God as the author of such grotesque horrors as are described in this chapter and the next (see, for example, Pippin 1992). But Flannery O'Connor saw clearly that "any Christian writer, even a writer of fiction, will find in modern life distortions which are repugnant to him, and his problem will be to make these appear as distortions to an audience which is used to seeing them as natural; and he may well be forced to take ever more violent means to get his vision across to this hostile audience . . . you have to make your vision apparent by shock—to the hard of hearing you shout, and for the almost-blind you draw large and startling figures" (O'Connor 1988:805-6).

John in his time knew that in a world distorted by sin, the abrupt invasion or visitation of the good is every bit as grotesque and terrifying as the onslaught of evil—and that human nature by itself is ill equipped to know the difference. Perhaps those who regard the book of Revelation as repulsive, sub-Christian or somehow unworthy of the God of the Bible need to call their own world into question with the same rigor they bring to these disturbing oracles out of their Christian past.

The Bright Angel's Announcement (18:1-3) The interpreting angel's speech ends with chapter 17. Suddenly he is replaced by *another angel coming down from heaven*. This angel *had great authority, and the earth was illuminated by his splendor* (18:1). He recalls the "mighty angel" John had seen long before, "coming down from heaven . . . robed in a cloud, with a rainbow above his head; his face was like the sun, and his legs were like fiery pillars" (10:1). The two do not have to be the same, yet they are alike in radiating the visible brightness, and consequently the authority, of the sovereign God they both represent. The angel here is not explicitly said to be "mighty," but he does speak with a *mighty voice* (v. 2).

With the coming of the bright angel, the time frame changes. John has been hearing the fall of "Babylon," or Rome, predicted as a future event (17:16). For the present, she is still "the great city that rules over the kings of the earth" (17:18). Now suddenly it is as if John himself is transported into the future, where he can look back on the city's fall as something already accomplished. The message is a familiar one: *Fallen! Fallen! is Babylon the Great!* (v. 2) because *all the nations have drunk the maddening wine of her adulteries* (v. 3). But there are two new elements here: a glimpse of the city's utter desolation and a view of what she has lost.

Rome's desolation is painted in colors taken from Isaiah's description of the ruin of old Babylon (Is 13:19-21) or Edom (Is 34:11-17). Rome, the new Babylon, has become *a home for demons, a haunt of every evil spirit, a haunt for every unclean and detestable bird* (v. 2). In a strange way, the grim announcement dramatizes the point that *the earth was illuminated* by the angel's splendor (v. 1). The message he brings is bad news for *Babylon,* but good news for the earth. The word repeatedly translated "haunt" (Greek *phylakē*) also means "prison," while the word "foul" is literally "unclean" (Greek *akathartos*). The message that *Babylon* will become a haunt or refuge for unclean spirits and unclean animals and birds means that the rest of the earth will be free of all such things. In particular, the three froglike "unclean spirits" that led the kings to assemble at Armageddon (16:13-14) will trouble the earth no more. The work of conquering unclean spirits, which Jesus began when he healed those who were demon possessed and continued in his resurrection, ascension and journey to heaven (1 Pet 3:18-19; Michaels 1988:206-11), is now complete. The stage is set for rejoicing over the earth's purification (see v. 20; 19:1-2).

The second new element in the bright angel's announcement is its emphasis on the economic power of the fallen city. Not only has she made the nations drunk and practiced immorality with *the kings of the earth,* but *the merchants of the earth grew rich from her excessive luxuries* (v. 3). With this the angel's oracle of judgment ends, leaving the

---

18:2 Some ancient manuscripts add the phrase "every foul beast" after *every unclean . . . bird,* attaching the words *and detestable* to this phrase rather than to the one about unclean birds (see NRSV). This longer reading may well be correct because the repetition of the

impression that Rome's real crime is not her drunkenness or sexual immorality, but her acquisition of wealth and luxury through trade and economic alliances with a host of client states and cities. Drunkenness and immorality, it turns out, are simply metaphors for Rome's economic—and consequently religious—imperialism.

The Voice from Heaven (18:4-20) The accent on Rome's economic power and material luxury continues in the next section, the longest direct address from heaven to John's readers since the end of chapter 3. With it the time frame shifts back to the present, as John is allowed to contemplate the worldly magnificence that will soon be gone. "Another angel coming down from heaven" (v. 1) gives way to *another voice from heaven* (v. 4)—a voice just as anonymous and just as mysterious as the angel that preceded it. The terms of address, *my people* (v. 4), suggest that the voice is God's voice, and yet it refers to God repeatedly in the third person (vv. 5, 8, 20). In this sense the voice is like the oracle of a prophet speaking for God without quite being God. The oracle is framed by twin appeals to the people of God, beginning with, *Come out of her, my people* [that is, out of Babylon] *so that you will not share in her sins, so that you will not receive any of her plagues* (v. 4). It ends, "Rejoice, saints and apostles and prophets! God has judged her for the way she treated you" (v. 20).

The First Appeal to the People of God (18:4-8) The first of these commands, perhaps more than any other in the entire book of Revelation, sums up the book's message: John wants his readers to make a clean break with the Roman Empire and everything it represents. He echoes the sentiments of the Jewish prophets about ancient Babylon (Jer 50:8; 51:6, 9, 45; compare Is 48:20; 52:11) and those of the apostle Paul about Graeco-Roman religion generally: "'Therefore come out from them and be separate, says the Lord. Touch no unclean thing, and I will receive you. I will be a Father to you, and you will be my sons and daughters, says the Lord Almighty'" (2 Cor 6:17-18).

What is surprising about the oracle as a whole is that most of it is

words *haunt* (three times) and *evil*, or "unclean" (three times), could have easily led a weary copyist's eye to drop down a line, leaving out the whole phrase.

unlike the beginning and the ending. It has more to do with the lost splendor of Babylon than with the obligations of the people of God. To be sure, there are four more imperatives addressed to Christian believers, all amounting to much the same thing: *Give back to her* [Babylon] *as she has given; pay her back double for what she has done. Mix her a double portion from her own cup* (v. 6). *Give her as much torture and grief as the glory and luxury she gave herself* (v. 7). These commands are rhetorical and are not to be taken literally. They refer to what *God* will do to ungodly Rome, not to what Christians must do. When taken literally, they violate the unambiguous teaching of Jesus: "Love your enemies, do good to those who hate you, bless those who curse you, pray for those who mistreat you" (Lk 6:27-28); of Peter: "Do not repay evil with evil or insult with insult, but with blessing" (1 Pet 3:9); and of Paul: "Bless those who persecute you; bless and do not curse" (Rom 12:14) and "Do not repay anyone evil for evil" (Rom 12:17).

In what sense can a voice from heaven in the book of Revelation command Christians to fly in the face of such teaching by taking double vengeance against fallen Babylon? The only possible answer is Paul's answer: "Do not take revenge, my friends, but leave room for God's wrath. . . . On the contrary; 'If your enemy is hungry, feed him; if he is thirsty, give him something to drink. In doing this, you will heap burning coals on his head.' Do not be overcome by evil, but overcome evil with good" (Rom 12:19-21; compare Prov 25:21-22).

In Revelation Christians "heap burning coals" on Babylon's head or *pay her back double for what she has done* precisely by nonretaliation, in obedience to the commands of Jesus, Peter and Paul, leaving room for God's wrath to accomplish its terrible purpose. For God's people, the oracle of 13:10 is still in effect: "If anyone is to go into captivity, into captivity he will go. If anyone is to be killed with the sword, with the sword he will be killed. This calls for patient endurance and faithfulness on the part of the saints." The paradox here is that the saints are able to participate in the judgment against Rome precisely by *not* taking up the sword against her. Like the slain Lamb (5:6), they are victors only

18:7 The translation *I sit as queen* is better than the NRSV "I rule as a queen." Babylon sees herself just as John saw her, as "sitting," whether on "many waters" (17:1, 15), or "on a

because, and only to the extent that, they are victims.

Yet the oracle is not *primarily* about the people of God or their responsibilities, even though it is addressed to them. Its more conspicuous purpose is to mourn (and ironically celebrate) Rome's impending downfall, setting forth in great detail the glory from which she will soon fall. This purpose is carried out in high rhetorical style, putting words into the mouth of Babylon herself (v. 7) and into the mouths of *the kings of the earth* (vv. 9-10), *the merchants of the earth* (vv. 11-17) and *every sea captain, and all who travel by ship, the sailors, and all who earn their living from the sea* (vv. 17-19).

As for Babylon, her judgment is in proportion to her own pretentiousness and self-sufficiency. Her words, spoken *in her heart,* are the only words attributed to her in all of John's visions: *I sit as queen; I am not a widow, and I will never mourn* (v. 7). Babylon is like the Christian congregation at Laodicea that said, "I am rich; I have acquired wealth and do not need a thing" (3:17). But God hates pretense, Christian or secular, above all else. The Laodiceans were pronounced "wretched, pitiful, poor, blind and naked," while "Queen" Babylon's *plagues will overtake her* in a single day—*death, mourning and famine. She will be consumed by fire, for mighty is the Lord God who judges her* (v. 8). With this death sentence, the voice from heaven reinforces the prophecy that the ten horns and the beast would humiliate the prostitute and destroy her with fire. This judgment would be the sovereign work of God (see 17:16-17).

The Three Laments over Babylon (18:9-19) The kings, merchants and seafarers of the earth mourn Babylon's demise with three variations, or stanzas, of the same song (18:10, 16-17, 19). Each group of mourners stands far from the city watching it burn, fearful for their own safety (vv. 9-10, 15, 17-18). The elements common to all three laments are identifiable in the dirge sung by the kings: *Woe! Woe, O great city, O Babylon, city of power! In one hour your doom has come* (v. 10).

The merchants and the seafarers elaborate the basic stanza in keeping with their respective interests. To the merchants, "the great city" had

scarlet beast" (17:3), or on "seven hills" (17:9). Wherever she is seated is her throne, corresponding to the throne of God. Here she "sits" as self-appointed queen of the world.

been *dressed in fine linen, purple and scarlet, and glittering with gold, precious stones and pearls* (v. 16). To the seafarers, it was *where all who had ships on the sea became rich through her wealth* (v. 19). All share the common opening line, *Woe! Woe, O great city,* and a concluding line introduced by the words *in one hour* (compare 17:12, "who for one hour will receive authority as kings along with the beast").

The merchants' dirge is the longest. They preface their formal lament with a long list of Rome's imports (18:11-13). These include not only the *fine linen, purple, silk and scarlet cloth,* the *gold, silver, precious stones and pearls* to be singled out in the lament proper (v. 16), but much more, starting with those luxury items and moving on to other luxuries as well as necessities—from silk, different kinds of wood, ivory, bronze, iron, marble, cinnamon and other spices, incense, myrrh, frankincense, wine, olive oil, fine flour and wheat, to cattle and sheep, horses, chariots, and finally slaves (that is, *bodies and souls*).

Despite the emphasis on slaves at the end of the list, with its moving reminder of their humanity, the list's primary purpose is not to highlight the evils of Roman slavery. More important is the light it sheds on John's first glimpse of "Babylon" at the beginning of his vision, where she was "dressed in purple and scarlet," and "glittering with gold, precious stones and pearls" (17:4). These are the items from the list singled out for special mention in the merchants' subsequent lament (v. 16). Now it is clear, if it was not before, that the prostitute's magnificent apparel is all imported. John himself would have recognized the purple and scarlet dyes that linked the seven cities of Asia economically to imperial Rome (see, for example, Ramsay 1904; Court 1979). To him, Rome and the provinces are interdependent, and implicated in the same crimes (remember the "cities of the nations" that fell when great Babylon fell according to 16:19). When the merchants have finished mourning the loss of their

---

18:13 Possibly the list avoids the usual word for "slaves" (Greek *douloi*) because it is the word used throughout the book of Revelation for "servants" of God (see, for example, 1:1; 19:2, 5, 9). The reference to "bodies"and human "souls" is one of John's few hints that Rome has been the oppressor of others besides Christians. For the notion of human beings as a trading commodity, see Ezekiel's denunciation of Tyre (Ezek 27:13).

18:18 There is irony in the seafarers' lament. The rhetorical question *Was there ever a city like the great city?* (literally, "Who is like the great city?") asked at the hour of her destruction echoes the earth's worship of the beast at the very height of its powers: "Who is like the beast? Who can make war against him?" (13:4).

profitable trade (vv. 11-13), they shed some tears for Rome herself. If they have lost their profits, Rome has lost all the luxuries world commerce brought her: The fruit you longed for is gone from you. All your riches and splendor have vanished, never to be recovered (v. 14). Worse, she has lost her life. The great city is no more (vv. 16-17).

In keeping with the judgments of the trumpets and the bowls, which affected earth and sea alike, the merchants of the sea take up the lament of the kings and merchants of the earth (vv. 17-19). *Was there ever a city like this great city?* they ask. Their motives, like those of the merchants of the earth, are economic: the place *where all who had ships on the sea became rich through her wealth* is gone in a single hour (v. 19). Their profits have withered and dried up. The seafarers do not know it yet, but before long the sea itself will be gone (21:1).

The Last Appeal to the People of God (18:20) The voice from heaven ends as it began, with a direct appeal to God's people: *Rejoice over her, O heaven! Rejoice, saints and apostles and prophets! God has judged her for the way she treated you* (v. 20). The use of *heaven* alongside three terms for Christian believers—*saints and apostles and prophets*—suggests that *heaven* refers here not to a place but to those who live there (as in 12:12, "Therefore rejoice, you heavens and you who dwell in them!"). In much the same way, "earth" can mean "the inhabitants of the earth" (as in 13:3-4, "the whole earth . . . followed the beast").

Heaven, therefore, includes all the angels, the four living creatures, the twenty-four elders and the great multitudes surrounding the throne of God. The cry *Rejoice over her, O heaven!* will be answered explicitly in 19:1-8. The presupposition of all John's visions is that angels and humans together form one community dedicated to the worship of God.

18:20 The phrase *saints and apostles and prophets* is literally "the saints and the apostles and the prophets." But some ancient manuscripts omit the *and* between *saints* and *apostles,* as well as the definite article before *apostles.* This turns the noun *saints,* or "holy ones," into an adjective, yielding the translation "the holy apostles and the prophets" and suggesting that the apostles in question are "the twelve apostles of the Lamb" (as in 21:14). The earliest and best manuscripts, however, have the reading presupposed by the NIV. There is no evidence that either the call to rejoice or the announcement of vindication applies only to revered figures of the past or to those in positions of church leadership.

As for the people of God on earth, they are commonly divided into *saints* and *prophets* (11:18; 16:6; 17:6); *apostles* are less often mentioned in the book of Revelation. *Apostles* here are not the twelve who traveled with Jesus, but missionaries sent out either to evangelize or to minister to existing congregations spread over a wide area (see 2:2, "those who claim to be apostles but are not"). The voice from heaven concludes by inviting all who belong to God on earth or in heaven to rejoice in their vindication.

The Angel with the Millstone (18:21-24) For the third time in John's visions, a *mighty angel* comes on the scene. The other angels so designated (5:2; 10:1) had something to do with a "scroll" or "little scroll" of destiny. The message of the scroll for John had been, "You must prophesy again about many peoples, nations, languages and kings" (10:11). Now John has done this, and Babylon's destiny is revealed. Again there is a *mighty angel,* but the angel plays a somewhat different role. Before, the contrast between the immensity of the angel and the smallness of the little scroll was almost comic. This angel carries a prop more suitable to his size and strength, *a boulder the size of a large millstone* (v. 21). He throws it into the sea, recalling Jeremiah's instructions to Seraiah the quartermaster regarding Babylon:

> Jeremiah had written on a scroll about all the disasters that would come upon Babylon—all that had been recorded concerning Babylon. He said to Seraiah, "When you get to Babylon, see that you read all these words aloud. . . . When you finish reading this scroll, tie a stone to it and throw it into the Euphrates. Then say, 'So will Babylon sink to rise no more, because of the disaster I will bring upon her. And her people will fall.'" (Jer 51:60-61, 63-64)

The curse on Babylon in Jeremiah's day is echoed in the words of the mighty angel: *With such violence the great city of Babylon will be thrown*

18:21 The verbal parallels between John's vision and the saying of Jesus about the millstone are not exact. The mighty angel takes up *a boulder the size of* [literally "like"] *a large millstone,* while Jesus refers to a stone actually used in grinding flour (in Mk 9:42 and Mt 18:6, literally "mule mill," or a millstone turned by mule power; in Lk 17:2, literally "mill stone").

18:24 The blood of prophets and saints is said to be found *in her,* not "in you" (as in the NRSV). The NIV has correctly translated the angel's speech as beginning in the third person

down, never to be found again (v. 21). The parallel is striking because Jeremiah had written of Babylon's judgment on a scroll, and a scroll was used to introduce all the judgments in the book of Revelation. Yet Jeremiah's stone was not like a millstone; it did not take a *mighty angel* to lift it, and it was thrown into the Euphrates, not the sea. Here the angel takes on the role of prophet and, like the ancient prophets of Israel, prophesies by actions as well as words. It is a new prophetic action, however, not just a reminder of Jeremiah and Seraiah in the time of the exile.

The image of the millstone has yet another source, closer to John's time than the prophecies of Jeremiah. Jesus said to his disciples that if anyone "shall offend" (KJV) or "put a stumbling block" (NRSV) before one of Jesus' "little ones," it would be better for that person "to be thrown into the sea with a large millstone tied around his neck" (Mk 9:42). Rome has not exactly "put a stumbling block" before Jesus' disciples or "caused them to sin" (see Mk 9:42 NIV). She has deceived the rest of the world instead. But to them she has done something far worse, for *in her was found the blood of prophets and of the saints, and of all who have been killed on the earth* (v. 24). The prostitute in John's vision was guilty of many crimes and boundless self-indulgence, but what condemns her above all is that she "was drunk with the blood of the saints" and "those who bore testimony to Jesus" (17:6). Because she offended the "little ones" who belong to Jesus, she is thrown into the sea, to sink like a stone and never be seen again.

Like the raven in Edgar Allan Poe's famous poem that could say only the one sad word, "nevermore," the mighty angel echoes and reechoes (six times in all) the grim refrain that *the great city Babylon* will disappear, *never to be found again* (Greek *ou mē . . . eti*). The music of harps and flutes and trumpets *will never be heard in you again;* no skilled crafts *will ever be found in you again;* industry, represented by the millstone

(v. 21), shifting to the second person ("you") as if speaking to Babylon herself (vv. 22-23), and then shifting back to the third person again (v. 24). *In her* probably does not refer to Babylon as a woman (that is, inside her dead body, based on the notion that she was "drunk with the blood of the saints," 17:6), but as a city (that is, within her precincts). The contrast between things that will not be "found" (Babylon herself, v. 21, and her industries, v. 22) and the one thing that will be *found* (responsibility for the death of the martyrs, v. 24) is striking.

itself, *will never be heard in you again;* even lamplight *will never shine in you again,* and the happy voices of bridegroom and bride *will never be heard in you again* (vv. 21-23). With this, the mighty angel reinforces and drives home the earlier lament of the merchants of the earth to Babylon that "all your riches and splendor have vanished, never to be recovered" (v. 14).

Finally the angel speaks of these merchants explicitly, calling them *your merchants* and *the world's great men,* and implicitly linking them to Rome's *magic spell* (Greek *pharmakeia*) by which *all the nations were led astray* (v. 23). This mention of magic, or sorcery (compare 9:21, 21:8, 22:15), recalls ancient prophetic denunciations of Babylon (Is 47:9) and Nineveh (Nahum 3:4), the latter linked explicitly to the deception of nations ("the mistress of sorceries, who enslaved nations by her prostitution and peoples by her witchcraft"). Magic here, like drunkenness elsewhere (14:8; 17:2; 18:3), is simply an image for the notion that Rome has deceived and corrupted the nations of the world.

Here as throughout the latter half of the book, John is answering the question of the psalmist, "Why do the nations conspire and the peoples plot in vain?" (Ps 2:1). Rome's crimes are, first, that she has deceived the nations that trade with her (v. 23) and, second, that she has killed Christian prophets and saints (v. 24). These were also the twin crimes of the dragon (12:9-10, 17) and the beast (13:3, 6-7, 12-15), but to John the more serious of the two is the second. Babylon falls like a millstone into the sea because she has shed the blood of God's people, and (almost as an afterthought) of *all who have been killed on the earth* (v. 24). The effect of verses 21-24 is to reinforce the conclusion that *God has judged her for the way she treated you* (v. 20).

The Rejoicing of Heaven and Earth (19:1-8) Emotionally there is no greater commentary on this passage than the famous Hallelujah Chorus

---

19:3 The statement that *the smoke from her goes up for ever and ever,* while not a direct allusion to hell, has the same finality as the fiery torment of those who worshiped the beast (14:11), of the two beasts themselves, and finally of the dragon in the lake of fire (20:10). It shows that Babylon's punishment is eternal. She has fallen, never to rise again (compare the announcement of Edom's eternal doom in Is 34:10).

19:6 The angel's interpretation of "many waters" as "peoples, multitudes, nations and languages" (17:15) is no longer in effect here. The comparison is not to "waters" as such,

from Handel's *Messiah,* yet the only word this piece has in common with the passage is "hallelujah," the ancient Hebrew expression for "praise the Lord" (see, for example, Ps 104:35; 106:48; Tob 13:17). The destruction of Rome is still in view, and the passage is best understood as a response to the command of 18:20: "Rejoice over her, O heaven!" The rejoicing comes first from *the roar of a great multitude in heaven* (vv. 1-2), from the great multitude again (v. 3), then from the *twenty-four elders and the four living creatures* (v. 4). The first two exclamations are introduced by *Hallelujah!* (vv. 1, 3) and the third one with *Amen, Hallelujah!* (v. 4). All these voices are from heaven in keeping with the command addressed to heaven to rejoice. The fourth voice is also from heaven, *from the throne,* but it is addressed to the people of God on earth: *Praise our God, all you his servants, you who fear him, both small and great!* (v. 5).

The fifth voice is the earth's response, *like a great multitude, like the roar of rushing waters and like loud peals of thunder* (v. 6). The rejoicing spreads from heaven to earth, in keeping with the movement in 18:20 from "heaven" to "you saints and apostles and prophets" on earth. The earth's *hallelujah* (v. 6) answers to the multiple "hallelujahs" in heaven. The announcement that *our Lord God Almighty reigns* is no news to heaven, but on earth it is an announcement of eschatological victory: the *Lord God Almighty* has taken direct control of the earth and has begun to reign anew. This is the visible realization of what was announced seven chapters earlier in connection with the seventh trumpet: "The kingdom of the world has become the kingdom of our Lord and of his Christ, and he will reign for ever and ever" (11:15).

The visible signs are now in place. If the time has come "for destroying those who destroy the earth," it is also the time "for rewarding your servants the prophets and your saints and those who reverence

---

but to a sound—the overpowering sound of a mighty waterfall (as in 1:15; 14:2; Ezek 1:24). This is shown through the parallelism with the sound of thunder.

In the phrase *our Lord God Almighty reigns* the verb *reigns* is aorist tense (Greek *ebasileusen*), suggesting that God has begun a new, distinctly eschatological reign over the earth (compare 11:17, "you have taken your great power and have begun to reign"; the Greek verb is similarly aorist).

your name, both small and great" (11:18). Babylon and her doom have gradually faded from the vision of rejoicing John sees in this chapter. She is never mentioned after verse 3. Rejoicing over Babylon gives way to rejoicing over the establishment of God's rule, and specifically over *the wedding of the Lamb* (v. 7). Suddenly a very different "woman" is in the picture—the Lamb's *bride,* or wife. In contrast to Babylon, who was "dressed in fine linen, purple and scarlet," with "gold, precious stones and pearls" (18:16), she is dressed only in *fine linen* that is *bright and clean* (v. 8).

At this point an interpretation is given: *(Fine linen stands for the righteous acts of the saints.)* This identifies not only the *fine linen* but also the woman who wears it. If the bride's fine linen stands for *the righteous acts of the saints,* then the bride herself represents *the saints,* the people of God whose blood has been avenged (18:24; 19:2) and who have joined in the chorus of rejoicing (18:20; 19:5). But who is giving the interpretation? It seems we are momentarily back in the world of chapter 17, in which "one of the angels who had the seven bowls" (17:1) interpreted, detail for detail, the vision of the evil woman on the scarlet beast.

John and the Angel (19:9-10) The interpreting angel has not been heard from since 17:18, yet no other angel has provided John with any interpretations since then. That same angel, therefore, is probably the one who concludes the vision with the command *Write: Blessed are those who are invited to the wedding supper of the Lamb!* and the assurance, *these are the true words of God* (v. 9). The vision ends as it began with a private encounter between John and this interpreting angel. Impressed by the fulfillment of the *words of God* (compare 17:17, "until God's words are fulfilled"), John falls at the angel's feet to worship. But

19:7 Because of the context, the Greek word *gynē* is commonly translated as *bride.* But the word means literally "woman" or "wife." Each of the three women in the book of Revelation—the mother threatened by the dragon in chapter 12, Babylon the prostitute in chapter 17 and the Lamb's bride here and in chapter 21—is first of all a "woman" (see 12:1; 17:3). "Woman" here is used abruptly after the destruction of the evil "woman" Babylon—as if the Lamb's pure and holy wife rises out of Babylon's ashes!

19:10 The command *Worship God!* cannot be understood as excluding the worship of the Lamb. If God is "worthy" of worship (4:11), the Lamb is equally so (5:11). Sometimes God and the Lamb are worshiped together in the book of Revelation, and sometimes God alone

he is told, *Do not do it! I am a fellow servant with you and with your brothers who hold to the testimony of Jesus. Worship God!* (v. 10). Once again he falls victim to the temptation of false worship. In one sense his desire to worship the angel is less serious than his admiration for Babylon the prostitute (17:6-7), for the angel is God's agent, not God's enemy. Yet in another sense it is more serious, since John actually falls down to worship someone other than God. The angel's warning is therefore more urgent: *Do not do it!* (literally "see not" or "see that you don't," v. 10).

In telling the story, John does not hesitate to make himself a negative example. He is as ignorant as Cornelius was when he fell down to worship Peter and was told, "Stand up . . . I am only a man myself" (Acts 10:26) or as the people of Lystra when they tried to offer sacrifices to Paul and Barnabas and were told, "We are only men, human like you" (Acts 14:11-15). John's angel, who obviously cannot claim to be a mere mortal, reminds John instead that they share a common position as servants of God and custodians of *the testimony of Jesus,* and God's servants do not worship each other. God alone is worthy of their worship.

The angel offers one last interpretation: *For the testimony of Jesus is the spirit of prophecy* (v. 10). The form of the pronouncement matches exactly that of the interpretation given in verse 8 (literally, "for the fine linen is the righteous acts of the saints"). The apparent meaning is that those who have *the testimony of Jesus*—the angel, John and John's *brothers* (fellow believers)—are all prophets. Prophets are bearers of the word of God, and in this book "the word of God" and "the testimony of Jesus" are inseparable (see 1:2, 9; 20:4). We learn now that *the testimony of Jesus* is not only a message *about* Jesus but also a message *from* Jesus the risen Lord. His is the one voice behind the many prophetic

is mentioned. Probably the angel's concentration here on God as his servants' sole object of worship is an echo of verse 5: "Praise our God, all you his servants, you who fear him, both small and great."

19:10 If *spirit* is read as lower case, it suggests that the *testimony of Jesus* is the essence or core of true prophecy, or of this prophecy in particular. If it is capitalized, it becomes "the Spirit of prophecy," or the Spirit of God speaking through prophets (for example, 14:13). The voice would then be identifying *the testimony of Jesus* with the voice of the Holy Spirit. Virtually all English versions, quite correctly, read *spirit* as lower case.

and angelic voices echoing through the pages of this book. So *the testimony of Jesus* is the spirit or essence of Christian prophecy. Whether it is also "the spirit of *the* prophecy," referring to the book of Revelation itself (1:3; 22:7, 18-19), is more difficult to say (it does have the definite article in Greek). If it is, then *the testimony of Jesus* is virtually equivalent to the title "revelation of Jesus Christ" at the beginning of the book (1:1). In any event, we have finally come to know the "angel" so mysteriously introduced in the opening verse of the book. Angels and humans function together here as prophets, just as their voices join together in John's visions in the worship and praise of God.

□ The Battle (19:11-21)

For the last chapter and a half, John's vision has been more auditory than visual. Not since the bright angel of 18:1 has he focused on something about which he said, "I saw" (Greek *eidon*). Instead he has attended to voices and messages from heaven that he quotes verbatim, sometimes explicitly claiming, "I heard" (Greek *ēkousa,* 18:4; 19:1, 6).

Now the visual aspect surfaces again. The account of the long-awaited battle between good and evil, as well as the millennium, the last judgment, and the new heaven and earth (19:11—21:8), is punctuated repeatedly by the expression *I saw* (19:11, 17, 19; 20:1, 4, 11, 12; 21:1, 2). The first three of these occurrences divide the battle story as follows: the mounted general and his armies (vv. 11-16), the invitation to birds of prey to feast upon the slain (vv. 17-18) and the battle itself (vv. 19-21). The invitation and the battle will be viewed together.

The Mounted General (19:11-16) One of Flannery O'Connor's short

19:11 The expression *called Faithful and True* could imply that these words, like "the Word of God" and "King of kings and Lord of lords," constitute a proper name (especially when capitalized, as in the NIV). But the single best ancient manuscript (Codex Alexandrinus) lacks the participle *called,* suggesting that *Faithful and True* are intended simply as a characterization or description of the rider. The same two words (translated differently as "trustworthy and true" in the NIV), are used in 21:5 and 22:6 to characterize or describe the "words" John has heard. To read them as an additional title only adds to the reader's confusion. As readers, we may feel that we already have more "names" here (vv. 12, 13, 16) than we know what to do with!

stories is about Walter Tilman, whose mother worried about him because, she thought, "He read books that had nothing to do with anything that mattered now." One day she found such a book in his room, open to a passage from St. Jerome's letter to Heliodorus: "Listen! the battle trumpet blares from heaven and see how our General marches fully armed, coming amid the clouds to conquer the whole world. Out of the mouth of our King emerges a double-edged sword that cuts down everything in the way. Arising finally from your nap, do you come to the battlefield! Abandon the shade and seek the sun."

Walter's mother's reaction was that "this was the kind of thing he read—something that made no sense for now. Then it came to her, with an unpleasant little jolt, that the General with the sword in his mouth, marching to do violence, was Jesus" (O'Connor 1988:800). Truly the "General" in John's vision is an extraordinary figure, not exactly marching as Jerome said, but riding *a white horse.*

Is this figure Jesus? Yes, but a better way of putting it is that he is "the testimony of Jesus"—and consequently "the spirit of prophecy" (v. 10)—displayed in visible form. His name, after all, is *the Word of God* (v. 13), a phrase elsewhere linked closely to "the testimony of Jesus" (1:2, 9; 20:4). Moreover, he is *Faithful and True* (v. 11), attributes as appropriate to a prophecy or a testimony as to a person (compare v. 9, "These are the true words of God"; 21:5; 22:6). Finally, he recalls a figure described in the Wisdom of Solomon in connection with the death of Egypt's firstborn in the time of the Exodus: "For while gentle silence enveloped all things, and night in its swift course was now half gone, your all-powerful word leaped from heaven, from the royal throne, into the midst of the land that was doomed, a stern warrior carrying the sharp sword of your authentic command, and stood and filled all things with death, and touched heaven while

19:12 The statement that the rider *has a name written on him that no one knows but he himself* is confusing because he is explicitly given at least two other names (not counting "Faithful and True"). These are "the Word of God" (v. 13) and "King of kings and Lord of lords" (v. 16), the second of which is also said to be "written" on him. Here we have still another name that is *not* revealed, so that one aspect of his being remains a mystery (compare 2:17; 3:12). Alternatively, the unknown name could be the one subsequently revealed in verse 16 (that is, "King of kings and Lord of lords"). But that is less likely because John disclosed this name, or title, already in 17:14.

standing on the earth" (Wis 18:14-16 NRSV).

Almost every detail in John's description of the mysterious rider on the white horse matches something that occurred earlier in his visions. The white horse recalls the horse John saw under the first seal (6:1-2), whose rider carried a bow and wore a crown. The two are introduced with exactly the same words (literally, "and behold, a white horse, and he who sat upon it," 6:1; 19:11). If the rider in chapter 6 represented either false prophecy or the spirit of antichrist (see above), it is appropriate that the rider here represents both true prophecy ("the testimony of Jesus") and Jesus Christ himself. Two other features, eyes like blazing fire (v. 12) and the sharp sword coming from the mouth (v. 15), correspond to John's opening vision of the figure who dictated to him the seven messages to the churches. The promise that this warrior will use the sword to strike down the nations so as to rule them with an iron scepter (v. 15) echoes the earlier description of the male child born of the woman and caught up to heaven (12:5; see also 2:26-27).

The grim statement that this figure *treads the winepress of the fury of the wrath of God Almighty* (v. 15) recalls the outcome of the bloody grape harvest carried out by angels "outside the city" (14:20). His robe is *dipped in blood* (v. 13), probably not his own, but the blood of his enemies. In this respect John's vision draws on the fearful dialogue of Isaiah 63:1-6:

> Who is this coming from Edom, from Bozrah, with his garments stained crimson? Who is this, robed in great splendor, striding forward in the greatness of his strength? . . . Why are your garments red, like those of one treading the winepress? "I have trodden the winepress alone . . . I trampled them in my anger and trod them down in my wrath; their blood spattered my garments, and I stained all my clothing. . . . I trampled the nations in my anger . . . and poured their blood on the ground."

19:14 While the vision of verses 11-16 concentrates intently on the one riding the white horse, John's attention here is momentarily drawn to the rider's armies. They, like him, are mounted on *white horses,* but in contrast to his bloodstained robe they are wearing *fine linen, white and clean,* recalling the "fine linen, bright and clean" worn by the Lamb's bride and interpreted as "the righteous acts of the saints" (v. 8). Here the wedding imagery gives way to that of military conflict, echoing 17:14, where the Lamb overcomes as "Lord of lords

This terrible judge and warrior wears on his head *many crowns,* or "diadems," (v. 12), a phrase strangely reminiscent of the seven crowns or diadems on the seven heads of the dragon (12:3) or the ten crowns on the ten horns of the beast (13:1). An almost comic touch is that the *many crowns* here rest on only one head! Probably in all three cases they represent spheres of rule or authority: the ten horns of the beast turned out to be "ten kings" (17:16), and while the dragon's seven heads were assigned no special significance, the corresponding heads of the beast were interpreted as a succession of kings or emperors (17:9-10). Here *many crowns* on a single head suggest many spheres of sovereignty under a single Lord, anticipating the inscription *KING OF KINGS AND LORD OF LORDS* finally made explicit at the end of the account (v. 16).

This inscription is a traditional formula (see 17:14) that is to be understood quite literally. The rider on the white horse is about to be seen precisely as a King victorious over all other kings, and as supreme Lord, victorious over "generals and mighty men" and their armies (v. 18). Victory in battle (presumably the same battle) was the point of 17:14 as well. There it applied to the Lamb, while here it applies to the rider on the white horse. Both clearly represent Jesus. Yet the Lamb was a silent warrior, as silent in his victory as in his redemptive death (compare Is 53:7). Jesus as the Lamb never speaks a word in the entire book of Revelation, while Jesus as the rider on the white horse is *the Word of God* (v. 13), the very embodiment of speech itself. John's vision now reveals that the great battle to follow is no literal battle at all (in spite of the bloodstained garments), but a divine decree in action. *The Word of God* simply speaks with the sword of his mouth, and victory is accomplished. The vaunted battle of Armageddon is no contest.

The Grim Invitation and Its Outcome (19:17-21) That the battle's outcome is a foregone conclusion is clear from the two scenes that follow

and King of kings—and with him will be his called, chosen and faithful followers." In both instances, the armies are made up of Christian believers (possibly along with their "fellow servants," the angels), yet in both instances their role is a minor one. They "overcome" (compare chapters 2-3) only because they are with Christ. The battle is his first of all, not theirs. *He* wields the sword; *he* rules the nations (but see 2:26-27); *he* treads the winepress of God's wrath (v. 15).

(each introduced by *I saw,* vv. 17, 19). John sees first *an angel standing in the sun* (and therefore beyond the sky), inviting all the birds in the sky to *come, gather together for the great supper of God, so that you may eat the flesh of kings, generals, and mighty men, of horses and their riders, and the flesh of all people, free and slave, small and great* (v. 18). This is the ghastly counterpart to the joyful "wedding supper of the Lamb" (v. 9). It anticipates the end of battle, when the ground is strewn with corpses, and the birds of prey claim their due. Already it is clear that the corpses are not those of the armies accompanying the rider on the white horse, but the armies arrayed against him. If the rider on the white horse evoked for John and his readers the traditional expectation of Jesus' return to earth as Son of Man, it is natural to wonder if perhaps this scene is intended to echo in some way the strange saying of Jesus in that connection, "Wherever there is a carcass, there the vultures will gather" (Mt 24:28; compare Lk 17:37).

Together the visions of the birds of prey in the sky (vv. 17-18) and the outcome of the so-called battle (vv. 19-21) form a kind of chiasm, that is, the same three elements are repeated in reverse order:

(a) the birds of the sky are invited to feast (v. 17)

(b) the doomed armies are described (v. 18)

(c) the beast gathers these armies for battle (v. 19)

(c′) the beast and false prophet are captured and thrown into the lake of fire (v. 20)

(b′) the armies are killed by the sword of the rider on the white horse (v. 21)

(a′) the birds feast on their flesh (v. 21)

The effect of the chiasm is to dramatize the inevitability of the outcome. The armies arrayed against the rider on the white horse are slaughtered by *the sword that came out of the mouth of the rider on the horse,* that is, "the Word of God." God speaks and it is done. The *angel standing in the sun* (v. 17) knows the end from the beginning. The *beast* has not been heard from since chapter 17, where his involvement in the conflict

19:20 John mentions *the fiery lake,* or "the lake of fire" (with the definite article), as if it were an image familiar to his readers. Yet this is his first use of the phrase (compare 20:10, 14, 15; 21:8). Possibly this *fiery lake of burning sulfur* is intended to recall 14:10, where worshipers of the beast were to be "tormented with burning sulfur in the presence of the

was made unmistakably clear (17:13-14). The *false prophet,* mentioned only once before in passing without further identification (16:13), is here explicitly said to be the one *who had performed the miraculous signs* on the beast's behalf and *had deluded those who had received the mark of the beast and worshiped his image* (v. 20). This identifies him as the second beast "coming out of the earth" who had enforced on the earth's inhabitants the worship of the beast from the sea (13:11-17). The false prophet played no role in the vision or the explanation by the angel in chapter 17, yet the two beasts are to John inseparable, and they go to their destruction together in this their final scene.

□ The Millennium (20:1-10)

Nine times out of ten, when people ask, "How do you interpret the book of Revelation?" what they mean is, "How do you interpret Revelation 20:1-10?" They want to know whether an approach is "premillennial," "amillennial" or "postmillennial," to use the jargon by which some evangelical institutions (and even individuals) define themselves. Although how we interpret these verses says little or nothing about how we interpret the book as a whole, our interpretation of them tends to become the litmus test by which our interpretation of the whole book is measured and classified.

The three terms come from the word *millennium,* meaning a period of a thousand years understood as a kind of utopia. Pre- and postmillennialism divide over the question of whether the second coming of Christ will take place before or after the thousand years mentioned repeatedly in this text (vv. 2, 3, 4, 5, 6, 7). Because there is a coming of sorts described in the previous chapter (when the rider on the white horse comes with his armies and destroys the forces of evil) and there is no discernible coming of Christ in chapters 20 or 21, it seems fairly clear on first reading that the coming is "premillennial" as far as *John* is concerned. The conqueror comes first (chap. 19), and the thousand years follow (chap. 20). But postmillennialism argues that what comes

---

holy angels and of the Lamb." That the beast and the false prophet are *thrown alive* into the burning lake suggests that the fire is for pain and torment, not simply destruction (compare 20:10).

in chapter 19 is not Jesus personally, but simply the triumph of "the testimony of Jesus" in the world, so that the millennium of chapter 20 is the result of the church's efforts in proclaiming the Christian gospel. This leaves us with no actual "second coming" of Jesus anywhere in the book—this in spite of repeated promises that "I am coming soon." Instead, we move from the triumph of the gospel to the destruction of evil and "the new heavens and new earth" without Jesus ever coming at all.

The third position, "amillennialism," *should* mean there is no such thing as a "millennium." But this makes no sense of the text as it stands because John claims, not once but six times, that he *saw* (or became aware of) a thousand-year period. Therefore most amillennialists do not deny the notion of a millennium. They argue instead that John's "millennium" is just another name for the age in which we now live, in which Jesus reigns as Lord by virtue of his resurrection and ascension. According to this scenario Christ will return after, or at the end of, the present age. Consequently, this "amillennial" view is a variation of postmillennialism.

Where does all this leave us? Above all, it demands that we distinguish carefully between what John experienced long ago in his vision on Patmos and what the world will experience someday in the near or distant future. *Within John's vision,* there is little doubt that his perspective was premillennial. It is only when his visions are viewed as a scenario for the actual future of the world that differing interpretations come into play, often because a literal premillennial reading is judged (rightly or wrongly) to conflict with conclusions derived from other parts of the Bible. Because of this, it is wise to deal with the text first of all simply as John's vision before attempting to explore its possible bearing on how our world is actually going to end. Such an approach is "premillennial" because this is the framework in which John saw the vision. The second stage of interpretation—the text's implication for *our own* future—can be addressed only afterward, and much more briefly,

---

20:2 Why *a thousand years?* The most striking thing about this number is the enormous contrast it creates with all other (much shorter) time periods in the book. All pale in comparison to this *thousand years.* John's point is similar to Paul's in Romans 8:18 ("I consider that our present sufferings are not worth comparing with the glory that will be

because less can be said about it with certainty.

What are we to think of a vision in which the seer is conscious of the passing of *one thousand years?* We are way beyond "half an hour" here (8:1), and the other longer periods of time mentioned in the book ("three and a half days" in 11:9, 11; "five months" in 9:5; "1,260 days" in 11:3 and 12:6; "42 months" in 11:2, 13:5) are periods John is told about or infers from his visions, not periods he actually sees or experiences. But in this vision he is given a taste of time travel, in that he is fastforwarded and allowed to see what happens when the thousand years are finished (vv. 7-10).

The Imprisonment of the Dragon, or Satan (20:1-3) The thousand-year interval is used in two connections in this passage: the imprisonment of Satan in the *Abyss* and his subsequent release (vv. 1-3, 7-10) and the reign of God's martyrs and saints (vv. 4-6). Although the view of J. A. Bengel (1877:5:368-69) that the text pointed to two distinct thousand-year periods, one after the other, cannot be sustained, we *are* dealing here with two distinct (though closely related) visions. If verses 4-6 were left out, a reader could move directly from verses 1-3 to verses 7-10 with scarcely a clue that anything was missing.

John gives Satan a very formal introduction as *the dragon, that ancient serpent, who is the devil, or Satan* (v. 2), almost exactly as in 12:9. The additional phrase in 12:9, "who leads the whole earth astray," is echoed here in the statement that Satan was imprisoned *to keep him from deceiving the nations anymore* (v. 3). This is part of a pattern of correspondence and contrast between this passage and 12:7-12. There the dragon was thrown down from heaven to earth (12:9, 12); here he is thrown from earth into *the Abyss*. There it was for only a short time (12:12); here it is for *a thousand years*. There his downfall meant deception and woe for the earth (12:12); here it means freedom from deception, and therefore peace and rest for the earth. Chapters 12 and 20 neatly frame the dragon's career. Chapter 12 marks the beginning of

revealed in us") or 2 Corinthians 4:17 ("For our light and momentary troubles are achieving for us an eternal glory that far outweighs them all"). In the immediate context, the *thousand years* of imprisonment contrasts sharply with the "short time" Satan will have afterward to work his mischief (v. 3; also 12:12).

his activity on earth, chapter 20 its end.

Two things are important in this connection. First, the language of verses 1-3 presupposes all that has transpired in chapters 12-19. The dragon is imprisoned so as not to deceive the nations *anymore* (Greek *eti,* v. 3). Second, there is an explicit recognition that the thousand-year imprisonment of the dragon is not quite the last word. Verse 3 (that is, *after this he must be set free for a short time*) anticipates verses 7-10 with their renewed outburst of activity and the dragon's final judgment in the lake of fire. This is a hint that the dragon is going to disappear from the scene in two stages rather than one.

The vision of the millennium begins when John sees an unidentified *angel coming down out of heaven,* like others he has seen before (10:1; 18:8). The angel, like the fallen star of 9:1, holds *the key to the Abyss,* not to release powers of evil (as in 9:1-11), but to seal up the terrible place with the source of all evil bound within (vv. 1-3). This first stage of the dragon's disappearance marks a time of temporary relief for the troubled earth. The battle is over. The beast and the false prophet are gone (19:20). But otherwise we are told nothing about this worldwide utopia. John knows only that God is in control. Later, in connection with the second stage, we will learn that "the camp of God's people" and "the city he loves" are on earth during the thousand years (v. 9), but for now all we know is that Satan and his cohorts are gone and the nations are no longer being deceived.

The Reign of the Martyrs (20:4-6) John's vision of the dragon's fate (Greek *eidon,* "I saw," v. 1) is interrupted by another vision (*eidon,* "I saw," v. 4) of "thrones, and those seated on them" (NRSV; literally, "thrones, and they sat on them"). In effect, all of verse 4 is the object of

---

20:3 The statement that the devil *must* be released (Greek *dei,* "it is necessary") reminds the reader again of the sovereignty of God, who controls the situation every step of the way (compare "the things which *must* take place," 1:1; 4:1; 22:6; "you *must* prophesy again," 10:11; anyone who harms the two witnesses *must* be killed," 11:5; the seventh king "*must* remain for a little while," 17:10).

20:4 To find two separate groups here, those who sat on thrones (perhaps the twenty-four elders of chapter 4) and *the souls of those who had been beheaded,* is to complicate unnecessarily an already complex scene. Verses 4-6 deal with only one group—*the souls* who had been martyred—and with their vindication. If there are other anonymous figures seated on the thrones, they play no part in the vision, and John's reason for including them

I saw (see Michaels 1992:90-91). John sees thrones first, then actions (literally "they sat" and "a judgement was given for them"). Only then does he recognize the people involved (*the souls of those who had been beheaded because of their testimony for Jesus and because of the word of God*). The scene recalls the vision in chapter 4, where John saw a throne being set up with an indefinite "someone" sitting on it (4:2), and a brief description followed of the one seated there (4:3). Even more strikingly, it resembles the opening of the fifth seal in chapter 6, where John saw "under the altar the souls of those who had been slain because of the word of God and the testimony they had maintained" (6:9). These "souls" had cried out, "How long, Sovereign Lord, holy and true, until you judge the inhabitants of the earth and avenge our blood?" (6:10).

The present passage is God's answer to their prayers. The point of verse 4 is not that they were now "given authority to judge" (NRSV) or that at some previous time they *had been given authority to judge* (NIV), but (literally) that "a judgment was given for them," that is, a divine verdict was handed down in their favor. Their prayer was, "How long . . . until you judge," and now, finally, God has stepped in to pass judgment on their behalf. Nothing in the text suggests that *they* are given the right to judge others. These martyrs are *priests of God and of Christ* (v. 6). In a sense they are kings for a thousand years, but not judges. That prerogative is reserved for God and the Lamb.

The martyrs in chapter 6 were said to be "slain" or "slaughtered." Here they have been *beheaded*. They are actual martyrs because in John's visions *all* faithful Christians have been killed. They are not an elite group that is more "spiritual" than other believers. The further description of them as those who *had not worshiped the beast or his*

---

remains unclear (Beckwith 1922:739).

20:5 The entire parenthesis (*The rest of the dead did not come to life until the thousand years were ended*) is missing in some ancient manuscripts (notably the fourth-century Codex Sinaiticus). This is probably because certain scribes judged it to be a marginal gloss added by earlier scribes. Certainly the comment does get ahead of the story John is telling, but no more so than the comment about Satan at the end of verse 3: "After that, he must be set free for a short time." In this case, scribes may have felt that the words should be left out because there is no explicit statement later (even in vv. 11-15) about *the rest of the dead* "coming to life." The manuscript evidence is not sufficient to justify leaving the verse out.

image and had not received his mark on their foreheads or their hands (v. 4) places the accent not on their martyrdom as such but on the faithfulness that made martyrdom inevitable.

Throughout the book of Revelation the Greek word *martyria* refers to faithful testimony, not necessarily violent death. Those who reign are not martyrs because they were slain or beheaded. On the contrary, they were killed because they were *already* "martyrs" in the sense of bearing faithful testimony to the truth about Jesus. They are simply the "victorious" Christians of chapters 2-3 (see especially 3:21, "to him who overcomes, I will give the right to sit with me on my throne, just as I overcame and sat down with my Father on his throne"). They are those who "follow the Lamb wherever he goes" (14:4), who are therefore "his called, chosen and faithful followers" (17:14). To John, they are the *true* Christians, and he seems to know of no other kind.

John continues his brief description of these "souls" by explaining what brought them to these thrones of honor. Once dead, *they came to life and reigned with Christ a thousand years* (v. 4). The rest of the dead, John adds parenthetically, *did not come to life until the thousand years were ended* (v. 5). How he knows this is uncertain. It is as if he anticipates what will come later in his vision (vv. 11-15).

Nothing is said of the location of the martyrs' reign. Some commentators assume it is in heaven, since in Revelation heaven is the appropriate place for thrones, whether God's throne or those of the twenty-four elders (4:2, 4). Yet the "souls" in 6:9-11 were "under" the heavenly altar, therefore presumably on earth. Moreover, the promise held out in chapter 5 to the redeemed "from every tribe and language and people and nation" was a promise of becoming "a kingdom and priests to serve our God, *and they will reign on the earth*" (5:9-10, italics

20:5-6 M. G. Kline (1975:366-75; 1976:110-19) argued that *the first resurrection* in these two verses is not a literal resurrection, but simply the death of the believer and the ensuing "intermediate state." There are two objections to his view: first, if he is right, then these verses represent no advance beyond the situation portrayed in 6:9-11; second, if this is *not* literally "the resurrection of the body and the life everlasting" of which the creeds speak, then where in the book of Revelation *is* this blessed hope to be found? Clearly not in 20:11-15, which has in view only "the second death" or "the lake of fire." It would be strange indeed if this revelation of the risen one (see 1:5, 18) had nothing to say of the future bodily resurrection of Christian believers (see Michaels 1976:102-9).

mine). In the present context, when John refers to "the camp of God's people, the city he loves" (v. 9), it is fair to assume that this is the place on earth where the martyred saints have reigned a thousand years on their thrones. Presumably "the city he loves" is Jerusalem, only partially destroyed in the "severe earthquake" of 11:13 and spared in the bloodbath of judgment "outside the city" in 14:20.

John now interprets and summarizes what he has just seen: *This is the first resurrection. Blessed and holy are those who have part in the first resurrection. The second death has no power over them, but they will be priests of God and of Christ and will reign with him for a thousand years* (vv. 5-6). The contrast between *first resurrection* and *second death* (compare 2:11) is striking. *First* resurrection seems to imply a "second": *the rest of the dead* will come to life (v. 5). Yet when they do (vv. 12-13), it is not called "the second resurrection," only "the second death," or "lake of fire" (vv. 14-15). *The first resurrection* is the only true resurrection John knows, and *the second death* is the only death that matters. If others are raised to eternal life after the thousand years (vv. 11-15), we learn nothing about them. At most we can speculate that if the martyrs are in some sense *priests of God and of Christ* (v. 6), they might mediate salvation to others on the earth, but we have no explicit evidence that this is the case.

The Release of Satan (20:7-10) Having seen the vindication of the martyrs, John now picks up where he left off in verse 3. At the end of the thousand years, Satan (no longer disguised as a dragon) is released from his prison to do what he did before: *deceive the nations* of the world (v. 8). This time he has no beasts or evil Babylon to help him. The nations he deceives are given little-known foreign names out of the biblical past, *Gog*

20:6 *Blessed* (Greek *makarios*) marks the fifth of seven beatitudes in Revelation (the first four being found in 1:3; 14:13; 16:15; 19:9). This beatitude corresponds most closely to 14:13, "'Blessed are the dead who die in the Lord from now on.' 'Yes,' says the Spirit, 'they will rest from their labor, for their deeds will follow them.'" In the millennium the passive "rest" of the martyred saints (compare 6:11) gives way to active "reigning" with Christ. John adds to "blessed" the adjective *holy* (Greek *hagios*), which clearly identifies those who reign as "saints" or "holy ones" (as in 5:8; 8:3-4; 11:18; 13:7, 10; 14:12; 16:6; 17:6; 18:20, 24; 19:8). In the present context, "the camp of God's people" (v. 9) is literally "the camp of the saints." Being *holy,* they share in the character of "the Holy One" who redeemed them (see 3:7; 4:8; 6:10), and their home is "the holy city" (11:2; 21:2, 10; 22:19).

and Magog (see Ezek 38—39). In Ezekiel's visions, "Gog, of the land of Magog" was an evil prince, "chief prince of Meshech and Tubal," while Magog was the land from which he came (Ezek 38:2). Here both words seem to denote lands or nations (compare the Jewish *Sibylline Oracles* 3.319, "Woe to you, land of Gog and Magog"; Charlesworth 1983:369).

Those who see no literal millennium in this passage regard Satan's deception of *Gog and Magog* as simply a retelling of the events leading up to the battle of Armageddon in chapters 16 and 19. They point to the similarity between verse 8 (*to gather them for battle*) and 16:14 ("to gather them for the battle") or 19:19 ("gathered together to make war"). But the absence of the beast and the false prophet is a crucial difference. To John it is not a case of the same story being told twice, but of history repeating itself. The repetition does not have the same immediacy for John or the reader that the conflict with the beast and the false prophet had. The obscure names *Gog and Magog* give the reader a sense of distance or remoteness, even unreality. As G. B. Caird once wrote, when Gog and Magog's armies are destroyed, John's "emotional attitude to them is very much that of a modern reader of science fiction, who can contemplate with equanimity the liquidation of Mars-men with a ray gun, because they do not belong to the ordered structure of human existence. Like the four earthly winds of an earlier vision (vii.1), they come from the four corners of the earth, the outlandish territory beyond the bounds of civilization" (Caird 1966:258).

The brief outbreak of evil at the end of the thousand years is John's way of saying that Satan's activity is not limited to the immediate threat to Christians from the Roman Empire in his own time. It can happen at any time and under a variety of circumstances. But the outcome is always the same. Satan is always defeated, whether thrown down from heaven

---

20:9 For *the breadth of the earth* as a place crossed by invading armies, we may compare Habakkuk 1:6, where Chaldeans are seen marching "through the breadth of the earth" (NRSV). The apocryphal book of Sirach distinguishes three spheres that are also significant in Revelation: "the height of heaven," "the breadth of the earth" and "the abyss" (Sir 1:3 NRSV). In our chapter this earth, which will pass away (20:11; 21:1), has only *breadth,* while in the visions that follow the "new earth" (21:1) will become coextensive with a three-dimensional holy city, whose length and breadth and height are equal (21:16). Only here is the city called *the city he loves* (compare Ps 87:2; Jer 12:7). Probably John is anticipating already the identification of "the Holy City, Jerusalem" with "the bride, the wife

(12:9), bound in the abyss (20:1-3) or thrown into the lake of fire (v. 10). Although the battle (v. 9) is not Armageddon, it is similar to it in one important respect. Like Armageddon, it is no real battle at all. When the armies *marched across the breadth of the earth and surrounded the camp of God's people, the city he loves,* the outcome was that *fire came down from heaven and devoured them* (v. 9). *The city he loves* (evidently Jerusalem) is protected again, and presumably the reign of the martyred saints continues (see 22:5, "and they will reign for ever and ever").

After the armies of the nations are destroyed, Satan himself is thrown into the lake of fire, *where the beast and the false prophet had been thrown* (v. 10; see 19:20). Again John makes it clear that he is not just retelling the story of the defeat of the beast and false prophet at the battle of Armageddon. The beast and the false prophet are *already* in the lake of fire. This is another conflict a thousand years later, even though the result is the same. The powers of evil were introduced one by one: first the dragon (chap. 12), then the two beasts (chap. 13), then Babylon the prostitute (chaps. 14-16). Now they have disappeared one by one in reverse order: first Babylon (17:1—19:10), then the two beasts (19:11-21), finally the dragon, or Satan (20:1-10). The battles are over. The stage is now set for the creation of a new world.

So much for John's premillennial vision of the triumph of good over evil. Now what of the reality toward which it points? Are we to conclude that the reality we should expect today in connection with what we call Christ's second coming is also premillennial? Not all "premillennial" commentators have thought so. I. T. Beckwith, for example, wrote, "When once we apprehend the fact that the essential truth of prophecy, as distinguished from its form, is not the revelation of a chronological program in the world's history, we cease to find there the prediction of an *eschatological era,* however closely the apocalyptist himself may have associated form and

---

of the Lamb" (21:9-10; compare 19:7-8; 21:2).

The words *fire came down from heaven and devoured them* echo word for word the language of 2 Kings 1:12, where fire came down from heaven and destroyed a captain and fifty men sent from King Ahaziah to challenge the prophet Elijah (compare also Lk 9:54, as well as the fire from the mouths of the "two witnesses" in Rev 11:5). The common feature in these accounts is that true prophets supposedly have the power to destroy their enemies with fire. This is not the case here, for no prophet calls down fire on the armies of Gog and Magog. God alone protects *the camp of God's people, the city he loves.*

substance" (1922:737). And according to Robert Mounce (1977:359), "John taught a literal millennium, but its essential meaning may be realized in something other than a temporal fulfillment."

In John's visions, the world goes on for a thousand more years *after* the coming of Christ, yet the prophet seems to know nothing of what that world will be like. His "millennium" simply provides a cushion of sorts between the demise of the Roman Empire, which threatened the Christian church in his own day, and the end of the world. This is appropriate because the Roman Empire did in fact pass from the scene many centuries ago, and yet world history continued, with ever new tyrannies and ever new threats to the people of God, from outside the church and from within. The church's conflict with the beast and false prophet and evil Babylon has become a precedent and a paradigm for conflicts with institutional authority in numberless times and places since the first century. If the story repeats itself once in Revelation 20 in the deception of Gog and Magog, it has repeated itself again and again in actual history.

In short, a careful reading of the book of Revelation from where we sit now, at the threshold of the third millennium, suggests an interpretation that is premillennial because that is what John saw in his visions, but not completely literal because Christ did not literally return and dead martyrs were not literally raised to life when the Roman Empire came to an end. What was future to John—the coming of Jesus to earth, the resurrection of the faithful, and the defeat of the powers of evil—is still future to us. We have no way of knowing what form the realization of these promises will take because the book of Revelation is a book of hope and encouragement, not a handbook of chronology or a blueprint for the future. We stand pretty much where John stood, and perhaps that is just as well. The "revelation of Jesus Christ" (1:1) is a revelation of some, but by no means all, of what awaits us. Let the mystery be.

□ From the Old Creation to the New (20:11—21:8)

A crucial difference between biblical Christianity and all "new age"

20:11 Twice in the book of Revelation John has seen a white horse with someone seated on it (6:2; 19:11), and once he has seen an angelic "son of man" seated on a white cloud (14:14). In each case there was a certain ambiguity as to who the seated figure was: Christ or antichrist? (6:2), the Son of Man or an angel? (4:14), Jesus or the testimony of Jesus? (19:11). Here again we have someone *seated* on something *white,* not a horse or a cloud

movements, including witchcraft (black or white) and paganism (ancient or modern) is that Christianity is not preoccupied with protecting "Mother Nature." Reverence for nature is *not* Christian teaching, even though respect for God's creation is. To misquote slightly a well-known saying of Jesus, "The natural world was made for human beings, not human beings for the natural world." Ecology, or the protection of the human environment, is important to Christians only when it is precisely that—the protection of the *human* environment. The world is not ours to abuse, for when we abuse it we abuse one another and, in the long run, ourselves. Yet the world emphatically is ours to use. "Be fruitful and increase in number; fill the earth and subdue it," God told Adam and Eve. "Rule over the fish of the sea and the birds of the air and over every living creature that moves on the ground" (Gen 1:28). It is no accident that technology has flourished in the "Christian" West more than anywhere else in the world.

The Judgment of the Old Creation (20:11) Mother Nature has taken a beating in the Revelation. We need only remember the terrible judgments on earth, sky, sea and fresh water in chapters 8 and 16. In the present passage we find that her troubles are not over. Preachers customarily refer to this *great white throne* judgment as a judgment on humankind (specifically on those who do not believe in Jesus), but John describes it first of all as a judgment on the natural world (v. 11), and only then on "the dead, great and small" who inhabited that world and who, at its end, lie buried within it (vv. 12-15). As soon as we see the *great white throne and him who was seated on it,* we are told that *earth and sky fled from his presence, and there was no place for them* (v. 11). John's language anticipates that of 21:1, "Then I saw a new heaven and a new earth; for the first heaven and the first earth had passed away." Ironically, movements that today call themselves "new age"are the very ones clinging

this time, but a *throne.* Rather consistently, "the one seated on the throne" has been God the Father, or so we have assumed (4:2-3, 9-10; 5:1, 7, 13; 6:16; 7:10, 15; 19:4; 21:5), but here again *white* suggests ambiguity. The figure could be God or Jesus the Lamb. In either case the work of judgment is a divine work.

nostalgically to an old natural order that is "passing away" (compare Heb 1:10-12; 1 Cor 7:31; 2 Cor 4:18; 1 Jn 2:15-17).

The Greek word *ouranos* can be translated as either "heaven" or "sky." When in doubt, most English versions prefer the translation "heaven." It makes no sense, however, to claim that "heaven" in the sense of God's dwelling place will disappear at the last judgment. The NIV's *earth and sky fled from his presence,* therefore, is better here. John refers here to the visible world around him, the *earth and sky* he could see from Patmos with his own eyes.

The Judgment of the Dead (20:12-15) John goes on to describe a universal judgment on *the dead, great and small* (v. 12). These *dead* must be "the rest of the dead" (v. 5) who did not come alive to reign with Christ in "the first resurrection." Consequently they are not "blessed and holy" nor immune to "the second death" (v. 6). After *books* are opened, and above all *the book of life,* the dead are judged *according to what they had done as recorded in the books* (v. 12). As to the distinction between the plural *books,* or "scrolls," not mentioned before in the Revelation (see Dan 7:10) and the singular "book of life" (see Rev 3:5; 13:8; 17:8; 21:27), Beckwith comments, "The former contain the record of . . . deeds, whether good or bad, which form the ground for judgment; the latter contains the list of those destined for life. There is no incongruity between the two ideas, for the deeds determine whether names are inserted in the book of life" (1922:748).

But things are not quite that simple. Names cannot be "inserted" in the book of life, for every name was either written or not written there "from the creation of the world" (13:8; 17:8). Salvation to John is by divine election, grounded in the mystery of God's grace. At the same time, salvation is the *outcome,* if not the reward, of good works ("I know your deeds," 2:2, 5, 19, 23, 26; 3:1, 8, 15; "for their deeds will follow them," 14:12). John made no attempt to reconcile the two ideas, probably because (like most apocalyptic writers) he saw no conflict between

20:12 Occasionally in evangelical Christian preaching and piety the so-called Great White Throne judgment is understood as a judgment of Christians according to their works, not to determine their salvation (which is by grace through faith), but to decide what their heavenly rewards will be (see also Mt 25:19-23; Lk 19:16-19; 1 Cor 3:12-15). Whatever its

them. It was Paul who taught us to see the conflict, and Paul's classic solution—that good works are the outward evidence of divine grace—is the solution most Christians have adopted and the one John probably would have adopted too, had he seen the problem.

The striking thing about this judgment according to deeds, or works, is that John does not mention any among the dead whose works were found acceptable to God. He tells us only that *if anyone's name was not found written in the book of life, he was thrown into the lake of fire* (v. 15). His terse language leaves many questions unanswered. Were the martyred saints who reigned a thousand years the only ones redeemed? Did the rest of the dead come to life only to die again in the lake of fire? Was anyone on earth redeemed during the thousand years? If not, what was the millennium's purpose? What about the prophets and saints of the Hebrew Bible? Are they raised to life in John's scenario? If so, is it before or after the thousand years? John answers none of these questions because he is recording a single vision with a single purpose, not providing a blueprint for the history of human salvation. His emphasis is on judgment here, not salvation: those whose names are not written in the *book of life* will not live. They will die forever in *the lake of fire*. John has already told us who they are: "the inhabitants of the earth" who worshiped the beast and the dragon (13:8; 17:8). Now that the beast and false prophet and the dragon are in the lake of fire (v. 10), their followers must inevitably join them there.

Yet even *the second death*, or *the lake of fire* (v. 14) has its positive side. It is not made first of all for human beings, but for supernatural entities and institutions that oppress human beings—Babylon implicitly (17:16; 18:9-10; 19:3), and the beast, the false prophet and the dragon explicitly. It is, as Jesus said, "prepared for the devil and his angels" (Mt 25:41). More important, the lake of fire swallows up *death and Hades* (compare Is 25:8; 1 Cor 15:54). After *the sea gave up the dead that were in it, and death and Hades gave up the dead that were in them,* and after all the dead were judged, says John, *death and Hades*

merit in the other passages, this interpretation has little basis in the text of Revelation. Those being judged here are not Christians, but "the rest of the dead" (v. 5), and the only *stated* outcome of this judgment is condemnation in the lake of fire (v. 15). If there are any exceptions, we know nothing about them, for they are outside the scope of John's vision.

were thrown into the lake of fire (vv. 13-14).

This is all very confusing for modern Christians who were taught that "Hades" is a biblical word for hell (see the KJV "death and hell were cast into the lake of fire") and that "hell" in the book of Revelation is itself the lake of fire. How can hell be thrown into hell? The eighteenth-century Welsh hymn writer, William Williams, captured the meaning in the third verse of his great hymn, "Guide Me, O Thou Great Jehovah":

When I tread the verge of Jordan,
Bid my anxious fears subside;
Death of death, and hell's destruction,
Land me safe on Canaan's side.

Quite a number of hymnals, unable to make sense of Williams's bold imagery, substituted "bear me through the swelling current" for the third line. But Williams himself saw clearly that the "death of death and hell's destruction" described in Revelation 20:14 is what opens the way for new life and salvation in chapter 21. The confusion stems from the fact that "Hades" is not "hell" as understood in Christian tradition, but the grave, corresponding to "Sheol" in the Hebrew Bible. It is never mentioned by itself in the book of Revelation, but only as the companion of "Death" (see, for example, 6:8). When John says that *death and Hades gave up the dead that were in them* (v. 13), he means the graves were opened and the dead were raised. This is the language of resurrection, the "second" resurrection if you like, corresponding to "the first resurrection" of verse 6. But instead of "the second resurrection" he calls it "the second death" (v. 14), for two reasons: (1) because his emphasis is not on being raised to life but on being raised only to die again in the lake of fire; and (2) because it is the death of death itself, and of death's grim companion, the grave.

20:15 If the fiery lake is a place of torment for the beast, the false prophet and the dragon (19:20; 20:10), but a place of destruction or nonexistence for death and Hades (20:14), which is it for persons who are *not found written in the book of life* and who are *thrown into the lake of fire?* The question of eternal torment versus annihilationism has been debated by theologians for centuries, and it cannot be settled on the basis of one verse. Yet the close link between the destruction of death and Hades in the lake of fire and this, the only mention of humans going there, suggests that annihilationism cannot be ruled out in this passage (Rev 14:11, where the lake of fire is not mentioned at all, is perhaps more difficult

The notion that death and the grave are thrown into the lake of fire characterizes the lake here not as a place of torment (contrast 19:21 and 20:10), but as a place of destruction or nonexistence. Death and Hades are not tortured or punished, they simply cease to exist. The message of this vivid scene is a simple one: "there will be no more death" (21:4). In Paul's words, "Death has been swallowed up in victory. Where, O death, is your victory? Where, O death, is your sting?" (1 Cor 15:54-55). The way is cleared for the triumphant visions of chapters 21-22.

The New Creation (21:1-8) The series of visions that began at 19:11 (each introduced by "I saw") now draws to a close. The positive benefits of "the second death" become explicit in John's vision of a new world. Here we find an answer to the question, If those whose names were not written in the book of life were thrown into the lake of fire, what about those whose names *were* written there? The answer given to this question is visual (vv. 1-2) and audible (vv. 3-8). John sees a new world and then learns its significance.

What John Saw and Did Not See (21:1-2) John's vision is of *a new heaven and a new earth* (v. 1), reminding him that *the first heaven and the first earth had passed away.* John had seen *the first heaven and the first earth* "pass away" just five verses earlier: "Earth and sky fled from his presence, and there was no place for them" (20:11). As we have already observed, "heaven" and "sky" are the same word in Greek. The NIV, which translated that word appropriately as "sky" in 20:11, has here obscured the similarity between the two passages by translating it as "heaven." John's point is that the "earth and sky" that disappeared (20:11) are now replaced with "a new sky" and "a new earth," in other words, a new world—a whole new human environment.

---

for the annihilationists to explain).

21:2 The rendering of the NIV, *coming down out of heaven from God,* is redundant: to come from heaven is to come from God. ("Heaven" is often used in Jewish literature to mean God.) But if the translation "sky" is used, the redundancy disappears: John saw the holy city coming down out of the sky (the "new sky" of the preceding verse), and he knew that in fact it was coming not just from the visible sky but from the very presence of God. Every time the holy city is mentioned in the book of Revelation, it is described with exactly the same expression, "coming down out of the sky from God" (compare 3:12; 21:10).

Something is different, however: *there was no longer any sea* (v. 1). Nothing was said in the preceding section about the sea disappearing with the sky and the earth. The sea remained and, with death and Hades, "gave up the dead" that were in it (20:13). As soon as the dead were judged, death and Hades were thrown into the lake of fire (20:14). But what about the sea?

Because it would be incongruous to have the sea thrown into the lake of fire, John contents himself with the observation that *there was no longer any sea.* The sea, like Hades, was to him a realm of death. Millions of dead are buried at sea, just as millions are buried in the earth. John was told of a beast coming out of the Abyss, or bottomless pit (11:7), but what he himself later saw was the beast coming out of the sea (13:1). From his perspective the sea, the Abyss and Hades all amount to much the same thing. What is more natural for a man imprisoned on a lonely island than to view the waters separating him from his companions on the mainland as waters of death? His perception that *there was no longer any sea* is simply another way of saying that in the new creation there is *no more death* (v. 4). It is possible, in fact, by ignoring the chapter divisions, to draw 21:1 into the orbit of the preceding chapter, as the concluding element in a four-part chiastic structure:

(a) "the sea gave up the dead that were it"

(b) "death and Hades gave up the dead that were in them"

(b′) "death and Hades were thrown into the lake of fire"

(a′) "there was no longer any sea"

John's new creation, then, consists of a new sky and a new earth, without the sea and what the sea represents. Above all it consists of *the Holy City, the new Jerusalem, coming down out of heaven from God, prepared as a bride beautifully dressed for her husband* (v. 2). John has no interest in the new sky and new earth for their own sake. They merely set the stage for the real center of his attention: the new Jerusalem (see 21:9—22:5). His priorities are the same as Isaiah's, from whom he draws

21:3 The *loud voice from the throne* is comparable to other anonymous voices throughout the book, either from heaven or specifically from the throne or temple or altar in heaven (for example, 9:13; 12:10; 16:7, 17; 18:4; 19:5). These are not literally God's own voice (for sometimes they call forth praise to "our God," 12:10; 19:5), yet they are voices that speak with divine authority.

Behold, I will create
new heavens and a new earth.
The former things will not be remembered,
nor will they come to mind.
But be glad and rejoice forever
in what I will create,
for I will create Jerusalem to be a delight
and its people a joy.
I will rejoice over Jerusalem
and take delight in my people;
the sound of weeping and of crying
will be heard in it no more." (Is 65:17-19)

The new Jerusalem is *prepared as a bride beautifully dressed for her husband* (v. 2). This city is also personified as a woman, not a prostitute like evil Babylon, but a pure and holy bride. The bride was mentioned in passing once before (19:7-8), when she represented "the saints," or people of God, the redeemed "virgins" who followed the Lamb wherever he went (14:4-5. They have now ruled with him on earth for a thousand years (20:4-6). *The Holy City, the new Jerusalem,* is not so much a place as a people (Gundry 1987:254-64), specifically a people meeting their God, as John is about to learn from two heavenly voices.

What John Heard (21:3-8) If there is one speech that captures in a nutshell the meaning of the entire book of Revelation, this is it. John hears *a loud voice from the throne* announcing (in the third person) the significance of what he has just seen (vv. 3-4). Then *he who was seated on the throne* continues, speaking in the first person (vv. 5-8). The message is one, in spite of the changing voices. The voice from the throne begins by calling John's attention to the vision he has just seen: *Now the dwelling of God is with men* (that is, with humankind). This means that "he will dwell with them as their God; they will be his peoples, and God himself will be with them" (v. 3 NRSV). As the speaker

The gender-exclusive language of the NIV, *now the dwelling of God is with men,* gives way in the NRSV to "see, the home of God is among mortals." This move avoids one problem only to create another: the redeemed in the new Jerusalem are hardly "mortals" if they have been raised from the dead (20:4-6). Therefore the translation "humans" (for the Greek *anthrōpoi)* is preferable to both the NRSV and the NIV.

shifts from present to future tense, we get the impression that John no longer stands at the scene of the last judgment, fastforwarded into the future with a new sky and a new earth, but back in his own time, on Patmos on the Lord's Day (as in 1:9-10).

The message is intended for him and the seven congregations in their day, and equally for us today. Its future-oriented language is the language of God's ancient covenant with the Jewish people. God told Moses to tell Israel, "I will put my dwelling place among you, and I will not abhor you. I will walk among you and be your God, and you will be my people" (Lev 26:11-12). Ezekiel wrote, "I will make a covenant of peace with them; it will be an everlasting covenant. I will establish them and increase their numbers, and I will put my sanctuary among them forever. My dwelling place will be with them; I will be their God, and they will be my people" (Ezek 37:26-27). Ezekiel added, "Then the nations will know that I the LORD make Israel holy, when my sanctuary is among them forever" (v. 28), suggesting that God's covenant with Israel signified hope for the Gentiles as well. Zechariah went a step further: "Many nations will be joined with the LORD in that day and will become my people" (Zech 2:11; compare Is 56:7). Yet nowhere in the Hebrew Bible are the Gentiles drawn fully into God's covenant with Israel.

This changes in the New Testament, where Paul reminds a *Gentile* congregation at Corinth: "For we are the temple of the living God. As God has said, 'I will live with them and walk among them, and I will be their God, and they will be my people'" (2 Cor 6:16). Similarly in Revelation the ancient covenant promises are for "his peoples," not simply the people of Israel (Bauckham 1993:137; see 5:9; 7:9). John has not forgotten that Jerusalem is a Jewish city, but he sees it here as representing all the cities and all the people of the world. Yet John is no universalist. His point is not that all humans will be saved, for he has already seen "the inhabitants of the earth" thrown into the lake of fire. The bride, or new Jerusalem, is simply his metaphor for those who are redeemed. They are the new humanity. The destiny of others is "the second death" (20:14), but for this group there is *no more death* (v. 4). The voice from the throne echoes the imagery of Isaiah 25:6-8: "On this mountain the LORD Almighty will prepare a feast of rich foods for all peoples . . . On this mountain he will destroy the shroud that enfolds all peoples, the sheet that covers all nations; he will swallow up death forever. The Sovereign LORD will wipe away the tears from all faces; he will remove the disgrace of his people from all the earth."

When the voice from the throne announces, *There will be no more death or mourning or crying or pain, for the old order of things has passed away* (v. 4), it recalls an earlier voice. The poignant phrase *no more* (Greek *ouk . . eti*) echoes the refrain of the angel who pronounced doom on Babylon (18:21-23), but with a glorious difference. There the things that would be "no more" were good things like music, trade, "the sound of a millstone," "the light of a lamp," "the voice of bridegroom and bride" (18:22-23). Here they are sad things like death, mourning, crying and pain (compare "no longer will there be any curse," 22:3, and "no more night," 22:5). In the earlier vision, all the joys of life sank with Babylon like a millstone into the sea (18:21); now the sea itself, and with it death, mourning, crying and pain, is *no more* (v. 4).

The transition from *the old order of things have passed away* (v. 4) to *I am making everything new* (v. 5) corresponds to a change in speaker. Instead of *a loud voice from the throne* (vv. 3-4), we now hear from the one *who was seated on the throne* (vv. 5-8). This is one of only two places in the entire book where God speaks personally and directly (Aune 1983:280), the other being 1:8, "'I am the Alpha and the Omega,' says the Lord God, 'who is, and who was, and who is to come, the Almighty.'" Here too God identifies himself with *I am the Alpha and Omega, the Beginning and the End* (v. 6) and here too gives the impression of speaking to John in his own time and immediate situation on the island of Patmos.

The good news at the heart of the book of Revelation is the announcement *I am making everything new* (v. 5). This is not something God does only at the end of time, but something going on already in the present age, whether in the seven congregations to which John wrote or in our troubled world today. It is a *trustworthy and true* pronouncement, so crucial to the message of the book that John is immediately commanded, *Write this down* (v. 5). A similar conviction lies at the root of Paul's bold affirmation that "if anyone is in Christ, there is a new creation; everything old has passed away; see, everything has become new" (2 Cor 5:17 NRSV). Whether John was familiar with Paul, or whether Paul was simply using an expression already common among early Christians, it was not a huge step to conclude that a God who remakes individuals is at work remaking the world as well. In the mind of God, if not yet in human experience, *it is done* (v. 6).

The voice continues to speak to John and his readers in their own time. The divine self-identification, *I am the Alpha and the Omega, the Beginning and the End,* combined with a promise (or promises) recalls several of Jesus' sayings in the Gospel of John, for example, John 6:35 ("I am the bread of life. He who comes to me will never go hungry, and he who believes in me will never be thirsty"), 8:12 ("I am the light of the world. Whoever follows me will never walk in darkness, but will have the light of life") and 11:25-26 ("I am the resurrection and the life. He who believes in me will live, even though he dies; and whoever lives and believes in me will never die"). Here the speaker seems to be God rather than Jesus, although at this point the two have become virtually interchangeable (see 22:13, where Jesus identifies himself as "the Alpha and the Omega, the First and the Last, the Beginning and the End"). Two promises are attached to the self-identification. First, to the thirsty *I will give to drink without cost from the spring of the water of life* (v. 6; compare John 4:14; 6:35; 7:37-38). Second, anyone *who overcomes will inherit all this, and I will be his God and he will be my son* (v. 7; compare the repeated promises in the seven messages of chapters 2-3 to those who "overcome").

These promises should be read as invitations to all who hear John's long letter read in the congregations of Asia. John assumes there will be some outsiders or inquirers sitting in on Christian worship assemblies

---

21:5 The voice tells John, *Write this down.* But what is he to write? Probably not just that *these words are trustworthy and true.* More likely John is to write down what he is hearing at the moment (whether the saying "I am making everything new," or all of vv. 3-5, or all of vv. 3-8), precisely because they are true and trustworthy words. Although John is supposedly writing down all that he sees and hears as he goes along (1:11, 19), the explicit command, "Write," is a device calling attention to sayings of special import (such as prophetic messages in chapters 2 and 3, or beatitudes in 14:13 and 19:9, or the words from heaven recorded here).

21:6 *It is done* (Greek *gegonan*) is literally "they are done," that is, all the words of God are accomplished (compare Mt 5:18, "until everything is accomplished"). The similar phrase

(1 Cor 14:23-25). They are the *thirsty* who are urged to drink of *the water of life* that is the Christian message. As for the believers in the assembly, their responsibility is to "hear" and "take to heart what is written" (1:3), and above all to "overcome" in the face of ridicule, social pressure and impending persecution, and so become God's *son,* or child. As we have seen (in connection with 1:6), knowing God as Father in the book of Revelation is more of a promise for the future than a present experience, even for those who "overcome." For the present, God is Jesus' Father, not ours, and even in this future setting the promise to God's son or child is, *I will be his God,* not his "Father."

Last comes a warning to all who reject such invitations, whether they call themselves Christians or not. The grim ending is a list of those whose *place will be in the fiery lake of burning sulfur,* which is *the second death* (v. 8; compare 20:14-15). Most of the classes of people there come as no surprise: *the vile, the murderers, the sexually immoral, those who practice magic arts, the idolaters.* They stand outside and are hostile to the Christian communities to which John is writing. But some are more surprising. The reference at the beginning of the list to *the cowardly* (Greek *deiloi*) and *the unbelieving* (Greek *apistoi,* literally "the faithless") recalls Jesus' rebukes to his disciples, "Why are you so afraid?" (literally, "Why are you such cowards?"). "Do you still have no faith?" (Mk 4:40; compare Mt 8:26).

Such terms seem to refer not to those outside the Christian movement but to those within the seven congregations who are cowards, unwilling to stand firm in the face of trouble and testing. They are not so much "unbelievers" as unfaithful Christians (compare Rev 2:10, "Be faithful, even to the point of death"; 17:14, "his called, chosen and faithful followers"). Similarly at the end of the list there is emphasis on *all liars,*

---

in 16:17, "it is done" (Greek *gegonen,* singular), stands in sharp contrast, for it signals the destruction of evil Babylon, not the birth of a new world.

21:7 The NIV's gender-exclusive rendering, *I will be his God and he will be my son* (like that of the KJV), quite literally follows the Greek (which uses the word *hyios,* "son"). The NRSV (legitimately) goes to the plural ("I will be their God and they will be my children") in the interest of inclusive language. The male-oriented language of the Greek may be explained by the fact that to the early Christians such words were as applicable to the man Jesus of Nazareth individually (Heb 1:5) as to the people of God corporately (though see 2 Cor 6:18, where Paul shows sensitivity to gender with the expression, "you will be my sons and daughters").

recalling Gentile Christians who "claim to be Jews though they are not, but are liars" (3:9; compare 2:9) and those "who claim to be apostles but are not" and are similarly found to be "false," or liars (2:2; 14:5; 22:15). If the purpose of these lies was to avoid persecution, then *the cowardly* and *liars* are the same. Never is it assumed anywhere in the Revelation that all those in the Christian congregations are necessarily "overcomers." Some inside as well as outside the church are destined for *the second death*. This sobering conclusion to God's voice from the throne leaves it to us to decide where we wish to stand at the last judgment.

□ Jerusalem and Her Destiny (21:9—22:15)

All of us have experienced, at one time or another, a sense of déjà vu, a feeling that what we are doing or seeing is something we have seen or done before. This can happen in our dreams or our waking moments and can raise in us troubling questions about where dreams end and reality begins. This phenomenon is evident in Revelation 21:9-10: *One of the seven angels who had the seven bowls full of the seven last plagues came and said to me, 'Come, I will show you' . . . And he carried me away in the Spirit to a mountain great and high.*

The attentive reader can look back to 17:1-3 to see where something similar to this happened before: "One of the seven angels who had the seven bowls came and said to me, 'Come, I will show you' . . . Then the angel carried me away in the Spirit into a desert." John expresses no such déjà vu. He never says, "This happened to me before," as he did, for example, in 4:1, when he identified the voice speaking to him as the "first" voice that he had heard earlier (in 1:10). Here he simply takes things as they come. Later, when the angel has shown him all there is to show (22:8-9), John falls down to worship the angel exactly as he did before (19:10). Again he is told not to do so, but to worship God alone. Yet nothing is made of the fact that this is happening for the second time or that John has not learned his lesson.

These features suggest that the repetition is for our benefit, not John's. The repetition establishes for the reader a sharp contrast between two cities personified as women—Babylon the prostitute and Jerusalem the bride. The framing of the two visions with similar introductions and conclusions could lead us to expect that the visions themselves will parallel each other in form or structure all the way through, so as to keep the contrast between the two cities always before us. But this is not the case. Aside from the introduction and conclusion, parallels are few.

The Vision of the City (21:9-21) Is *one of the seven angels* the same angel who showed John the vision of Babylon in chapter 17? There is no way to be sure. The reference to a single angel in 1:1 and 22:16 suggests that it is, yet the angel now plays a somewhat different role. The vision of the holy city, unlike that of Babylon and the beast, is not a cryptogram that needs decoding. Consequently the angel is not an interpreting angel (as in 17:7-18). Instead, John supplies the interpretation himself (21:22-27; 22:3-5).

The angel promises to show John *the bride, the wife of the Lamb* (v. 9), but what then appears is a city, not a woman (v. 10). From this point on, the bridal imagery is dropped, to surface again only in 22:17. The image of the city as a woman is not carried through consistently, as it was in chapters 17 and 18. The angel shows John the holy city (vv. 9-14) and then measures it (vv. 15-21). The *mountain great and high* (v. 10) to which John is taken *in the Spirit* (that is, in his vision) is more than a vantage point from which to view the holy city. It is Mount Zion itself (14:1), on which the city stands, or rather "lands" in its descent from the sky.

The impression of enormous height in the reference to the *mountain great and high* is confirmed shortly when John sees *a great, high wall* surrounding the city (v. 12). In contrast to Babylon, situated in a "desert" (17:3), and in contrast even to "the city he loves," standing on "the breadth of the earth" at the millennium's end (20:9), this is a three-dimensional city, with length, breadth and height all equal. The traditional city *laid out like a square* becomes in John's vision a giant cube. The city is *12,000 stadia in length, and as wide and high as it is long* (v. 16). Translated into modern measurements, this means almost fifteen hundred miles long, fifteen hundred miles wide and fifteen hundred miles high. Such a city defies both logic and imagination. Edwin A. Abbott, in his classic Victorian fantasy, *Flatland: A Romance of Many Dimensions* (1884), wrote of a two-dimensional world in which women were lines, working-class men were triangles, professional men were squares and priests were circles. The hero, "A Square," has a mystical experience in which a spherical Stranger ushers him into "the Land of Three Dimensions," transforming his flat world forever (Abbott 1952:80). John too looks into a city far beyond his comprehension or powers of description.

The angel's measurement (vv. 15-21) reveals that the city's *great, high wall* rises to a height of 144 cubits (about 216 feet), which is impressive enough for an ordinary city, but ridiculously small for a city 1500 miles high! Consequently the NIV renders the measurement as *144 cubits thick* (see also Beckwith 1922:761). This is unlikely because (1) the first mention of the wall (v. 10) called attention to its great height, not its strength or thickness, and because (2) the wall is not built for protection or to keep people out, for its gates are always open (v. 25). Moreover, the word "thick" is not in the text, which says simply "144 cubits." The correct interpretation is "144 cubits high" (as in the NIV margin).

Despite the comparative modesty of 144 cubits, the intended effect is great height, as opposed to smallness or inadequacy. The measurement is not given for the sake of comparison with anything else. The *great, high wall,* like the *great and high* mountain of verse 10, simply calls attention to the strange fact that this city is three-dimensional. It has height as well as length and breadth. Such numbers as twelve thousand (stadia) and 144 (cubits) recall the 144,000 of chapter 7, with twelve thousand from each of the tribes of Israel: "a great multitude that

---

21:14 Logic and theology might have led us to expect that the Jewish twelve tribes would have been the foundations of the walls (because they came first in time), and the Christian twelve apostles, the gates (because their message determines who enters the city). In fact the opposite is true. The reversal of expectations has the effect of integrating the two groups so that each depends on the other. Moreover, the reversal of order between verses 12-14 (gates/foundations) and 19-21 (foundations/gates) forms what is known as a chiasm (a device we have already noted in Revelation), furthering the impression that neither group takes priority. Both are essential to the city's existence and identity. Although "apostles" or Christian missionaries are mentioned in 2:2 and 18:20, the Twelve appointed by Jesus are mentioned only in this vision. The author writes as one who did not himself belong to their number.

21:15 *The angel who talked with me* is literally "the one who talked with me," echoing verse 9. Yet the angel says nothing between "come, I will show you the bride, the wife of the Lamb" (21:9) and "these words are trustworthy and true" (22:6). The angel here, in contrast to chapter 17, waits until the vision is concluded to engage John in dialogue (see 22:6-15).

21:16 The notion that ancient cities were often *laid out like a square* (Greek *tetragōnos*) is supported not only by Ezekiel's prophecies of a renewed Jerusalem (Ezek 45:1; 48:20, 30-35)

no one could count, from every nation, tribe, people and language, standing before the throne and in front of the Lamb" (7:9). The huge cubical city has more than enough room for the 144,000 from Israel or even for a crowd without number from all nations. It encompasses the whole people of God. In some sense it *is* the people of God (Gundry 1987:254-64).

The notion of the city as people is conspicuous both in John's first sight of the city (vv. 9-14) and in the angel's measurement (vv. 15-21). First the angel shows John *twelve gates* in the city wall, three on each side, with twelve angels at the gates (vv. 12-13), and then, more briefly, the wall's *twelve foundations* (v. 14). On the gates John sees inscribed *the names of the twelve tribes of Israel* (v. 12) and on the foundations *the names of the twelve apostles of the Lamb* (v. 14). When the city is measured, the order is reversed: the twelve foundations are described first and at greater length (vv. 19-20), and then the twelve gates (v. 21). Each of the foundations is decorated with a different kind of precious stone, but there is no way to correlate these stones with whatever specific "apostles" John may have had in mind (John has no list of "the twelve apostles of the Lamb" comparable to his list of the "sons of Israel" in 7:5-8). As for the twelve gates, there is no differentiation among them. Each gate is a single pearl, all apparently alike and all evidently of enormous size. The "peoples" of God (see 21:3) have become a single people, one holy city.

---

but also by Greek historians describing Babylon (Herodotus *History* 1.178), Nineveh (Diodorus Siculus *History* 1.3), and Nicaea (Strabo, *Geography,* 12.4.7). Caird (1966:274) finds especially close similarities to Herodotus's description of ancient Babylon (see also Mounce 1977:380). But Caird's conjecture (1966:273) that the city somehow represents, on a gigantic scale, the holy of holies in King Solomon's temple ("twenty cubits long, twenty wide and twenty high," 1 Kings 6:20) is less plausible. John is quite explicit later that the city as such is not a temple or a sanctuary; rather, "the Lord God Almighty and the Lamb are its temple" (v. 22).

21:17 John makes clear that the "cubit" he is using is the standardized unit of measurement so designated—the distance from a man's elbow to his fingertip. The height is 144 cubits *by man's measurement, which the angel was using* (literally, "by the measure of a man, that is, of an angel"). Caird (1966:273-74) argues that John "does not mean the standard cubit," but rather the (unknown) length of an angel's forearm, making it impossible to calculate in human terms. John's point is just the opposite: the cubit is the normal one because the angel is the size of an ordinary man and measures as a man would measure. ("Man" is as appropriate as "person" or "human being" in this instance because of the likelihood that the cubit was originally measured by the length of the male forearm.)

Another conspicuous element both in the angel's presentation of holy Jerusalem (vv. 9-14) and in the act of measuring the city (vv. 15-21) is that the city reflects the character and the splendor of God in heaven. The city comes, after all, *from God* (v. 10). When John first sees it descending, it has *the glory of God, and its brilliance was like that of a very precious jewel, like a jasper, clear as crystal* (v. 11). When the angel has finished measuring the city, we learn that the city wall is *made of jasper,* while the city itself is *pure gold, as pure as glass,* with a street of *pure gold, like transparent glass* (vv. 18, 21). The comparison to jasper, with its indeterminate color, recalls the "someone" sitting on the throne in John's first vision of heaven (4:3, like "jasper and carnelian"). The phrases *clear as crystal, as pure as glass,* and *like transparent glass* echo the description of "what looked like a sea of glass, like crystal" in front of the throne in the same early vision (4:6). These varied expressions all make the point that the city radiates through and through the glory and purity of God, who made it and adorned it as the place for God and humans to dwell together in a world made new (see v. 3).

John's Interpretation of the Vision (21:22-27) This vision, unlike the one in chapter 17, is no "mystery" (see 17:5, 7). John is not amazed or beguiled by what he has seen (as in 17:6), nor does he need to have anything explained to him (as in 17:7-18). As a prophet, he is given the correct understanding to pass along to his readers. Curiously, the interpretation rests first of all on what he does *not* see. No "holy city," least of all Jerusalem, should be without a temple, but John sees no temple and concludes from this that *the Lord God Almighty and the Lamb are its temple* (v. 22). With these few words he gathers up Ezekiel's elaborate prophecy of a renewed temple in Jerusalem (Ezek 40—48) into its concluding disclosure of the city's name: THE LORD IS THERE (Ezek 48:35; compare Rev 3:12). If God and the Lamb are the temple of the holy city, they are also its light (vv. 23-25). There is no need of *the sun or moon,* either as sources of light or as objects of worship, no special

21:27 The addition of the conjunction "but" in the NRSV (for the Greek *kai,* normally translated "and") at the beginning of the verse is a helpful translation in the context. The point of verse 26 is that Gentile nations will bring their gifts into the city; verse 27 adds that *nevertheless* this Gentile wealth and tribute will not pollute the city or make it unclean (as

feasts determined by solar or lunar calendar, no more cycle of day and night. Normally a city's gates are open during the day for commerce and closed at night against enemy attack. But because there is *no night there* (v. 25), this city's gates are always open. Far from being a fortress, the new Jerusalem is an open city without enemies (contrast 20:9), for its enemies are in the lake of fire (see 20:15; 21:8).

To be sure, there are former enemies in the picture who are not residents of the holy city. They are *the nations* and *the kings of the earth,* who appear as friendly vassals (v. 24). The *kings of the earth* had earlier been deceived into immorality with Babylon the prostitute (17:2; 18:3, 9) and had fought (unsuccessfully) against God and the Lamb (16:14; 17:12-14; 19:19-21). Now at last they have given their allegiance to the true "ruler of the kings of the earth" (1:5), who is "King of kings and Lord of lords" (19:16). The *nations,* or "Gentiles," were similarly deceived more than once (14:8; 18:3, 23; 20:3, 8) and were thrown into turmoil (11:18). Yet all along their destiny has been that Jesus and those who follow him would "strike down" (19:15) and ultimately "rule" (12:5; 19:15) them "with an iron scepter" (fulfilling Ps 2:1-2, 8-9).

In short, John finds in this vision the realization of the "song of Moses the servant of God and the song of the Lamb" sung by the redeemed in chapter 15: "All nations will come and worship before you, for your righteous acts have been revealed" (15:4). Here too the hopes of the biblical prophets for Jerusalem have come true, above all Isaiah 60:3: "Nations will come to your light, and kings to the brightness of your dawn" and 60:11: "Your gates will always stand open, they will never be shut, day or night, so that men may bring you the wealth of the nations—their kings led in triumphal procession."

John concludes his interpretation with a reminder that while Jerusalem is open to *the kings of the earth* and *their splendor* (v. 24), as well as to *the glory and honor of the nations* (v. 26), it is not open to anything unclean or to *anyone who does what is shameful or deceitful* (v. 27).

---

it might have done under other circumstances; see, for example, Josh 7:10-13). Even though the city's gates stand open to everyone day and night, it remains always and unmistakably "holy" (see vv 1, 10).

Only those *whose names are written in the Lamb's book of life* will enter the city. The implication is that both the residents of the city and the Gentiles who bring their wealth and tribute into it *are* those who are *written in the Lamb's book of life.* John's vision includes not only the redemption of Christian saints and martyrs, but in some sense the redemption of the rebellious and often deceived Gentile nations as well (see Bauckham 1993:98-104). The two groups are allied in that both worship the God of Israel and the Lamb, but the precise relationship between them is left to our imagination.

The Vision of the River of Life and Its Interpretation (22:1-5) The second stage of John's vision begins with the words *then the angel showed me* (v. 1; compare 21:9, 10). Having seen the holy city, John is now shown *the river of the water of life, as clear as crystal, flowing from the throne of God and of the Lamb down the middle of the great street of the city* (vv. 1-2). The river reflects the crystal-like quality of the city itself (v. 11) or of the glassy "sea" in front of the throne in John's first vision of heaven (4:6). The *great street* (Greek *plateia*) is the wide main street of the city, emphasizing the river's centrality to the city as a whole and its visibility to all residents. Ironically, the same broad street or plaza that had been a place of death where the bodies of two martyred prophets lay in public view for three and a half days (11:8-9) is now a place of life, where the river of life irrigates *the tree of life* for the benefit of the city's inhabitants and the nations that live by its light (v. 2; compare 21:24). Just as the city had twelve gates and twelve foundations, the tree of life yields *twelve crops of fruit,* corresponding to the twelve months of the year.

The vision plays on two biblical themes, "the tree of life" in the Garden of Eden (Gen 2:9), to which Adam and Eve were denied access

---

22:2 The phrase "in the middle of the street" should be understood not as defining the location of the throne of God and the Lamb, but as indicating where the river flowed, that is, *down,* or "through" (NRSV) the middle of the city's main street. Another interpretation takes the phrase with what follows rather than what precedes (that is, "in the middle of the street *and* on either side of the river is the tree of life"), but this creates a picture that is hard to visualize. If the tree of life is "on either side of the river" (suggesting rows of trees along both banks of the river), how can it also be "in the middle of the street"?

The *tree of life* echoes the promise to those who "overcome" at Ephesus, where the tree

after the Fall (Gen 3:24), and Ezekiel's vision of water flowing down from the restored temple in Jerusalem all the way to the Dead Sea (Ezek 47:1-12). That John's interpretation of the Genesis passage is shaped decisively by Ezekiel was recognized already in the eighteenth century by the Oxford scholar Benjamin Kennicott (1747:93-97). John's *tree of life* is indeed located in a garden (more precisely, it *is* a garden), but the garden now stands in the heart of a city. In Ezekiel's vision, a river flows eastward from the temple "down into the Arabah, where it enters the Sea. When it empties into the Sea, the water there becomes fresh. . . . There will be large numbers of fish, because this water flows there and makes the salt water fresh; so where the river flows everything will live. . . . Fruit trees of all kinds will grow on both banks of the river. Their leaves will not wither, nor will their fruit fail. Every month they will bear, because the water from the sanctuary flows to them. Their fruit will serve for food and their leaves for healing" (Ezek 47:8-9, 12).

The shift from the vision of *the river of the water of life* (vv. 1-2) to John's interpretation of it (vv. 2-5) is even more abrupt than in the case of the vision of the holy city. John sees the river only within Jerusalem itself, and he links Ezekiel's trees lining the river with the tree of life from Genesis. Instead of "all kinds" of fruit trees, he is shown one kind of tree, *the tree of life,* bearing *twelve crops of fruit,* presumably for the city's inhabitants. As in Ezekiel, the leaves are for healing, but in John's vision specifically for *the healing of the nations* (v. 2). The tree of life is the reason why the bruised and battered Gentile nations will walk in the light of the holy city, "and the kings of the earth will bring their splendor into it" (21:24). Whether or not they "eat from the tree of life" (2:7), they clearly have some kind of a share in its benefits (see 22:14, 19). In their own way they too are redeemed.

was said to be in "the paradise of God" (2:7). That phrase was used in the LXX for "the garden of God," or Eden (see Gen 13:10; Ezek 28:13; 31:8-9). By placing the tree of life in the holy city, John in effect locates paradise there as well. Access to both is reserved for those who enter the city (see vv 14, 19).

22:3 Zechariah 14:11, often cited as a parallel to "nothing accursed" in the holy city, is actually not a close parallel. Zechariah's "no more curse" (RSV) is not a promise of holiness or purity, but of safety or immunity from destruction (see both NIV and NRSV on Zech 14:11). This issue does not come up in John's vision.

The remainder of John's interpretation (vv. 3-5) mainly reinforces what was said earlier. *No longer will there be any curse* in the city, and *no more night* (Greek *ouk. . . . eti,* vv. 3, 5), just as there will be no more death or crying or pain (21:4). The *curse* is probably concrete rather than abstract. It is not the curse of Gen 3:14 (although the image of the tree of life may have called to mind that universal curse on humanity), but specifically "nothing accursed" (NRSV) or "no accursed thing" (Greek *pan katathema*). The point is much the same as in 21:27, where "nothing impure" (Greek *pan koinon*) is to enter the city. In a similar way, *no more night* (v. 5) echoes the language of 21:25, "there will be no night there."

Having already described the river of life *flowing from the throne of God and of the Lamb* (v. 1), John now adds, somewhat belatedly, that *the throne of God and of the Lamb will be in the city* (v. 3). He stated earlier that God and the Lamb are the city's "temple," or "sanctuary" (Greek *naos,* 21:22), and now the temple is understood as a throne in the new Jerusalem, just as it was in heaven (see chap. 4). His mention of the throne-as-temple affords John the opportunity to reflect briefly on the relationship between God and the people of God: *and his servants will serve him. They will see his face, and his name will be on their foreheads* (vv. 3-4; compare 7:15, "they are before the throne of God and serve him day and night in his temple"). For the first time in the entire book, John holds out the possibility of seeing the face of God. Strictly speaking, this was contrary to Jewish belief (see Ex 33:20; also Jn 1:18; 6:46; 1 Jn 4:12). Yet there was a strand of Jewish and early Christian piety that allowed such a possibility in a metaphorical sense (for example, Ps 11:7; 17:15; 42:2; also Mt 5:8; 1 Jn 3:2). This is what is meant in the present passage. To see God's face is to belong to God, to have God's name written

22:3-4 There is no way (and no need) to determine whether the pronoun "his" (as in *his servants, his face,* and *his name*) refers to God or to the Lamb. The two are so closely identified in this whole passage that they stand together as the single object of worship. It cannot be argued, for example, that we will see Christ's face but not God's (compare 1 Jn 3:1-2, where the Father and the Son are similarly indistinguishable).

22:6-7 The NIV, NRSV and most English versions place all of verse 6 in quotation marks, making the whole verse part of the angel's pronouncement. It is more likely that the angel says only, *These words are trustworthy and true* (as, for example, in the NASB). It would be an awkward bit of self-reference for the angel to say that the Lord *sent his angel.* Instead,

on the forehead (compare 14:1), and to live in the light of God's presence (compare 21:23).

John's reflection on his vision ends with the declaration that the servants of God in the holy city *will reign for ever and ever* (v. 5). The prophecy of the twenty-four elders that saints "from every tribe and language and people and nation" would "reign on the earth" (5:9-10) is not exhausted in the thousand-year reign of 20:4-6. Their reign "on the earth" (now a new earth) with God and the Lamb continues forever. The point is not that the redeemed are kings and queens individually, but that just as they participated with the Lamb (rather passively, it seems) in victory over the powers of evil, so they will participate with God and the Lamb in ruling over the new creation. The victory at Armageddon belonged first of all to "the Lord of lords and King of kings" and only secondarily to his followers, and the same is true of the rule of God over the earth. The promise that they will reign for ever and ever cannot be separated from its premise that the Lord God will give them light (v. 5).

John and the Angel (22:6-15) The angel's conclusion, *these words are trustworthy and true* (v. 6), recalls a similar statement by the angel at the end of the vision of Babylon and her destiny ("these are the true words of God," 19:9). It also repeats word for word the pronouncement of the one "seated on the throne" in 21:5. Both previous passages were accompanied by commands to "write this," referring to something John was being told. This time there is no explicit command to write, but there are three clear references to *this book* (vv. 7, 9, 10), the book John was told to write in his very first vision (1:11) and is now bringing to completion.

What words are meant when the angel says, *These words are trustworthy and true* (v. 6)? The angel's own words? Not unless they

---

the voice is that of either the anonymous narrator of 1:1-3 or John himself. Because the pronouncement stands within the long letter attributed to "John" (1:4—22:21), the speaker is probably John reflecting on what the angel has shown him in 21:9—22:5 (perhaps in 17:1—19:10 as well). In this case it is John who then delivers the prophetic message of verse 7 (*see, I am coming soon*), finally identifying himself by name in verse 8. The words *see, I am coming soon!* are abruptly inserted to explain the phrase *the things that must soon take place* in verse 6. The rest of verse 7 simply continues the thought of verse 6 (roughly corresponding to the flow of thought in 1:1-3).

were left unrecorded. The angel has said nothing to John between 21:9 and 22:6. John has been "shown" a great deal (21:9; 22:1), but as far as we know has heard no words spoken (contrast the vision of Babylon in 17:1—19:10; also the vision of the new creation in 21:1-8). Therefore the pronouncement *these words are trustworthy and true* must have a wider reference—probably to the entire book of Revelation, which is now drawing to a close. This is supported by the fact that what immediately follows in verse 6, *The Lord, the God of the spirits of the prophets, sent his angel to show his servants the things that must soon take place,* echoes a number of phrases from the book's title (notably "to show his servants," "what soon must take place" and "by sending his angel," 1:1).

At this point John, speaking as a prophet in Jesus' name, delivers words from Jesus reinforcing the notion that Jesus' coming will be *soon.* Then he pronounces a blessing on whoever *keeps the words of the prophecy in this book* (v. 7; compare 1:3). John identifies himself by name for the first time since 1:9 when he says, *I, John, am the one who heard and saw these things* (v. 8). The reference to hearing as well as seeing (reiterated in the next clause, *when I had heard and seen them*) suggests once again that the visions and voices of the entire book are in view, not merely the wordless vision of 21:9—22:5. Although *these things* (Greek *tauta*) must include the things the angel has just shown John, ultimately (like *these words* in v. 6) they encompass everything John has seen and heard (and written down) from the beginning of his series of visions until now.

Verses 8-9 are a reenactment of 19:9-10, where John tried to worship the angel and was told in no uncertain terms to back off, to worship God alone. Here he seems to have forgotten that the incident ever took place. As we have seen, the repetition is for the sake of the reader. For the second time we (as well as John) are commanded, "Worship God!" (v. 9; compare 19:10). There is a finality to verses 8-9 that was not evident in 19:9-10. The concluding imperative of the book of Revelation is to

22:6 *The spirits of the prophets* are probably the "seven spirits" before the throne of God (1:4; 4:5; 5:6), for they are the only "spirits" (plural) other than unclean spirits (16:13; 18:2) mentioned anywhere in the book. As in 1:4, they serve to underscore the power and majesty of God. They also establish God, the Lamb and the Spirit together as the source and authority

worship God (and Jesus the Lamb) *now,* not waiting until that wonderful future time (*soon* though it may be) when we will "serve him" and "see his face" in the new Jerusalem (vv. 3-4).

Whether the worship of angels was a specific problem or a danger in the seven congregations of Asia is difficult to say (see Col 2:18; also perhaps the effort to put angels in their place in Heb 1:4-14). Certainly the view of angels here is similar to the conclusion reached by the author of Hebrews: "Are not all angels ministering spirits sent to serve those who will inherit salvation?" (Heb 1:14). The angel tells John (again) that he is John's *fellow servant,* but instead of associating John with "your brothers who hold to the testimony of Jesus" (19:10), the angel speaks here of *your brothers the prophets,* together with *all who keep the words of this book* (v. 9). The meaning is the same, for in 19:10 the angel had added, "The testimony of Jesus is the spirit of prophecy." Yet the concluding reference to *the words of this book* and those who take its words to heart reminds us that John's *book* is now virtually complete. The angel's words acquire a solemnity and a finality they did not have before (compare 1:3 with its solemn blessing on the reader and the hearers of the written prophecy).

In keeping with this finality, the angel adds, *Do not seal up the words of the prophecy of this book, because the time is near* (v. 10). The contrast with the book of Daniel appears to be deliberate. "Go your way, Daniel," that prophet was told, "because the words are closed up and sealed until the time of the end. . . . You will rest, and then at the end of the days you will rise to receive your allotted inheritance" (Dan 12:9, 13). There is no such waiting period in the book of Revelation. The announcement made at the very beginning (1:3) is repeated word for word: *the time is near* (v. 10). The difficulty for us living at the end of the twentieth century is that we have learned that the time was *not* near, at least not as we customarily measure time. The book of Revelation is to us what the book of Daniel must have been to John and his contemporaries: a sleeping giant waiting to be awakened. Reading it

---

for Christian prophecy in the seven congregations of Asia. Probably the *servants* (Greek *douloi*) who receive the revelation are those who will one day live in the holy city (see v. 3), not just Christian prophets. They are the same "servants" mentioned in 1:1.

awakens the giant and puts us at the threshold of the coming of Jesus: *Behold, I am coming soon* (vv. 7; 12).

What is the angel's message to those who stand at the threshold of Jesus' coming? Not what we might have expected: *Let him who does wrong continue to do wrong; let him who is vile continue to be vile; let him who does right continue to do right; and let him who is holy continue to be holy* (v. 11). Throughout the New Testament, starting with the proclamation of John the Baptist and Jesus, the nearness of God's kingdom and the end of the age serves as an incentive for repentance or moral reform: "Repent, for the kingdom of heaven is near" (Mt 3:2; 4:17; compare Mk 1:15; Rom 13:11-13; Jas 5:8; 1 Pet 4:7). Here, by contrast, no such possibility is in view. The moral condition of good and bad alike seems fixed and unlikely to change. To some extent this picture is consistent with the book of Revelation as a whole. The wicked do *not* as a rule repent of their idolatry or immorality (9:20-21; 16:11). Most often, those called to repentance are those who already belong to communities assumed to be "righteous" or "holy" (2:4, 16, 21-22; 3:3, 19). For them to "repent" is simply to become what they already are.

But is this the correct interpretation of the angel's pronouncement? Do these words in fact have anything to do with individual repentance? Probably not. The point is rather that good and evil are never transcended. The dualism so evident to John in Roman society between the godly and the wicked is not going to change in the short time that remains before Christ's coming. Individuals may change (in either direction), but two groups will continue forever—those who *do wrong,*

22:13 Jesus' formula of self-identification echoes similar formulas in 1:8, 1:17 and 21:6. The attributes of God and Jesus Christ are so intertwined here that they cannot be separated, yet there can be no doubt that the speaker here is Jesus. Not only is Jesus clearly the one who "comes" (v. 12; explicitly so in v. 20), but he proceeds to identify himself by name in verse 16.

22:14-15 The NRSV, NEB and REB all end the quotation of Jesus after verse 13 so that verses 14-15 are attributed to John. There is no real warrant for doing so. Rather (with the NIV), the prophetic oracle should be understood as continuing through these verses. Jesus identifies himself as "the Alpha and the Omega, the First and the Last, the Beginning and the End" (v. 13) and then, on the basis of his divine identity, pronounces a beatitude (just as he does in the Gospels) on the righteous (v. 14) and a curse of sorts on the ungodly (v. 15). On such a reading, the quotation extends still further, as Jesus goes on to identify himself in verse 16.

or the *vile,* on one side, and those who *do right,* or are *holy,* on the other. One group's names are inscribed in the book of life; the other's are not. In the words of Jesus' parable of the wheat and the weeds in Matthew's Gospel, "Let both grow together until the harvest. At that time I will tell the harvesters: First collect the weeds and tie them in bundles to be burned; then gather the wheat and bring it into my barn" (Mt 13:30). In the end, as we have seen, certain things will be "no more" (Greek *ouk . . . eti*) for the wrongdoers (18:21-23), and other things will be "no more" (*ouk . . . eti*) for the righteous (21:1, 4, 25; 22:3, 5). But the wrongdoers and the righteous themselves, the vile and the holy, will *not* similarly disappear. They will continue as two distinct groups "still" or "evermore" (Greek *eti*), the wrongdoers in the lake of fire (20:15; 21:8), the righteous and holy, appropriately enough, in the holy city.

The angel's self-identification as *fellow servant* to Christian prophets (v. 9) implies that the angel shares the prophetic function of delivering messages from God or the risen Jesus to Christian congregations. In verses 12-15 the angel begins speaking prophetically in Jesus' name, *Behold, I am coming soon,* (v. 12), just as John did in verse 7. Whether the voice belongs to a human prophet or an angel makes no difference, for in either case the real speaker is Jesus, who identifies himself with the words, *I am the Alpha and the Omega, the First and the Last, the Beginning and the End* (v. 13). Within the pronouncement, the solemn promise, *My reward is with me, and I will give to everyone according to what he has done* (v. 12), reinforces the dualism of verse 11. There are two kinds of people in the world, and there always will be. Each group goes to its fitting reward. Here as in 21:6-8, an Alpha and Omega saying

---

22:14 The tenses suggest that this verse is addressed to John's readers in their own time (and therefore to us as well). The present participle *those who wash* (or "those washing") their robes refers to something a person does now, before it is too late, so *that they may have the right to the tree of life and may go through the gates into the city.* It has nothing to do with martyrdom, but echoes the reference in 7:14 to those who "have washed their robes and made them white in the blood of the Lamb." It is a metaphor for trusting in the death of Jesus for salvation (compare Jn 1:29; 1 Jn 1:7; Heb 9:14; 1 Pet 1:2).

22:15 The list of those *outside* the holy city corresponds rather closely to the list of those who end up in the lake of fire (21:8). The main difference is that here the list begins with *dogs,* a widely used metaphor in the ancient world for "anything unclean" (Greek *pan koinon,* 21:27) or under a curse (*pan katathema,* 22:3). For this metaphor in early Christianity, see Philemon 3:2, Matthew 7:6 and *Didache* 9.5.

(v. 13) introduces a brief description of two contrasting destinies (vv. 14-15). The righteous will have access to the holy city and the tree of life, while the fate of the wicked is simply to be *outside* (Greek *exō*). The grim understatement reminds us once again that the ungodly will end up *in the fiery lake of burning sulfur,* or *second death* (21:8).

Mark Twain's Huck Finn, on reading John Bunyan's *Pilgrim's Progress,* commented, "It was interesting, but tough." In a similar way the book of Revelation is "tough" for believers and unbelievers alike, and it is at least as tough today as it was in the first century. Twain is also supposed to have said, "I don't worry about the parts of the Bible I can't understand. I have enough trouble with the parts I can understand." Among the most difficult passages in Revelation are some whose meaning is actually quite clear—the warnings of eternal punishment.

It is not fashionable today, nor popular, to scare people into the kingdom of God, least of all from the pulpit. Church is a place people go to find comfort and reassurance. Yet four sections in the latter part of John's prophecy end on the same note of stern warning (20:15; 21:8, 27; 22:15). Ironically, John's vision of evil Babylon ended with a cry of triumph on behalf of the people of God (19:6-10), while his vision of blessed Jerusalem ends with a solemn picture of those outside. Despite all the glories of the holy city, we cannot feel comfortable or complacent. Instead, we must ask ourselves the same question we posed when reading the seven messages of chapters 2-3: Which side am I on? Where will I be found?

There is a place for fear in Christian ministry and Christian experience, and yet fear cannot be the last word. As John Newton wrote, "'Twas grace that taught my heart to fear, and grace my fears relieved." In the book of Revelation, fear is the next-to-last word, not the last. The last word is a word of hope and expectation, the "Amazing Grace" that Newton celebrated.

22:16 The plural *you* (Greek *hymin*) is rarely used in the book of Revelation, aside from the seven messages (2:10, 13, 23, 24)—only in 1:4, 1:9, 12:12 and 18:20. More often a singular "you" is used, referring either to John himself or to the "angel" of one of the churches. Except for 12:12, where it refers to "the earth and the sea," the plural has in mind Christian believers in the seven churches, those for whom the book is intended. Here, however, the group designated as *you* is distinguished from the churches by being given a message *for* the churches. The exact meaning of *for* [Greek *epi*] is difficult to fix. *Epi* could mean "on" in the sense of "about" (compare 10:11, where John was told to prophesy *about* "many

☐ Conclusion (22:16-21)

Certain syllables, ordinary in themselves, become sacred by repetition and familiarity. For generations, devout Christians at worship have sung "Jesus, Jesus, Jesus, Sweetest Name I Know" and "How Sweet the Name of Jesus Sounds." Charismatic believers with hands uplifted have been known to repeat the name "Jesus" a dozen times or more as a prayer, without elaboration or specific petition. No sound, no word, no name is more sacred to Christians than "Jesus."

On only two occasions in the Bible does Jesus identify himself by that sacred name. To Saul of Tarsus on the Damascus road he said, "I am Jesus, whom you are persecuting" (Acts 9:5; also 22:8; 26:15). At the end of the book of Revelation he announces, I, Jesus, have sent my angel to give you this testimony for the churches (v. 16). These words continue without a break the speech of Jesus that began with the promise, "Behold, I am coming soon" (vv. 12-15). They are Jesus' own restatement of the words of the long title at the book's beginning (1:1-2) and of John's words in 22:6: "The Lord, the God of the spirits of the prophets, sent his angel to show his servants the things that must soon take place."

The "angel" mentioned in these passages is probably not to be limited to the angel present in any particular context (for example, the angel of 21:9—22:6 or of 17:1—19:10). Rather, John's Revelation comes to him through a variety of angelic figures and voices—from the humanlike figure of chapter 1 who turned out to be Jesus himself, to the "mighty angel" of 5:2, 10:1 and 18:21, to the seven angels who completed the harvest of chapter 14, to the angels with the seven last plagues in chapters 15-16. In some sense, when Jesus claims to *have sent my angel to give you this testimony for the churches*, he means all these and more, even though in the present context the angel most immediately in mind is the one that showed John the holy city.

---

peoples, nations, languages and kings"), or it could even mean "against." But Revelation (aside from chapters 2—3) is not a description of the churches, much less an oracle against them. Therefore the common translation is preferable, with *epi* as "for" in the sense of purpose (that is, to deliver to the churches, which is what John is doing in the book of Revelation; see Bauer 1979:287). The distinction between *you* and *the churches* strongly suggests that Jesus is addressing a community of Christian prophets (John included) who minister to *the churches* (see Aune 1989:103-16).

Throughout this last chapter the reader encounters great difficulty in determining who the speaker is. A good rule to follow is that the one speaking remains the same unless there is a clear signal to the contrary. Verses 16-19 are best understood as a continuous speech of the risen Jesus to John and his "brothers the prophets" (see v. 9), entrusting them with the whole book of Revelation (Greek *tauta,* literally "these things") as a *testimony* to deliver to *the churches* (the seven in Asia above all, but probably a wider circle as well). Having identified himself by name, Jesus further claims for himself the title of *the Root and the Offspring of David, and the bright Morning Star* (v. 16), implying, first, that he is the Jewish Messiah from David's line (compare 5:5) and, second, that his coming will mark the dawn of a new day (compare 2:28) and a new creation. The emphatic pronoun "I" (Greek *egō*) punctuates the whole of Jesus' concluding brief discourse: *I, Jesus* (v. 16), *I am the Root and the Offspring of David* (v. 16), and *I warn everyone* (v. 18). And although the "I" is not repeated in verse 17, there is no evident change of speaker.

Contrary to all modern translations, therefore, Jesus, not John, is the one quoting what *the Spirit and the bride* are saying, and inviting the thirsty to *take the free gift of the water of life* (v. 17). This is appropriate because only God or Jesus has the authority to give such an invitation to life (compare 21:6; also Jn 4:14; 6:35; 7:37-38). But are the explicit invitations to *come* (Greek *erchou*) directed to Jesus (as in v. 20, *Come, Lord Jesus*) or to *whoever is thirsty?* Are they prayers for Jesus' future coming, or invitations to the unbeliever to come and be saved?

The ambiguity divides commentators, but it is traceable to the imagery of the wedding supper. Verse 17 should be understood against the background of 19:7, "for the wedding of the Lamb has come, and his bride has made herself ready," and 19:9, "blessed are those who are invited to the wedding supper of the Lamb." *Come* is the bride's word summoning her bridegroom, the Lamb, and at the same time a call to any who would be guests at the wedding. Instead of describing the actual banquet, Jesus limits himself to the simple metaphor of taking *the*

22:17 The reference to *him who hears* the voice of the Spirit and the bride recalls the expression, "He who has an ear, let him hear what the Spirit says to the churches." Mention of the one *who hears* serves a rhetorical purpose. We might have expected, "The Spirit and the bride say, 'Come,' so let the hearer come," but instead the hearer's job is to echo the *free gift of the water of life* (compare 21:6 and 22:1). Because the marriage metaphor is never expanded into a full-fledged parable or allegory (in the manner of Mt 22:1-14 or 25:1-13), the heralded "wedding of the Lamb" is nowhere described. The joy of the wedding gives way to the immeasurable joy of an abundant stream of water for those who are dying of thirst, in the tradition of Isaiah 55:1: "Come, all you who are thirsty, come to the waters; and you who have no money, come, buy and eat! Come, buy wine and milk without money and without cost."

The joyous summons to life is in keeping with the fact that the gates of the holy city are always open (21:25) and the leaves of the tree of life are "for the healing of the nations" (22:2). It is also in keeping with Jesus' plea at the end of the seven messages to the churches: "Here I am! I stand at the door and knock. If anyone hears my voice and opens the door, I will come in and eat with him, and he with me" (3:20). Jesus' concluding invitation to come and *take the free gift of the water of life* is similarly directed to anyone. The only exception is those who are truly "outside" (v. 15)—in the lake of fire (20:15; 21:8, 27). Just as in the parables of Jesus (above all in Mt 22:1-14), there is an unmistakable tension between the universal offer of life and the rejection of those who have not prepared themselves to receive life. This tension pervades the entire book of Revelation, in fact, the entire Christian religion. Christianity preaches a universal gospel of salvation, but not a gospel of universal salvation. All are invited to come, but not all do come. God respects human freedom to the extent that evil never disappears, even though it is defeated.

We are reminded of this once more in the next two verses. The *I* who bears testimony in verses 18 and 19 is clearly Jesus, not John (see Mounce 1977:396). By omitting quotation marks, most English translations give the mistaken impression that this is John solemnly testifying to the truth of the book he has just written. The Revised English Bible goes so far as to translate the beginning of verse 18 as "I, John, give this warning to everyone who is listening to the words of prophecy in this book."

---

invitation (to bridegroom and wedding guests alike), giving it urgency and emphasis. The Spirit (that is, the prophets in each congregation) speaks for the bride (that is, the people of God corporately). The prophetic voice is echoed by the people of God individually, and Jesus then directs it beyond them to *whoever is thirsty* (v. 17).

But the name "John" is not in the text, and verse 20 (even in the REB) makes such an interpretation nearly impossible: "He who gives this testimony says, 'Yes, I am coming soon!'" (REB). Clearly Jesus, not John, is the one who is *coming soon,* and just as clearly Jesus, not John, is the one with the authority to lay down the severe sanctions about adding to someone *the plagues described in this book* (v. 18) or taking away someone's *share in the tree of life and in the holy city* (v. 19).

The warning stands in the tradition of Moses' speeches to the people of Israel (Deut 4:2, "Do not add to what I command you and do not subtract from it, but keep the commands of the LORD your God that I give you"; see also Deut 12:32). Like the warnings of Moses, this warning is directed "to the hearer . . . before whom the book is read in the congregation, not to a copyist" (Beckwith 1922:778-79). Robert Mounce agrees: "It is addressed not to future scribes who might be tempted to tamper with the text (nor to textual critics who must decide between shorter and longer variants!) but to 'every man that heareth,' that is, to members of the seven churches of Asia where the book was to be read aloud. The warning is against willful distortion of the message" (1977:395). Jesus goes beyond Moses by invoking a stern sanction heightened by a play on words: if anyone adds anything to the Revelation, God will add to that person the plagues described in this book, not only the "three plagues" of 9:18 or the "seven last plagues" of 15:1, but all the plagues. If anyone takes away anything, God will take away that person's share in the tree of life and in the holy city, which are described in this book (vv. 18-19). The closest New Testament parallel to Jesus' grim play on words here is the sanction attached to his own commands in the Sermon on the Mount: whoever breaks one of the least of "these commandments" and teaches others to do so will be called least in "the kingdom of heaven" (Mt 5:19). The warning in Matthew appears to be a deliberate understatement, the real point being that "unless your righteousness surpasses that of the Pharisees and the teachers of the law, you will certainly not enter the

---

22:18-19 For the idea of a curse on anyone who adds to or takes away from a document, see the early Jewish *Letter of Aristeas* 310-11, referring to what was supposed to have happened after the Hebrew Bible was translated into Greek: "'Since this version has been made rightly and reverently, and in every respect accurately, it is good that this should remain exactly so, and that there should be no revision.' There was general approval of

kingdom of heaven" (Mt 5:20). This one at the end of Revelation is less subtle and even harsher. It amounts virtually to a curse.

We who presume to write commentaries on the book of Revelation—or any other book of the Bible, for that matter—are assuming a serious, even frightening responsibility. The same is true of those who teach the Bible in the church or preach it from the pulpit. Few can say what the apostle Paul said to the Ephesian elders at Miletus, "I did not shrink from declaring to you the whole counsel of God" (Acts 20:27 RSV). Yet the burden is not limited to the commentator, the pastor or the teacher. The point of the "curse" at the end of the book of Revelation (thus at the end of the whole Bible) is that the same responsibility rests on *every* reader or hearer of the word of God.

Not everything in the Bible is to be "kept" or "obeyed"; much of it is purely descriptive, and the reader's or hearer's responsibility is to pay attention, follow the story and give thanks for what God has done. But every book of the Bible has imperatives as well as indicatives. What God has done demands a moral response, and in every book, including Revelation, there is something to "keep" and something to "obey." The hearers cannot pick and choose what to obey and what to ignore, or they do so at their peril. That is the thrust of Jesus' last warning. To restate the warning positively, as a benediction, we need only go back to the beginning: "Blessed is the one who reads the words of this prophecy, and blessed are those who hear it and take to heart what is written in it, because the time is near" (1:3).

Jesus' final words, *Yes, I am coming soon* (v. 20) reaffirm the earlier pronouncement, "Behold, I am coming soon!" (v. 12). Children brought up in fundamentalist or evangelical homes sometimes have nightmares about the Second Coming of Jesus. These nightmares result from sermons or Sunday school lessons that pose the question, Where will you be when Jesus comes, in the Lord's house or in some den of iniquity? Christians are taught to pray "Thy kingdom come" and "Come, O Lord!" (1 Cor 16:22). But sometimes we are not so sure that we really want the

---

what they said, and they commanded that a curse should be laid, as was their custom, on anyone who should alter the version by any addition or change to any part of the written text, or any deletion either" (Charlesworth 1985:33). The parallel is not exact, for *Aristeas,* unlike the book of Revelation, is a written translation, not a newly given "original," and the curse is directed to scribes, not hearers.

Lord to come, either because life on earth has so much to offer or because of childhood fears.

To be honest, there is some ground for our childhood fears and bad dreams, painful though they may have been to us psychologically. Through much of the book of Revelation, the coming of Jesus is as much a threat as a promise. "If you do not repent, I will come to you and remove your lampstand from its place" (2:5). "Repent therefore! Otherwise, I will soon come to you and will fight against them with the sword of my mouth" (2:16). "But if you do not wake up, I will come like a thief, and you will not know at what time I will come to you" (3:3). "Behold, I come like a thief! Blessed is he who stays awake and keeps his clothes with him, so that he may not go naked and be shamefully exposed" (16:15). At the end of the Old Testament in the Christian canon, the coming of God himself is a threat, not a blessed promise. Malachi prophesies the coming of Elijah, who "will turn the hearts of the fathers to their children, and the hearts of the children to their fathers; or else I will come and strike the land with a curse" (Mal 4:6).

At the very end of the New Testament, however, the coming of God is the coming of Jesus, and its meaning is at last transformed. *Yes, I am coming soon* is no longer a threat, but a promise. The bad dream is over. "Amen. Come, Lord Jesus." There is both curse and blessing in the book of Revelation, but blessing has the last word. As the reader makes peace with the coming of Jesus, the long letter comes to a close. In the manner of the letters of Paul, John ends with the closing salutation, *The grace of the Lord Jesus be with God's people. Amen* (v. 22).

Bibliography

Abbott, Edwin A.
1952 *Flatland: A Romance in Many Dimensions*. New York: Dover Publications; first published anonymously in 1884.

Aune, David E.
1983 *Prophecy in Early Christianity and the Ancient Mediterranean World*. Grand Rapids, Mich.: Eerdmans.

1989 "The Prophetic Circle of the John of Patmos and the Exegesis of Revelation 22.16." *Journal for the Study of the New Testament* 37:103-16.

Bauckham, Richard
1993 *The Theology of the Book of Revelation*. Cambridge: Cambridge University Press.

Bauer, Walter
1979 *A Greek-English Lexicon of the New Testament and Other Early Christian Literature*. 2nd ed. Revised by W. F. Arndt and F. W. Gingrich. Chicago: University of Chicago Press.

Beasley-Murray, George R.
1974 *The Book of Revelation*. London: Oliphants.

Beckwith, Isbon T.
1922 *The Apocalypse of John*. London: Macmillan.

Bengel, J. A.
1877 *Gnomon Novi Testamenti* 5:172-389. Edinburgh: T. & T. Clark.

Bierce, Ambrose
1947 *The Collected Writings of Ambrose Bierce*. New York: Citadel.

Boring, M. Eugene
1989 *Revelation*. Louisville, Ky.: John Knox.

Caird, G. B.
1966 *A Commentary on the Revelation of St. John the Divine*. New York: Harper and Row.

Case, Shirley Jackson
1920 *The Revelation of John: A Historical Interpretation.* Chicago: University of Chicago Press.

Charles, R. H.
1920 *A Critical and Exegetical Commentary on the Revelation of St. John.* 2 vols. Edinburgh: T. & T. Clark.

Charlesworth, J. H., ed.
1983 *The Old Testament Pseudepigrapha.* Vol. 1. Garden City, N.Y.: Doubleday.

1985 *The Old Testament Pseudepigrapha.* Vol. 2. Garden City, N.Y.: Doubleday.

Court, John M.
1979 *Myth and History in the Book of Revelation.* London: SPCK.

Danby, H.
1933 *The Mishnah Translated from the Hebrew.* Oxford: Oxford University Press.

Elliott, E. B.
1847 *Horae Apocalypticae; or, A Commentary on the Apocalyse, Critical and Historical.* London: Seeley, Burnside and Seeley.

Farrer, Austin
1964 *The Revelation of St. John the Divine.* Oxford: At the Clarendon Press.

Feuillet, André
1966 "Le premier cavalier de l'Apocalypse." *Zeitschrift für die neutestamentliche Wissenschaft* 57:229-59.

Finegan, Jack
1981 *The Archaeology of the New Testament: The Mediterranean World of the Early Christian Apostles.* Boulder, Colo.: Westview.

Ford, J. Massyngberde
1975 *Revelation.* Garden City, N.Y.: Doubleday.

Giblin, C. H.
1994 "Recapitulation and the Literary Coherence of John's Apocalypse." *Catholic Biblical Quarterly* 56:81-95.

Grant, Robert M., ed.
1966 *The Apostolic Fathers: A New Translation and Commentary.* Vol. 4, *Ignatius of Antioch.* Camden, N.J.: Thomas Nelson.

Gundry, Robert H.
1987 "The New Jerusalem: People as Place, Not Place for People."

Novum Testamentum 29:254-64.

Hall, Robert G.
1990 "Living Creatures in the Midst of the Throne: Another Look at Revelation 4.6." *New Testament Studies* 36:609-13.

Hawthorne, Gerald F.
1975 "A New English Translation of Melito's Paschal Homily." In *Current Issues in Biblical and Patristic Interpretation*. Edited by Gerald F. Hawthorne. Grand Rapids, Mich.: Eerdmans.

Hendriksen, William
1939 *More Than Conquerors: An Interpretation of the Book of Revelation*. Reprint, Grand Rapids, Mich.: Baker, 1973.

Keener, Craig S.
1993 *The IVP Bible Background Commentary: New Testament*. Downers Grove, Ill.: InterVarsity Press.

Kennicott, Benjamin
1747 *Two Dissertations*. 2nd ed. Oxford: At the Theatre.

Kerkeslager, Allen
1993 "Apollo, Greco-Roman Prophecy, and the Rider on the White Horse in Rev 6:2." *Journal of Biblical Literature* 112:116-21.

Kiddle, Martin
1940 *The Revelation of St. John*. New York and London: Harper and Brothers.

Kline, Meredith G.
1975 "The First Resurrection." *Westminster Theological Journal* 37:366-75.

1976 "The First Resurrection: A Reaffirmation." *Westminster Theological Journal* 39:110-19.

Ladd, George Eldon
1972 *Commentary on the Revelation of John*. Grand Rapids, Mich.: Eerdmans.

Mazzaferri, F. D.
1989 *The Genre of the Book of Revelation from a Source-Critical Perspective*. Berlin: Walter de Gruyter.

Melville, Herman
1931 *Romances of Herman Melville*. New York: Tudor Publishing.

Metzger, Bruce
1971 *A Textual Commentary on the Greek New Testament*. London and New York: United Bible Societies.

Michaels, J. Ramsey
1976 "The First Resurrection: A Response." *Westminster Theolog-*

ical Journal 39:102-9.

1988 *1 Peter.* Waco, Tex.: Word Books.

1991 "Revelation 1.19 and the Narrative Voices of the Apocalypse." *New Testament Studies* 37:604-20.

1992 *Interpreting the Book of Revelation.* Grand Rapids, Mich.: Baker Book House.

Mounce, Robert H.
1977 *The Book of Revelation.* Grand Rapids, Mich.: Eerdmans.

Munck, Johannes
1950 *Petrus und Paulus in der Offenbarung Johannes.* Copenhagen: Rosenkilde og Bagger.

O'Connor, Flannery
1988 *Collected Works.* New York: Library of America.

Pippin, Tina
1992 *Death and Desire: The Rhetoric of Gender in the Apocalypse of John.* Louisville, Ky.: Westminster/John Knox.

Ramsay, William G.
1904 *The Letters to the Seven Churches of Asia and Their Place in the Plan of the Apocalypse.* London: Hodder and Stoughton.

Rissi, Mathias
1966 *Time and History: A Study on the Revelation.* Richmond: John Knox.

Schwartz, Hillel
1980 *The French Prophets. The History of a Millennarian Group in Eighteenth-Century England.* Berkeley: University of California Press.

Sharrock, Roger, ed.
1987 *The Pilgrim's Progress: John Bunyan.* London: Penguin Books.

Stonehouse, Ned B.
1957 "The Elders and the Living-Beings in the Apocalypse." In *Paul Before the Areopagus and Other New Testament Studies.* London: Tyndale.

Stuart, Moses
1845 *A Commentary on the Apocalypse.* Andover, Mass.: Allen, Morrill and Wardwell.

Swete, Henry Barclay
1908 *The Apocalypse of St. John.* Grand Rapids, Mich.: Eerdmans.

Tenney, Merrill C.
1957 *Interpreting Revelation*. Grand Rapids, Mich.: Eerdmans.

Theron, D. J.
1957 *Evidence of Tradition*. Grand Rapids, Mich.: Baker Book House.

Thompson, Leonard
1990 *The Book of Revelation: Apocalypse and Empire*. New York: Oxford University Press.

Vos, Louis Arthur
1965 *The Synoptic Traditions in the Apocalypse*. Kampen: Kok.

Wall, Robert W.
1991 *Revelation*. Peabody, Mass.: Hendrickson.

Wilder, Amos Niven
1972 *Grace Confounding*. Philadelphia: Fortress.

Wilson, Stephen G.
1992 "Gentile Judaizers." *New Testament Studies* 38:605-16.

Yarbro Collins, Adela
1976 *The Combat Myth in the Book of Revelation*. Missoula, Mont.: Scholars Press.

1984 *Crisis and Catharsis: The Power of the Apocalypse*. Philadelphia: Westminster.